FI

THE FEAR OF THE WORD:
Censorship and Sex

by
ELI M. OBOLER

The Scarecrow Press, Inc.
Metuchen, N. J.   1974

Library of Congress Cataloging in Publication Data

Oboler, Eli M
   The fear of the word: censorship and sex.

   Bibliography: p.
   1. Censorship--United States. 2. Censorship.
3. Obscenity (Law)--United States. 4. Obscenity (Law)
I. Title.
KF4770.O2   363.3'1'0973   74-6492
ISBN 0-8108-0724-6

To Marcia, Leon, and Carol

severest critics
and
most beloved inspirations

".. .an overwhelming case can be made out for the statement that no nation can prosper or even continue to exist without heretics and advocates of shockingly immoral doctrines. "

--George Bernard Shaw, Preface to The Shewing-Up of Blanco Posnet, 1909.

"Dogmas are at their best when nobody denies them, for then their falsehood sleeps, like that of an unconscious metaphor, and their moral function is discharged instinctively. "

--George Santayana, Reason in Religion, 1905.

".. . the slaughter-houses and indecencies without end on which our life is founded are huddled out of sight and never mentioned, so that the world we recognize officially in literature and in society is a poetic fiction far handsomer and cleaner and better than the world that really is. "

--William James, The Varieties of Religious Experience, 1902.

iv

FOREWORD

Such a work as this--which at least impinges on so many different and varied intellectual disciplines--needed (and received) the advice of scholars in many fields. For such help--and without in any way ascribing to them responsibility for what appears in print, which is certainly my own doing--may I herewith thank the following, all valued colleagues at Idaho State University (the institution where I have worked for nearly a quarter-century, and the institution which granted me a most welcome sabbatical leave, during which much of this volume was written):

Dr. Glen O. Allen
Prof. Wilbur Huck
Dr. Sven Liljeblad
Dr. Shanna McGee
Dr. William Shields
Dr. David Stewart
Dr. Earl Swanson

In addition, community legal expert and good friend, attorney Chilton Phoenix, and Pocatello's Presbyterian minister, Dr. Jo Austin Lininger, were most helpful in advising on material in their respective fields.

Finally, appreciation is due to a group of departed worthies--Mozart, Vivaldi, Bach, Telemann, Gluck, Purcell, Haydn, Handel, Beethoven, Schubert, and Satie--whose creative genius provided essential aural background for the writing of what follows. I hope it turns out to be neither too baroque nor too classical nor too romantic; yet, equally, neither aleatory nor dissonant.

Eli M. Oboler

Pocatello, Idaho
Idaho State University
October 1, 1973

ACKNOWLEDGMENTS

Passages are quoted from The Encyclopedia of Sexual Behavior, edited by Dr. Albert Ellis and Dr. Albert Abarbanel, by permission of Hawthorn Books, Inc. Copyright (c) 1961 by Hawthorn Books, Inc. All rights reserved.

Quotations from The Ethics of Sexual Acts, by René Guyon (copyright (c) 1935 by Alfred A. Knopf, Inc.) are included by permission of Alfred A. Knopf, Inc.

Simon & Schuster, Inc. granted permission to quote from Caesar and Christ, by Will and Ariel Durant (copyright (c) 1944 by Will Durant) and from The Renaissance, by Will and Ariel Durant (copyright (c) 1953 by Will Durant).

Thanks are also due to John Wilson, for permission to quote from his Logic and Sexual Morality (Penguin Books, 1963); and to Faber & Faber, Ltd., for permission to quote from Reason and Emotion by John MacMurray.

CONTENTS

1. THE BASES OF CENSORSHIP

"... no one knows what is good
Who knows not what is evil;
And no one knows what is true
Who knows not what is false."

---Edgar Lee Masters,
Spoon River Anthology, 1916

Chapter 1

THE BASES OF CENSORSHIP

Of the writing of books about censorship there will presumably be no end, for nothing about books seems to be of such perennial interest as the tales of when and where and how someone or some group or some governmental body tried--successfully or otherwise--to eliminate or, at least, to expurgate them. The sense in censorship has always been more widely accepted than the nonsense; the errors of the censor are rarely, if, indeed, ever admitted to be such; and the conventional wisdom concerning the eternal verity of censorship is so conventional and so generally accepted as supernal wisdom that few have even ventured to mention the clay feet of the Great God Censorship. There is evidence that the permissive attitudes of some citizens have not influenced the majority. Regardless of how people behave privately, they can be counted on to act in public as solid citizens. The conventional wisdom remains unchanged.

"Everyone knows" that pornography is corrupting, degrading and, always and everywhere and for everyone, a direct incitement to illegal and immoral actions related to sex. "Everyone knows" that without legal and actively enforced restraints on what may be read about sex, all that will be written or read will be the immoral and indecent and corrupting and degrading and libidinous and lustful and defiling and coarse and vulgar and appealing to prurient interest and--oh, just plain "dirty," in the usual parlance of "everyone." "Everyone knows" there are hundreds and hundreds of millions of dollars worth of obscene and pornographic literature sold every year in America. "Everyone knows" that such reading is the greatest single cause of juvenile delinquency, rape and homosexuality, and an indirect cause of a great deal of, if not of all, other crime. "Everyone knows" that the widespread use of "dirty" words will soon cause the moral fiber of our civilization to deteriorate to the level of Sodom and Gomorrah at their worst--and, of course, will cause us to risk the same severe divine

2

punishment wrought upon those two sinks of iniquity.

In short, what "everyone knows" is surely hardly worth examining or disputing. Like the conventional wisdom on so many other topics, it is so because "everyone knows" it is so. Never mind proof of any of the propositions about censorship and its relationship to writing about sex; forget about logic and evidence and reason; "everyone knows" why there is, why there has been, why there must always be censorship--or do they?

On the topic of the origins of censorship, any study is still more in the question-asking than the answer-giving state. All of the explanations given in the rest of this book are not really reasons for, but rationalizations for censorship of publications dealing with human sexual activity. There are too many variables, too many imponderables connected with the essentially heuristic problems of moralistic investigation to permit even such a volume as this to claim definitiveness. As Joseph Wood Krutch has written, "As long as man seeks answers he is a human being. Once he abandons the search he is in danger of ceasing to be what we recognize as such. If history proves how unreconcilably men may differ in their moral judgments it demonstrates also that a belief in the importance of such judgments is a persistent characteristic of the human mind."[1]

Sometime, somewhere, there is a human necessity to try to find human, reasonable answers to some of what will probably eventually no longer be unanswerable questions concerning the fundamental human motives and justifications for trying to keep other humans from seeing what they want to see, writing what they want to write, and reading what they want to read.

The democratic philosophy is based on man's presumed ability to reason, to decide for himself in his own best interest. It relies on man's educability and his free exercise of conscience in moral issues. Censorship represents the complete denial of all of these, and is, therefore, both anti-democratic and pro-totalitarian. The more totalitarian the state, the greater the amount of opprobrium given to free expression, and the more severe the penalties attached to failure to heed censorship.

Some questions seem to be basic in considering the origins of censorship. The following list is not exhaustive,

but is intended to include most of the more significant
questions:

    1.   What are the cultural bases of censorship?

    2.   Does the inherently sexual nature of man as a
biological being require the kind of restraint on his mental
activity represented by censorship of reading about sex?

    3.   Is censorship of printing, publishing, dissemina-
tion of, and reading about sexual matters required to protect the innocence of children? If so, up to what age?

    4.   Does government, does any church, does any
individual have the right to limit artistic creativity in any
way?

    5.   Could the power of public opinion replace govern-
mental censorship as a brake on excessive amounts or types
of erotically frank writing? Should it?

    Sometimes the censors have worked through the appa-
ratus of the duly constituted law, sometimes with theological
sanctions, sometimes through such extra-legal methods as
burning and boycott and pre-censorship. But almost all
censors seem to share a few common characteristics:

    1.   They know better than the prospective reader
what is "right" for him to read.

    2.   They themselves may read the censorable matter
without being deleteriously affected.

    3.   They know conclusively what bad effects reading
of "bad" stuff will have.

    4.   They can see no possibility of good results from
reading the fit-to-be-censored items.

    After a generation as a practicing academic librarian
and a good deal of varied activity in the field of writing
and working for intellectual freedom--particularly as it is
related to librarians and libraries--I became interested in
looking into what seemed a hitherto unexplored and significant area of the story of censorship--especially censorship
of writings dealing in any way with sex. This area of ex-
ploration was that of the whole complex of <u>causes</u>, of

sources, of the origins of censorship.

Why are men afraid of certain words, even though
the behavior they denote is generally accepted? Why will
most people react emotionally and passionately--even vio-
lently--to spoken or written words, while in many cases
having comparatively mild reactions to the actions described
by the words? As James Harvey Robinson wrote a half-
century ago, "...talk and writing are forms of conduct,
and, like all conduct, are inevitably disagreeable when they
depart from the current standards of respectable behavior.
To talk as if our established notions of religion, morality,
and property, our ideas of stealing and killing, were de-
fective and in need of revision, is indeed more shocking
than to violate the current rules of action."[2]

The obvious first place to look in research into the
cause, the origins of the censorship of written statements
concerning the sexual life of men--the basic theme of this
volume--was, of course, the field of linguistics. If we
are concerned with the fear of the word, then let us look
into why particular words have become imbued with a more
or less evil spirit of their own. But it soon became apparent, upon beginning this research, that much more fundamental to this study than the study of languages and of
word-origins were the related fields of anthropology and
psychology. Of particular significance in trying to plumb
the depths of the censor's mind was an attempt to relate
the modern mind to the primitive mind.

For the purpose of this volume, along with a rather
thorough study of pertinent writings in linguistics, anthropology and theology, there has been at least some research
into history, law, morals, ethics, aesthetics, general
philosophy, sociology, psychology, and related fields. Out
of all this has come at least a tentative set of conclusions,
of which the most significant, it is hoped, if there is general agreement with it, will be that censorship is neither
essential nor inevitable for man's progress or well-being--
only customary. From an examination of the human sciences, it is possible to conclude that censorship has no basis
in reason. If there were no intervention of human nature,
one could simply be logical; that is, postulate some reasonable, rather simple premises and state their more or less
obvious conclusions:

1.   The widespread dissemination of all possible

knowledge is a good thing for mankind.

2.   Censorship is clearly an attempt to narrow down,
if not eliminate, man's self-knowledge, as well as his
knowledge of extra-human activity.

3.   Therefore, censorship, no matter for what reason, is bad for humanity.

In the brief space of a single generation, we have
seen a Ulysses, a Lady Chatterley's Lover, and a Tropic
of Cancer emerge from underground illegality to newsstand
and library distribution with impunity. In a few more years
we may no longer find practically blasphemous the public
use of what is now called "obscenity," and language will be
relegated to its appropriate place as the medium of the
message. The true obscenities of our times--poverty,
hunger, gross inequality of economic, social and political
opportunity, needless disease, nationally-approved violence
(war), environmental pollution--all the death-related phenomena of our civilization--will be what we shall then en-
deavor to censor, rather than sex-related words and writings,
as if they were really of vital significance to our lives and
to our civilization's future.

Let us begin our inquiry into the origins of censorship, then, with the fundamentals on the anthropological
background of the fear of the word. The three key sentences
to remember on the general subject of the fear of the word
are these: (1) "In the beginning was the Word, and the
Word was made Flesh"; (2) "Ye shall know the truth, and
the truth shall make you free"; (3) "The fear of the Lord
is the beginning of wisdom."

2. TABOO: THE PRIMITIVE CENSOR

"To overcome the subjective terrors: that is an important aspect of the age-long struggle out of barbarism.... Our life is overwrought with tradition and panics, distorting superstitions and fantastic lures.... The regiment of bogeys is waiting for people at birth ... so we begin to build up the sense of sin and the furtiveness of sex. The body becomes the object of a sneaking curiosity, of a tingling and embarrassing interest. We surround the obvious with great wastes of silence, and over the simplest facts we teach the soul to stutter."

--Walter Lippmann, Drift and
Mastery, 1912

Chapter 2

TABOO: THE PRIMITIVE CENSOR

As far back as the early civilizations of Sumer and
Egypt, there was a widespread belief that marking a hard
stone--such as lapis lazuli--in a special, personal way was
an act of magic. Once a design was scratched on a gem,
this could be imprinted on soft clay, and the stamped object
became itself a magical object with a taboo on it. Placing
an imprinted clump of clay on the top of a pot or a jar,
once the clay was imprinted with your seal, meant that no
one could partake of whatever was inside the jar without
breaking a taboo and running the risk of the dire penalties
of such taboo-breaking. So, in the very earliest known
Assyrian Bronze Age settlements, engraved stones served
as effective seals, denying to the non-elect what was considered private, by means of what was soon to become
writing. [1]

This taboo of the written word may be the earliest
known example of censorship. It has all the earmarks of
such, except that it was an individual, rather than a group
or societal, action. Neolithic man had gone beyond Paleolithic man, in this respect, as in many others. But Paleolithic man too--in particular, those who lived in caves just
after the Ice Age--spent a fair share of his time in artistic
activity. The end of this artistic activity was control over
nature. Cave art had a magic purpose. [2]

What was that purpose? It was to satisfy the felt
need for repetition of the needs, the dreams, the desires
of the cave-man, just as much as our art and literature do
the same for today's city-dweller. And just as not everything can be depicted or written about now--not even of
what is, let alone of what may be--so there was undoubtedly
censorship as a significant element in the troglodyte's life-
pattern. Some artists surely wanted to limn objects and
activities which are not shown in the Aurignacian cave walls,
comparatively recently unearthed in Spain and France. But

8

their principal job was not to make representations of whatever they wanted, but rather to help the hunters catch bison.
So bison were drawn on the cave walls, and, as Childe says,
"As surely as the artist drew a bison in the dark caves,
so surely would there be a living bison in the steppes outside for his fellows to kill and eat. "3

       It was not only considerations of presumed economic
and societal utility which inhibited the artist, the creator--
then or later. Basic to the regulation of life in primitive
society was the taboo. Sigmund Freud's classic Totem and
Taboo gives ample evidence to prove that "the basis of
taboo is a forbidden action for which there exists a strong
inclination in the unconscious. "4 Why is this action forbidden? The semi-rational, semi-superstitious mind of
primitive man had to sanctify the social restrictions he had
put upon himself out of his fear of chaos. The taboo prohibitions lack all "reasonable" justification and are of unknown
origin. All we know for certain about taboos among primitive tribes is that they continue to exist and have existed
for a very long time. Who would have the temerity to question them? Once a taboo is broken, the wrath of the gods,
the tribesmen feel, is inevitable. So, even though this
power may seem incomprehensible to civilized man, its
existence and authority were taken as a matter of course
by those who lived under its sway.

       Fritz Steiner, who has conducted probably the most
thorough study of this subject, has given a sound anthropological basis for many of Freud's psychoanalytically-
oriented concepts. Steiner defines taboo as concerned
"with all the social mechanisms of obedience which
have ritual significance" and--more appropriately and use-
fully for the present study--"with specific and restrictive
behavior in supposedly dangerous situations. " Where violations or taboos occur, destructive powers are unleashed.
Committing a tabooed deed brings defilement and supernatural
punishment. Furthermore, Westermarck notes that "when
an object is taboo it is supposed to be charged with mysterious energy that will injure or destroy the person who comes
into contact with the forbidden thing, whether he does so
willfully or by mistake. "6

      Surely this is a direct precursor of the idea of cen-
sorship. The modern censor of writing about sex is as
much--if not more!--concerned with the dire and deadly consequences of the reputed bit of pornography as he is with

the writing itself.   Indeed, in our day censorship could not
last a minute if the general reading public did not feel that
those who read a particular story or poem or play might
well be injured or even destroyed (psychically, at least), if
they violate the taboo.   Thus, an understanding of the source
of taboos is of interest here.   As French philosopher
Georges Bataille has put it, "I do not think man has much
chance of throwing light on the things that terrify him before
he has dominated them....   But man can surmount the
things that frighten him and face them squarely. "[7]

        According to Freud, the two venerable and significant
taboos are those against killing the totem animal and against
sexual intercourse with totem companions.   Taboos in the
latter group are more pervasive, derived as they are from
an awesome or mysterious origin. [8]   Bataille enlarges on the
second of these, to find that everywhere and always" ... as
far as our knowledge goes, man is defined by having his
sexual behavior subject to rules and precise restrictions. "[9]
He lists quite a number of specific taboos or restrictions involving sexual behavior, but states unequivocally that "the
taboo within us against sexual liberty is general and universal; the particular prohibitions are variable aspects of it. "[10]

        Among primitive tribes, it is quite common to have
special rules involving sexuality for the leaders.   For example, among the hill tribes of Assam, according to Sir James
G. Frazer, "the head man must be chaste, the husband of
one wife, and he must separate himself from her on the eve
of a general or public observance of taboo ... the violation
of any of these taboos would bring down misfortune on the
whole village. "[11]

        Continence, according to Frazer, is also required
(for four days) of those who "handled a corpse and dug the
grave" (among the Thompson Indians of British Columbia);
of the Polynesian Maoris (and among other aborigines) when
they were preparing to go on the warpath; and for a whole
year among those men of the Kwakiutl Indians of British
Columbia who ate human flesh as part of their ceremonial
rites.   No sexual intercourse is permitted to hunters and
fishermen sent out by tribes in many places and times; nor
in what Sir James calls "... many cases in which the savage
bridles his passion and remains chaste for motives of superstition.... "[12]

        There are widespread taboos concerning menstruation

and loss of blood at childbirth. Freud has pointed out that
there are "countless" rules concerning taboos on savage
women relating to menstruation, and he is sure that it is a
superstitious fear of blood which causes such taboos. [13]

It should not, then, amaze anyone that it took until
1970 before the first printed advertisements to use the word
"vagina" were published in American nationally-distributed
magazines. All the years of oblique reference to "feminine
hygiene" were, of course, a form of censorship--imposed
by the manufacturers, the advertising agencies, and/or the
media in a desire to avoid "bad taste." But in 1970, along
with nationwide release of X-rated motion pictures, the presentation of nude actors and actresses on the Broadway
stage, and complete frankness in both fictional and non-fic-
tional printed works on sex, came the acceptance of the fact
that women do have special hygienic needs which can be explicitly described in print--and suddenly "bad taste" is no
longer a factor!

There is no question that sexual taboos have always
been important to the basic activities of all groups. As
Birket-Smith has proven, most customs connected with farm-
ing are sexually-related, because sexual activity was thought
to help crops grow by magic. [14] And required continence on
the part of hunters and soldiers, before going into action,
as already mentioned, is a well-evidenced phenomenon.

Birket-Smith, by the way, backs strongly the before-
mentioned theories about the relationship between taboo and
sex, saying that such turning-points in life as birth, menstruation and death bring man close to the supernatural, and
indeed that at these crucial times man is exposed to peril,
and also able and likely to transmit dangers to others. Under those circumstances, naturally man needs and gets (at
least from primitive tribes) many more restrictions and taboos than at other times.

In our civilization the fact that copulation during the
menstrual period is still considered unclean or even danger-
ous--despite the fact that there is no scientific evidence of
such "uncleanness" or that any "danger" exists--is one more
demonstration of the long life of sexual taboos. And written
discussion of such activity is, of course, censor-bait.

Birket-Smith describes this kind of reaction--referring
specifically to savages--as based on fear of sorcery, since

the savage sees the genitals as "the seat of one of life's
most powerful and mysterious instincts...," to be "...re-
garded as being especially exposed to magic and attacks by
evil spirits."[15] So, even today, sex is not to be talked or
written about, lest evil befall the speaker or writer or listener or reader.

Indeed, Birket-Smith sees clothing, especially covering or concealment of the genitals, as associated primarily
with the feeling of shame, rather than protection.[16] If
there is protection involved, it is from the wrath of the
gods. The whole Adam and Eve story (to be discussed in
detail later in this volume) bears on this.

One interesting corollary of taboo--briefly alluded to
earlier--is that its observance or lack of observance is considered of vital importance to the whole society involved,
rather than merely to the individual transgressor. Robert
Lowie tells us that "it is a cardinal tenet of Eskimo religion
that the transgression of any one of a legion of taboos en-
dangers the food supply; all efforts to hunt seals prove fruitless and the settlement is on the verge of starvation."[17]
According to this theory, the taboo-violator must either confess or suffer the death penalty, if group calamity is to be
avoided. This fits in with the general public acceptance of
the theory that the reading, writing, or distribution of sexually frank material hurts the whole community severely, and
is not a matter purely of individual importance. If this
were not so, and only the individual directly concerned were
affected, it would be rather difficult to sustain public opposition to the widespread distribution of material dealing with
sex.

There are very few examples of a complete absence
of taboos on sexual activity in any civilization. It is true
that the Trobriand Islanders, whose life was so meticulously
and scientifically chronicled by Bronislaw Malinowski, are
among the few exceptions. As Malinowski says, in these
islands "...there is no condemnation of sex or of sensuality." The only "repressing and moulding forces"--so far as
sexual activity is concerned--are "submission to matriarchal
tribal law" and "prohibitions of exogamy...."[18] Malinowski's penetrating studies gave experimental confirmation to
much of Freudian psychology (which will be discussed in a
later chapter). But the Trobriand Islanders' lack of sexual
taboos is certainly unusual--even rare. In country after
country, tribe or other group after tribe or other group, the
taboos on sexual relations are accepted and obeyed.

Religious asceticism originates in the basic acceptance of sexual taboos. There is a "negative cult" in primitive society, just as there is in civilized religion. Those who follow this consider themselves sacred and separated beings, as compared to the common run of individuals. Those who lead the "negative cult," says Durkheim, "...do not prescribe certain acts to the faithful, but confine themselves to forbidding certain ways of activity...."[19] Their choices are enforced by taboos.

Durkheim says, forthrightly, "There is no religion where there are no interdictions and where they do not play a considerable part...."[20] Certainly whole books of the Old Testament and a great many parts of the New bear witness to the Judeo-Christian ethics being largely based on taboos or interdictions. Asceticism is the apotheosis of the negative cult, where "...the system of interdicts swells and exaggerates itself to the point of usurping the entire existence."[21] But all religions contain at least some element of asceticism; they vary in the amount of emphasis or development afforded to this way of living. If it is true that a man does become more sacred, more like a god, "only by efforts made to separate himself from the profane," then certainly fasting, celibacy and chastity, silence, and various other self-deprivations and self-punishments are necessary to achieve even near-sainthood, let alone semi-divinity. Among the least of these, obviously, but certainly among those necessary, is deprivation of reading about sex.

Malinowski has supplied perhaps the best summation of the significance of taboo in society. He states that even in what appear to be completely licentious cultures, there is no evidence of anything like promiscuity. Without exception he finds that in every human culture there are "...systems of well-defined taboos which rigidly separate a number of people of opposite sexes and exclude whole categories of potential partners." Obviously, these taboos are most complex when they deal with the sexual relations of man and woman; "...there is no simple biological release mechanism in man, but instead there is a combined psychological and physiological process determined by cultural tradition. Associated with it and supplementing it is a system of cultural taboos which limit considerably the working of the sexual impulse."[22]

Or, as he put it in another context (a discussion of the significance of the absence of rut--purely biologically motivated mating--in man), "the sexual impulse is not confined to any season, not conditioned by any bodily process, and, as far as more physiological forces are concerned, it is there to affect at any moment the life of man and woman. " So, if it were not for the inhibiting social factors which control and restrict sexual desires, if it were not for man's self-imposed taboos, "this impulse, absorbing and pervading as it is, would ... interfere with all normal occupations of man, would destroy any budding form of association, would create chaos from within and would invite dangers from without. " Malinowski followed this fine flourish of rhetoric with the flat justification that "...this is not a mere phantasy; the sex impulse has been the source of most trouble from Adam and Eve onwards. "23

This argument has been made frequently, for it serves as a defense for practically every taboo ever imposed or yet to be thought of; indeed, it would serve as a powerful pro-censorship plea. If, as Malinowski says, "there must be taboos which prevent sex from constantly interfering in ordinary life" and if "man is endowed with sexual tendencies but these have to be moulded ... by systems of cultural rules ...,"24 surely censorship of the written word is one of the more reasonable of such "cultural rules. " It is obviously less final and punitive than asceticism (self-imposed chastity), emasculation, or limitation of copulation to procreative purposes only--all, at various times, approved by various "cultural rules. "

There is not complete acceptance of this explanation. For example, Georges Bataille's ideas may be of some corrective benefit in their emphasis upon the psychological aspects of sexuality. His separation of eroticism from "simple sexual activity" is clear from his definition: "Eroticism ... is a psychological quest independent of the natural goal: reproduction and the desire for children. "25 The progress of mankind, in relation to its attitude to sex, has been "...moving imperceptibly from unashamed sexuality to sexuality with shame, which gave birth to eroticism. "26 Sexual taboos are a product of this shame, rather than a cultural mechanism to keep the lid on rampant sexuality. While taboos in most cases are really religious taboos, the taboo on eroticism, as he describes it, has a dual significance. It is, of course, first of all a forbidding, a denial; but it is also an indication of a strong desire. Without the desire, why would the taboo be necessary?

While desire is one aspect of the psychology of

eroticism, shame is another, and can be understood by com-
parison to the human response to death. Bataille's lengthy
examination of the relationship between death and eroticism
leads him to the conclusion that "man is an animal who
stands abashed in front of death or sexual union. He may
be more or less abashed, but in either case his reaction
differs from that of other animals."27 Putting it very simply, man is afraid of both the act of sex and the certainty
of death, and will do almost anything to shield himself--and
other men--from the real facts of life and death. Man's
urge to live is basic, but it is so overweening an urge that
it assumes a primary importance that brings with it the taboo. Management of the urge to live then becomes a basis
for the control of eroticism. This theory, anchored in an
individualistic psychology, speaks against the idea of taboo
as social control.

     Malinowski and Bataille are in agreement on one
phase of the significance of sexual taboo, but with somewhat
different reactions in that agreement. Bataille does believe
that the function of sex taboos is to restrain the sex impulse and lead to its sublimation. He says, "work demands
the sort of conduct where effort is in a constant ratio with
productive efficiency. It demands rational behavior where
the wild impulses ... are frowned upon. If we were unable
to repress these impulses we should not be able to work."28
But taboos are not fixed and unalterable. Bataille goes so
far as to say that "the transgression does not deny the taboo
but transcends it and completes it."29 Very few taboos, if
any, are really absolute, so the taboo is modified, regulated,
explained, clarified, or, in Bataille's phrase, given "limited
licence." And, in the world of censorship, there has been
very little (except where specific titles were proscribed, as
in the Index Expurgatorius of the Roman Catholic Church)
that was really specific and definite--at least until the years
during which the U.S. Supreme Court insisted that federal,
state, and municipal laws dealing with obscenity and pornography be almost fantastically precise and in agreement.
(And that period ended with the decisions of June 21, 1973--
see Chapter 15.)

     The mere existence of a taboo, with all of its threat
to the individual and the group, as is obvious, does not mean
it will not be violated. For man, in his full measure, stands
in opposition to the dead hand of tradition. The Promethean
myth is repeated in various guises in many cultures, not that
it really requires mythic heroes to carry through on the

natural consequences of sexual desire, but the persuasive-
ness of tradition and its priestly allies foretold a tragic
destiny to any innovator.

The figures who have defied taboos are the heroes of
the humanist tradition, but not of the general populace. They
stand as victimized by the gods or by society, which would
like to hold for itself the disposition of the fearsome powers
these heroes release. We will not acknowledge these forces
because of the supposed peril they bring. But the forces
are there. One of the wisest books ever published on the
whole subject of Sex in Civilization (its title) states in the
preface that "the most significant aspect of our civilization
... is pretence. Pretence is the key to modern civilization...."30

And what was true of 1929 is surely as true of 1974,
indeed of practically any times of which we have record.
Primitive man said one thing and did another in the sexual
area, so far as we can ascertain; so, of course, did Assyrian man and Greek man and Hebrew man and Puritan man
and Victorian man. And so do we.

To say that we are human seems to be the same
thing as saying we are inconsistent. The thoroughgoing
saint is as infrequent in human history as the absolute sinner. When St. Augustine, in perhaps the most commonly
quoted section of his Confessions, begged of the Lord to
make him chaste and continent, he also added "...but not
yet. " It was a very human thing to do.

This raison d'être for the taboo is equally one of the
reasons for the existence of censorship. If reading about
eroticism encourages "the wild impulses, " then there will be
less time for the workaday world. The censor, then, in a
sense, supposedly assists the Establishment to maintain itself, for without an efficient, hard-working, general population, no nation can long endure. And the censor removes
the temptations to "waste" time in sexual activity--time
which, from an economic standpoint, could better be spent
in work or at least in serious activity.

Reading about eroticism, too, will carry a stigma of
guilt by association, and the language used will be judged by
the standards used to consider behavior. The idea of taboo
can be analyzed from this standpoint of the way taboo rules
work in practice among primitives. These obey the rules

of the language (often complicated enough) with the same
critical indifference as they display to the rules of society.
The power of the act becomes the power of the word. In
general, the logic is something like this: sexual intercourse
is a bad thing, so one abstains from the bad to achieve the
good in action, thought, and language. It is perfectly reasonable, therefore, for our modern censors to wish to deny
reading about copulation in order to achieve "good results";
thus censorship, from this viewpoint, is an enforced continence or abstinence, even if one step removed from actuality. This interplay can be considered as distinct from the
social character of certain words and sounds, which will be
treated in the following chapter.

It is this semi-automatic working of the taboo which
is reflected in the modern techniques of censorship. Just
as Lévy-Bruhl said of the primitive that he will not ask himself if it is demonstrably true that a taboo violation will result in utter ruin for his whole group; so the general public
today really is not willing to question the need for a multi-
level censorship. Like the primitive, who, Lévy-Bruhl
feels, does what he does because of what his ancestors always thought, most people, if asked, "why do we need censorship?" will wonder about the question, rather than about
the fact of censorship's existence. Censorship, like all taboos, has a built-in self-justification, composed of a combination of illogic, emotion, and at least a semi-religious
background.

Lévy-Bruhl's analysis of taboo points out that most
often primitive tribes "reason" from a result back to a
cause. [31] Surely the history of censorship gives a multitude
of examples of this "back-formation." Juvenile delinquency
has to be the result of reading sexy novels; rape follows
reading about rape; premarital sex relations must have as
their basic cause the reading of immoral books. What other
reasons could there possibly be for these social deviations?

The explanations of the modern censor and the mind
of the primitive may be far apart in time and space, yet
there are other quite recognizable likenesses. For example,
listen to Lévy-Bruhl's explanation of the difference between
the civilized view of a transgression, sin, or crime and
what this means to a primitive: "To us a transgression
signifies the violation of a rule, the infringement of a material or a moral law. To primitives, it is an abnormality,
something unusual and unheard of--a sinister omen, the

manifestation of a malign and unseen power ... our point of
view is juridical and ethical; that of the primitives is above
all mystic. "[32]

        In modern society, repression within the individual has
in large part taken over the role which taboo played in primitive societies. This kind of "repression" is really another
name for neurosis. But even if the individual is not neurotic, he is deterred from actions not acceptable to society by
what J. C. Flugel variously describes as conscience or rational restraint--which is really a sort of self-censorship.
Flugel claims that civilized man has his own set of taboos--
but he calls them laws, religious codes, superstitions, conventions, and even "good manners. "[33] Whether sexual taboos come up in consideration of who may marry whom, or
the timing of the sexual act itself, or in other matters related to man's sexual nature, they are all taboos, of which
evidences can be found far closer to home than among head-
hunters in the Celebes or in primitive man or in simply uncivilized man. If, as Leslie White has graphically demonstrated, civilized man can be said to have existed only since
the beginnings of metallurgy in the last less than one per
cent of cultural history, it should hardly be unexpected to
find that the influences of precivilization are still quite
strong. White categorically states that "a mature, urbane,
and rational civilization is not to be achieved in a mere million years from the anthropoid level. "[34]

        The fact that no divorced man has yet succeeded in
winning the Presidency of the United States should exemplify
the importance Americans, even of our comparatively "free"
generation, place on old taboos. It is the implied and covert
imputation of sexual immorality to a leading U. S. politician,
even more than the accusation of an extremely confused reaction to a stress situation, which makes what happened at
a rural bridge one night likely to affect our national politics
for decades to come. We can stand having our entertainers
and our littérateurs become taboo-breakers, but not our top
politicians. They must at least not be either blatant or care-
less in their sexual pecadilloes. Being suspected is almost
as bad as being caught, where non-permissible sexual activity is involved, especially for politicians.

        Any objective study of the vagaries of censorship of
writing about sex in the half-millenium or so of its recorded
history should serve to convince one that it is the censor,
as much as primitive man, who acts as if violation of his

rules is "the manifestation of a malign and unseen power, "
as if to read or write or distribute any erotic material were
as heinous a crime as violating a primitive taboo.   Surely
these are the kinds of transgressions which will bring down
the righteous wrath of God, let alone of man.   Taboo and
the consequences of their violation are not just primitive
ideas.   They are with us today.

       As Sir James Frazer wrote over sixty years ago,
"It seems most improbable that in our own rules of conduct,
in what we call the common decencies of life as well as in
the weightier matters of morality, there may survive not a
few old savage taboos, which, masquerading as an expression of the divine will or draped in the flowing robes of a
false philosophy, have maintained their credit long after the
crude ideas out of which they sprang have been discarded by
the progress of thought and knowledge. ... "35   This sounds
as if it were written for 1974--as if the Edwardian-era
anthropologist and folklorist was explaining the reasons for
modern censorship.

3. THE WORD AND THE FLESH

"We should have a great many fewer disputes in the world if words were taken for what they are, the signs of our ideas only, and not for things themselves."

> --John Locke,
> An Essay Concerning Human Understanding,
> 1960

Chapter 3

THE WORD AND THE FLESH

Since men communicate by means of words and language, once we are past the remote predawning of the beginnings of man, it is essential to understand the role of words in the control of men's thought. How one looks at this is, of course, dependent on how one looks at the place of the word in human life.

As far back as we can determine, and certainly attested to by the example of present-day primitive tribes, man has been afraid of the word. Father Walter J. Ong has written, "The word in its original habitat of sound ... is not a record at all. The word is something that happens, an event in the world of sound through which the mind is enabled to relate actuality to itself."[1]

In oral culture (to use Father Ong's terminology), "One can ask about something, no one can look up anything."[2] We today are in the alphabet and print stage of culture, rapidly developing into what Father Ong calls the "electronic" stage. Where we are in the varieties of communications media certainly determines a good deal of how we live.

Let us look for a moment at the way primitive, uncivilized man dealt with significant words. There is, of course, no question that even in civilized society, that is, among those who believe in the Judeo-Christian faiths, Islam, or Buddhism, for example, certain ineffable names of God are not permitted to be used or are at least reserved for very special occasions and special people to say or write. If you disagree with this, and you happen to be Jewish, consider the fact that even today no Orthodox Jew will read the two Hebrew letters which spell out "Jehovah" as such, but will rather look at letters which say one thing and read off another, "Adonai." Among Christians, as a comparable

21

phenomenon, the Catholic Holy Name Society has an aversion
to blasphemy.   There are many other examples of reluctance
to utter certain words.

Perhaps a clearer statement of all this is simply to
remind Christians of the fact that the New Testament states
unequivocally (in a new, modern version), "When all things
began, the Word already was.   The Word dwelt with God,
and what God was, the Word was.   The Word, then, was
with God at the beginning ... So the Word became Flesh. ... "3
This kind of unequivocal statement of the primacy of the
word has had a very strong effect on Christian acceptance
of the basic importance of what is written and what is said.

The lines at the beginning of the Fourth Gospel have
been a center of controversy and misunderstanding since they
were written, for, literally speaking, they identify Logos
(God's mind) with the Word, and the Word with the Flesh.
The Flesh referred to, of course, is God Incarnate--Jesus
Christ.   John, the disciple of Jesus, who wrote the Fourth
Gospel, used the word "Logos" (he wrote in Greek, of
course), but the best-known translation (the King James version) rendered this term--susceptible to a great many inter-
pretations--as "the Word." Logos has been interpreted in
many ways: as meaning the Second Person in the Trinity;
as referring to the power of God to affect actions by speaking; as meaning "God's communication to the Prophets and
others who are to speak out for him ... "; as referring to
the divine speech, to those who wrote the Bible; and, finally,
as what is actually written in the Bible. 4   Father Ong's discussion suggests the psychology that fostered the elevation
of the word.   The word is an event that captures actuality;
and as the sole representation of event in pre-literate cultures, it contains the full meaning of that event and assumes
a sacred import.   Historically this application of the word
came about through identification in the Hebrew wisdom literature of "word" with God's word or wisdom.   Wisdom then
was a manifestation of God, and Christians on this basis
proceeded to employ "logos" as representing God incarnate.

The reverence for God's words in both Testaments
and the related emphasis given to language by the first lines
of the Fourth Gospel combine to give words and language a
singular importance in the Judeo-Christian ethic.   Father
Ong, indeed, says that "the focal point of Hebrew, and, even
more, of Christian belief is found in a culture which for historical reasons makes so much of the word. ... "5   If

traditional Christianity has put such ultimate importance in the Word (or language) as to equate it with the Christian Deity, then certainly what gets said or written is of great consequence. The pious Christian, then, will be almost as intimidated from reading what is written or said about sexual conduct as he is from repeating what is generally accepted as the original sin.

Very simply put, this comes down to saying that it must be logical and reasonable, once one has accepted the premise that God is the Word, that anyone who "profanes" the word--by blasphemy, obscenity, or pornography--is really profaning the center of faith, the core of belief, the Holy of Holies. Getting back to the belief in the magical power of words among practically all men, S. J. Tambih, looking at this anthropologically, has made a most clear statement of the true significance of language: "There is a sense in which it is true to say that language is outside us, given to us as a part of our cultural and historical heritage; at the same time language is within us, it moves us, and we generate it as active agents. Since words exist and are in a sense agents in themselves which establish connections and relations between both man and man, and man and the world, and are capable of 'acting' upon them, they are one of the most realistic representations we have of the concept of force which is either not directly observable or is a metaphysical notion which we find necessary to use."[6]

The potency of words causes them to assume magic powers and so themselves become taboo. Certain words in primitive cultures are interdicted, because some utterance of words under certain circumstances is believed to effect certain consequences. Since the primitive savage cannot discriminate between words and things, the savage has a tendency to believe that there is a "real and substantial bond" between a name and the person or thing it stands for.[7] Thus the savage is very like the child, in seeing that all that he has to do is say something, and then consequences naturally ensue.

Primitive peoples have always put a special magic in words, sometimes ascribing a greater power for good--or, more commonly, evil--to the spoken or inscribed or written word than to the action it symbolized. Among the American Indians, for example, words have always been much more than a means of communication or self-expression. As anthropologist Margot Astrov has put it, to the Indian the

word really has what she describes as "creative potency."
She gives many examples to corroborate the fact that among
tribes all over the North American continent it was taken as
an article of faith that the word served in an important way
to maintain and to prolong the individual's life. [8]

The word, for the American Indian, has a palliative,
a healing, even a creative strength, a strength which cannot
be put into effect without the word. For most of us words
may not be quite as important as this; but probably for all
of us there are some words which do have a kind of a magic
or "creatively potent" effect.

Of course, for most of us words are simply means
of expressing ideas and exchanging facts, of communication.
But in all countries and times there has been a strong faith
in words as magic. Indeed, as John Condon has said, "At
the root of the attitude of magic is the assumption that words
are part of the thing to which they refer...."[9] Both as
symbol and in actuality, words, to the believer in magic,
come before the thing to which they refer, and are, as spells
and taboos, of prime importance in the business of living.
The ogre who said "fe-fi-fo-fum" would not have been able
to detect the Englishman, he knew very well, if he did not
say words--and they had to be the right words in the right
order to accomplish what he was after. This phenomenon
of hypostatization of the word (Ernst Cassirer's phrase)--the
idea that the name of a thing and its essence have a necessary and invariable relation to each other--is one of the
most basic considerations behind the whole idea of censorship. Once we grant that by referring to sex or its manifestations we are dealing with the actual phenomena connected with sex, we have arrived at an emotional and even
metaphysical impasse which is hard to solve without simply
proscribing the utterance of depiction or writing of the words
involved.

Taboos, as such, have already been discussed, but
verbal taboos deserve some separate attention. The fear of
the word is a phenomenon long predating the beginnings of
Christianity or even of Judaism. The great historian and
theoretician of language, Otto Jespersen, has written:
"...under certain circumstances, at certain times, in certain places, the use of one or more definite words is interdicted, because it is superstitiously believed to entail certain
evil consequences...."[10] And our modern-day censors, who
interdict the use of specific words (particularly those most

commonly referred to as "four-letter words," although it is really their content, rather than their length, which defines them as "obscene"), are simply following in historical footsteps whose marks can be traced back a long, long way.

The old folk dictum, expressed in the children's phrase, "Sticks and stones may break my bones, but words can never hurt me," is, unfortunately, not widely accepted once one is beyond childhood in age, if not in philosophy. Leaving aside even the laws on libel and slander, the laws against obscenity and pornography are quite clearly there to carry out the idea that words can indeed hurt one. This is nothing new in the history of civilization. "To Western Europe the peoples in the Mediterranean, accustomed for thirty centuries to an alphabet, the written word is something of a magical charm," says anthropologist Paul Radin. "In the beginning," he continues, "was the Word, i. e., the written word. In its manifold repercussions this worship of the written word finally included the unwritten word, extended itself until it ended in the deification of thought. Thus the word and thought became a thing in themselves, living in real entities, instead of retaining their old function of merely giving validity to certain reality."[11] It is far from proven, as we have already noted, that modern man is free of primitivism. Modern civilization has simply added the written word, whose advent, as Radin says, makes the real difference between the way that primitive man acted and the way that civilized man behaves.

Involved in verbal taboos is the verbal expression of sex. J. C. Flugel has said that "...the whole sphere of sex is, of course, still the most taboo-ridden of all subjects in the modern world...." In discussing verbal taboos he points out that "forbidden" words (those dealing with sex), despite prohibitions to the contrary, can be and are used quite frequently to serve as scapegoats on which hostile feelings can be vented.[12] Their forbidden character is sufficiently present to make these words serve in the role of vehicles for the displacement of our hostile feelings. We vent our frustration by using the tabooed words, even though, as we all know, the actual meaning of what we say may well be totally irrelevant to the situation as it exists. When one hits his finger with a hammer in the process of performing a humdrum household chore and reacts by saying a blasphemous, or scatological, or obscene term, it is a pretty normal way of verbalizing the resulting hurt and anger and frustration (and usually all of these are really reactions to one's

own incompetence) to say the "bad" word or words.   Surely
this is better than taking up the hammer and hitting oneself
or another person!

In the long history of verbal taboos it has been found
that obscene words are usually much closer to actual action
than the other kinds of commonly tabooed words.   Ferenczi,
an associate of Freud, stated that such words had retained
to a greater extent than others their original close connection with the things or actions they denoted. [13]   Flugel has
said that "... when we swear we enjoy a 'sudden glory' that
is derived from a temporary overthrow and defiance of our
super-ego, and of the social authorities from which our
super-ego is derived. "[14]   If the Flugel theory is correct,
the censor who denies the individual the chance to read or
speak so-called "safety-valve" words is really doing a great
disservice to both the individual and society.   He may be
keeping the taboo language away from so-called "innocent"
eyes and ears, yet he is almost certainly affecting adversely
the not-so-innocent who, these days, are not far from being
in the majority.

The general use of taboo words today has, as is well-
known, changed from even the customs of a decade ago.
Edward Sagarin, a sociologist who has probably done more
study on so-called "dirty words" than anyone else now writing, says (and it would be hard to dispute him), "no longer
are there any unprintables, except for those who do not care
to print them. "[15]   He says that the fact that our official culture finds much of what is now written, published, and read
to be immoral and outrageous is no proof that it really is
so. [16]

Given the powerful voices that reject the legitimacy
of expression about sex, even if printable, there is no as-
surance that literary permissiveness will never be curtailed,
for a most interesting paradox develops here.   Using Sagarin's definition that "pornography is the socially disapproved
appeal to the libido, "[17] or our own broad discussion of the
irrationalities of societal norms, there does evolve the possibility that an excess of public statement about sex will result in an actual negative reaction to the "pornography revolution. "   Thus, if not a new wave of Puritanism, at least a
quasi-Puritanical reaction may ensue.   Indeed, something
like this did happen after the brief, but certainly merry,
reign in England of Charles II.   The comparatively austere
period, culturally speaking, which followed may well have

been part of a normally to-be-expected cycle.

That the verbal taboo has a powerful religious connection is generally agreed by scholars. Among the ancient
Egyptians, for example, there was certainly widespread assumption that words were sacred things. The noted Egyptol-
ogist James Henry Breasted describes the ancient Egyptian
religious theory in this fashion: "The extraordinary basis
of this early system is the fundamental assumption that mind
or thought is the source of everything.... The agency by
which mind became creative force was the spoken word
which enunciated the idea and gave it reality. So the idea
becomes reality via the medium of the word." Furthermore,
"...the god himself is identified with the heart which thinks
and the tongue which speaks."[18]

Breasted suggests that this is possibly "the prehistor-
ical background of the Logos doctrine of New Testament
days...." He dates the manuscript from which he derived
these ideas of ancient Egyptian belief back to about 3400
B. C., and describes what is found therein as "...the oldest
thoughts of men that have anywhere come down to us in written form."[19] (And the Logos doctrine clearly bears a
strong resemblance to the beliefs of the First Dynasty in
Egypt).

British archaeologist V. Gordon Childe reminds us of
the sheer difficulty of writing in Egyptian hieroglyphic and
hieratic scripts, especially when their alphabet, added to the
ideograms and determinatives, required about 500 characters.
Reading in ancient Egypt was "...a mystery initiation into
which was obtainable only by a prolonged schooling." Under
these difficulties of writing and reading, it was, says Childe,
to be expected that "...words ... must seem to possess an
authority of their own. The immortalization of a word in
writing must have seemed a supernatural process...." And
what else could it be but magic that a dead man "...could
still speak from a clay tablet or a papyrus roll?"[20]

If the word is primal and basic for mankind as far
back as ancient Egypt, it is not unexpected that it is basic
in the Hebrew Old Testament and to the Judaic idea of law.
The fact that the Jews are known as "The People of the
Book" is significant. The origin of sacred words and the
idea of holiness in taboo is not quickly perceived. For example, at an early point in the history of the tribe the magical power of the name of Yahweh was recognized. To know

the name conferred on the user power over the enemy. If
Gentiles knew the name they could even use the power of the
Jews' own God against them! As was already stated, the
names could be no less powerful than the Being represented,
and God's pronouncements were always literally true, no
matter how puzzling they were as the centuries blurred their
original intent. The schools of mystical exegesis among the
ancient Hebrews professed to discover inner meanings and
created elaborate mystical systems while never casting in
doubt the literal truth of God's words. [21]

The Jewish-Greek philosopher, Philo of Alexandria,
who lived during the late first century B.C. and the early
part of the first century A.D., was the first to offer a doctrine of the logos in post-Biblical days. [22] But his reconcil-
iation of Platonic theory and Judaism did not influence the
Apostle John in the wording and thought in the beginning of
the Fourth Gospel, because Philo's logos was not God in His
essence but rather the means for His action.

What Philo was attempting to do was to combine the
Platonic doctrine of ideas, the Stoic "logoi spermatoikoi"
which permeate the cosmos, and Jewish angelology. For
Philo, the logos is "the unity of ideas, the simple source of
all cosmic powers, and the highest of the angels."[23] This
has been transmogrified, in Christian theology, to relate
mainly to the idea of the Second Person, "...the pre-existent
heavenly Christ of whom it is said that He was made flesh
in Jesus, the Christ born among men."[24] For Philo, a
Greek Jew who remained a Jew, the logos (with a small letter l) was a mediating force between God and man--literally
the word, communicating. For St. Paul, a Hellenistic Jew
converted to Christianity, "Jesus was God's Logos."[25] But
Paul went further than either Philo or the Apostle John, and
he used an older Jewish term (Messiah) as the appellation
for the Logos. This was certainly a brand-new way of looking at the Logos concept.

New Testament scholar Rudolf Bultmann has an important insight to contribute here. He sees Jesus as "...the
bearer of the word...." For, Bultmann says, it is the fact
that "man is constrained to decision by the word which
brings a new element into his situation, and the word therefore becomes to him an event...."[26] Bultmann has sought
to reconstruct the contemporaneous elements of the Christian
mythology and for him, "the Gospel of John cannot be taken
into account at all as a source for the teaching of Jesus...."

Bultmann's exclusion of everything in the synoptic gospels
which for various reasons, such as what they contained or
the language in which they were written, could have origin-
ated only in Hellenistic Christianity is, as he says, intended
to get back to the true historical Jesus. [27] This was the
Jesus who lived in Palestine, was Jewish, and spoke Ara-
maic (the Semitic language which dates from about 300 B.C.
until the seventh century A.D. and was the everyday language of a great part of Southeast Asia, including Palestine).
But Bultmann, in denying the significance of the Greek addition to the type of Christianity he is looking for, the basically Jesus-centered Christianity, still sees the vital importance
of the Word to the Christian religion. Although foreign to
the events of his own ministry, Christ as the Word has been
philosophically more influential than primitive Christology.

What is of import in all this, as related to the origins of censorship, is that there seems to be little change,
except in greater sophistication and complexity of thought,
from the savage to the Egyptian to the Jew to the Greek to
the Christian, in accepting, one way or the other, the absolute sacredness of the Word. And a Word which is sacred
invests almost all words with at least a magic power, if not
necessarily a sacred one. Magic reigns by fear--and the
censor lurks in the fear of the word and its powers.

Censorship, then, is a long-lasting operation built into
all societies which exalt the word. Thus we can easily understand why it has been so persistent. Especially where
the sense of sin has been a feature of conscience, words
are too portentous to be used with freedom. So, there has
never been any period in the Western world of the past two
thousand years or more when there has been a complete absence of sexual suppression. The clear danger of repressing
bad language perpetuates the tendency of such suppression.
Needless to say, the concept that certain words are so bad
or dangerous that they cannot or must not be used is at the
core of many attempts to limit the free expression not only
of words, but of ideas in speech and writing. If it were
recognized that the words themselves are no more than verbal symbols and can not work magic by forcing people to
commit presumably socially awkward or dangerous sexual or
other acts, this would go a long way toward solving the
problem of censorship.

It is pretty well-established that mankind has not pro-
gressed very far beyond what the Kronhausens refer to as

"the period of animistic worship,"[28] at least so far as our
nearly unquestioning acceptance of the intrinsic power of
words is concerned. The Kronhausens feel that no matter
what our good intentions, we still have a tendency to ascribe
to obscene words a certain mystery, a real power which is
fostered by keeping up a taboo against their use, especially
in print. "Thus," they say, "censorship turns out to be essentially an anxiety operation on the part of society. As
long as society feels itself threatened by the use of 'obscene' words, it will continue to exert some degree of censorship on this basis alone in literature and in speech."
They continue, "If freedom of expression is a sign of a mature society, then the frivolous suppression of words and/or
ideas by certain censorious groups must be recognized for
what it is: the symptom of a social neurosis defending its
own illness, and thereby contributing to a continuance of that
illness for the society as a whole."[29]

They go so far as to say that censorship is the main
weapon of attack to bring about the social repression of sexuality.[30] As Mark Twain said, long ago, "Man is mostly
and exclusively the immodest animal, for he is the only one
with a soiled mind, the only one under dominion of a false
shame." What Mark Twain implies is that man himself
must claim responsibility for this soiling, and the source of
his shame does not repose in language.

C. K. Ogden and I. A. Richards have probably been
more significant in the study of semantics than any critics
of our century; in their pioneering work, The Meaning of
Meaning, they devote an entire chapter to "The Power of
Words." After discussing at length the prevalence of "verbal
superstition" in primitive and classic Greco-Roman times,
they deplore what they see as the persistence of a "primitive
linguistic outlook," not only as significant among the whole
religious world, but in the work of the profoundest thinkers,
religious or not. They find this phenomenon "...one of the
most curious features of modern thought."[31]

In a supplement to the Ogden-Richards volume, anthropologist Malinowski cites what he calls "the innumerable
superstitions--the agnostic's fear of blasphemy or at least
reluctance to use it, the active dislike of obscene language,
the power of swearing [which show] that in the normal use of
words the bond between symbol and referent is more than a
mere convention."[32] This is pretty strong language, but research has indicated its truth.

It is not words which cause our troubles, but rather
the role in our lives which we permit them to have. Words
control us because of our desire, our willingness, to be controlled by them. It is unfortunate indeed that the words and
the wills over which we do have some control cannot be considered as fully responsible for whatever troubles we may
have; there is always the threatening figure of the Censor,
who (whether legally or extra-legally) does his best--or
worst--to see to it that we do not even have the opportunity
to read or see the words which a great many people would
like to use or read or see.

INTERLUDE

PORTRAIT OF A CENSOR:

1. CATO (234-149 B.C.)

"...the lash of his tongue might fall upon any man present, but it was pleasant to see it descend upon one's neighbor. Cato fought corruption recklessly, and seldom let the sun set without having made new enemies. Few loved him, for his scar-covered face and wild red hair disconcerted them, his big teeth threatened them, his asceticism shamed them, his industry left them lagging, his green eyes looked through their words into their selfishness ... when their [the farmers'] votes made him censor, all Rome shuddered.... He expelled Manilius from the Senate for kissing his wife in public; as for himself, he said, he never embraced his wife except when it thundered--though he was glad when it thundered.... After five years of heroic opposition to the nature of man, he retired from office ... he seems to have been sincere in his conviction that an education in Greek literature and philosophy could so rapidly dissolve the religious beliefs of young Romans that their moral life would be left defenseless against the instincts of acquisition, pugnacity, and sex. His condemnation ... took in Socrates; that prattling old midwife, Cato thought, had been rightly prisoned for undermining the morals and laws of Athens.... "

--Will Durant, <u>Caesar and Christ</u>, 1944.

"He was of ruddy complexion and grey-eyed; as the writer, who, with no good-will, made the following epigram upon him lets us see:

> Porcius, who snarls at all in every place,
> With his grey eyes, and with his fiery face,
> Even after death will scarce admitted be
> Into the infernal realms by Hecate. "

--Plutarch, "Marcus Cato," in: <u>The Lives of
the Noble Grecians and Romans</u>, tr. & rev., 1864.

32

4. HELLENISM, STOICISM, AND CENSORSHIP

"Who can change the opinions of men?   And without a change of sentiments what can you make but reluctant slaves and hypocrites?"

--Marcus Aurelius,
Meditations, 180 A.D.

Chapter 4

HELLENISM, STOICISM, AND CENSORSHIP

Of all civilizations which have exerted their influence
on modern man, perhaps the Greek--particularly during its
highest point, the Age of Pericles--best exemplified a civilization whose people at least attempted to live so that there
was a maximum of freedom (at least for Greek citizens) and
a minimum of repression, including censorship.

Any study of the relationship of ethics to sexual conduct, and especially of restrictive conduct relating to sex,
must begin with a study of what the ancient Greeks thought
and did. In the words of Professor Gilbert Murray, perhaps
the greatest of all authorities on ancient Greek civilization,
Hellenism was "...in the fullest sense a humane civilization. "[1]

In the Periclean Age of Greece (approximately 495-
322 B. C., from the birth of Pericles to the death of Aristotle), "the old rules and taboos and superstitions were gone, "
and "life must depend not upon force but upon free speech
and persuasion. "[2] Despite the existence of many gods,
Greece at its civilized peak was notable, Murray stresses,
for "the absence of authoritative orthodoxy and censorship. "
It was, after all, in ancient Greece that Lysistrata was written and then presented publicly. And Lysistrata put no author in prison, and caused no censorship stir. [3]

Murray gives what he calls a "causally connected"
series of qualities of Greek life, qualities which may well
be compared with those of today's American civilization:
"the wreck of ordered tribal traditions and taboos in the
Heroic Age, the unsacerdotal and un-superstitious background, the consequent absence of dogmatism and censorship,
the freedom of thought and speech, the consciousness that
our enemies have something to say for themselves and ought
to be understood, the enjoyment of drama and dialectic, and

34

lastly the use of both as instruments in the search for truth. "[4]

(It is not necessary to agree with Murray's interesting metaphor, which explains the comparative freedom of the Greek mind by pointing out that the Greek wore less clothing than most civilized men--at most a robe, an under-robe, a belt, and, on occasion, two sandals--and just as these did not hamper his body movements, so his lack of a ceremonial preconception let his mind go free, but it is a rather striking one. To carry this to our times would be to say that the ecdysiast, the member of the nudist cult, and the Oh! Calcutta! cast are, or should be, our leading philosophers!).

The basic difference between the Greek ethic and the Judeo-Christian ethic is that the first sees the good life, as Murray puts it, "as the performance of a function or duty by a member in an organism" or "...a free will working with God for the achievement of his unknown purpose, "[5] as compared to the modern, accepted Western civilization idea of a system of sins and punishments. Follow the first philosophy, and nothing is "wrong" to start with. It must be proven wrong by what it causes. The second philosophy must have some form of censorship as its adjunct, because without censorship a pre-conceived "wrong" will certainly be promulgated. Greek ethics (excepting Platonic ethics) is as experimental and humanistic as Christian ethics is rule-bound and authoritarian. The pre-Hellenistic Greek judged by praxis; modern man by fiat, by already set down rules and regulations. A modern-day Heraclitus, who would talk of never setting foot in the same stream of water twice, would be hard to find--and even harder to emulate.

In G. Lowes Dickinson's characterization, the Greek "...in the Puritan meaning of the phrase ... had no sense of sin. If an ancient Greek did something wrong, he would be punished for it; Aeschylus says, 'Blood calls for blood'. " Or, to put it another way, Dickinson contrasts the Greek and the Christian point of view on these matters by saying that the Greeks had a "...conception of sin as a physical contagion to be aired by external rites, " while today's conservative Christian moralists see sin "...as an affection of the conscience which only 'grace' can expel. " In classical Greece, if a man committed a misdeed, the Greek ethic told him that he would be suitably punished by something going wrong in his life--illness, or other personal misfortune. He suffered no pangs of conscience, felt no concern about

punishment from the gods; Dickinson avers that there is no
trace of either remorse or repentance in the Greek attitude
on sin. 6

Under these circumstances, how could the Greek pro-
fitably foster or encourage censorship? If he felt no sin had
been committed in whatever sexual activity he performed, he
could not reasonably countenance repression or denial on the
reporting of matters of sex, as in a play.   Certainly a language like classical Greek, which did not even contain in its
vocabulary a word which meant "chastity," was not an appropriate one for the censor.

Another aspect of Greek morality which was opposed
to censorship was the general acceptance of the middle way
as the right way to live.   Solon is credited with the apo-
thegm, "nothing in excess"; and Aristotle based his entire
ethical theory on this idea.   The basic classical Greek assumption was "...that it is not passions or desires in themselves that must be regarded as bad, but only their dispro-
portional or misdirected indulgence. "7   Where the Puritan
would give up all sensual pleasures, since they are entirely
and absolutely wrong, the moral Greek is temperate in his
actions concerning these matters, as in all his way of living.

Certainly asceticism was no part of the Greek ideal,
since it was obviously one extreme.   Equally, libertinism,
or license, was equally far from Greek ethical concepts.
As Dickinson phrases it, "...the ultimate test of true worth
in pleasure, as in everything else, is the trained judgment
of the good and sensible man. "8   So, if there was an accepted censorship among the Greeks of the Heroic Age, it
was self-censorship, the "trained judgment of the good and
sensible man. "   And he did not judge for others, nor did
his government; he did it himself, for himself.

The early Romans, according to one of the best modern chroniclers of the history of human morals, "...were
a people of steady habits, disciplined, hard-working...."
Brinton compares them to "...the early Jews ... the Spar-
tans ... the Scots and the early New Englanders. "9   They
were "moral"--in the sense we understand the word today--
simply because it was the thing for Romans to do.   It was
not until the fifth century B.C. that the office of censor was
deemed necessary in Rome.

The first institutional office ever to be set up by a

civilized government to regulate the morals of its citizens
was the Roman censorship, which began its activities in 443
B. C. Every fifth year two censors were chosen by the Cen-
turial Assembly (Will Durant calls this group "... a frankly
conservative and aristocratic institution") to serve for eight-
een-month terms. These censors had as a basic responsibility the quinquennial census of Roman citizens; to count the
citizens, they had to set standards for citizenship; among
these standards was the question of whether each reputed
citizen was guilty or not guilty of immorality or any other
crime.

For political and military purposes, and to determine
appropriate taxation, the censors had the obligation to mark
off the name of any man whose public or private conduct
they disapproved. It was each censor's own responsibility--
without even any veto power from his colleagues or from
the Roman Senate--to decide where every Roman individual
fit into the highly classified scheme of Roman life. And
certainly not every censor was another Cato, incorruptible
and scrupulously fair.

In some ways the Roman censorship was above even
the Consulship. The censors were, in a sense, above even
the Senate and the knights, since they were the ones who
issued lists of persons eligible for those particular offices.
If a Senator was notoriously profligate or licentious or dis-
honorable, it was the censor's duty to mark him as unfit
for office. [10] So the Roman censor, who policed the morals
of the Roman citizens, gave his name to his successors who
judged the morals of what was written and performed and
displayed for the edification and entertainment of all citizens
in the centuries to come.

The most famous of Roman censors was Cato, the
Elder, usually referred to as Cato the Censor (234-149
B. C.). Livy describes him as one who had a sharp temper,
used language that was "bitter and absolutely reckless.... "
Livy also says of him that "enmities in abundance gave him
plenty of employment, and he never suffered them to
sleep.... "[11] William Stearns Davis characterizes him as
"... cold-blooded, hard-headed, practical, abstemious.... "[12]
It is interesting to note that the presence and work of this
paragon among censors hardly seemed to change the Roman
way of life at the time when he lived. Will Durant describes
this very period in Roman history as one where "in the upper classes manners continued to be coarse and vigorous,

amusements often violent, language freely obscene...."[13]

The censors' work didn't seem to help much ... then
or now. Brinton says that "Rome at almost any time after
the end of the second century B.C. has long been a symbol
for moral looseness, for evil, not only in public but in private life." The important thing to note here is not what occurred, but why. Brinton comments briefly on what he calls
a "persistent theme in the moral history of the West"--
namely, that the imposition of what he calls "sumptuary,
prohibitory, 'blue law' legislation," accompanied by official
or semiofficial educational propaganda toward "a return to
'primitive' virtues," has seldom, if ever, in history seemed
to accomplish its purpose. Indeed, just as one example,
Brinton points out that the corpus of Greek and Latin writings together "...form the first and still one of the major
sources of pornographic pleasure available to the Western
reader...." Aristophanes, Lucian, Catullus, Propertius,
Ovid, Petronius, Martial, Juvenal--quite a group!

But Rome had its moralistic philosophers as well as
its censors and pornographers. The Stoic ideal is still admired today. Starting in Greece with Zeno, probably its
most noted Roman theoreticians and practitioners were Seneca, Epictetus, and Marcus Aurelius. Seneca, paradoxically, was Nero's tutor (on literature and morals, but not philosophy, we are told).[15] Will Durant describes the central
ideas of Stoicism as follows: "that man is part of a whole
and must co-operate with it--with his family, his country,
and the divine Soul of the world; that he is here not to enjoy the pleasures of the senses, but to do his duty without
complaint or stint." Fortunately, Durant says, the later
Roman Stoics did not demand either perfect virtue or an
ascetic disregard for what seemed good and fortunate in life.
Thus, Durant epigrammatically summarizes, "Stoicism became the inspiration of Scipio, the ambition of Cicero, the
better self of Seneca, the guide of Trajan, the consolation
of Aurelius, and the conscience of Rome."[16]

The Stoic, despite his love of pure reason, which he
saw as the highest faculty of man, clearly recognized the
humanity of man; indeed, pleasure and the "lower instincts"
were no less natural to man than human reason. So the
Stoic was by no means automatically a censor. Since, as
Bertrand Russell describes the Stoic philosophy, "...the individual will is completely autonomous, and no man can be
forced to sin for outside causes,"[17] it would be most un-
Stoical to encourage restriction of a censorial sort.

On censorship Marcus Aurelius, like a good Stoic on
any topic, was dispassionate. Among other relevant statements, he said, "... a man must learn a great deal to enable him to pass a correct judgment on another man's
acts... "; "neither in writing nor in reading wilt thou be able
to lay down rules for others before thou shalt have first
learned to obey rules thyself. Much more is this so in
life"; "... look not round at the depraved morals of others,
but run straight along the line without deviating from it. "[18]
Epictetus, in his Manual, said, "... there is nothing intrinsically evil in the world..., " and advised, "Avoid impurity
to the utmost of your power before marriage, and if you
indulge your passion, let it be done lawfully. But do not be
offensive or censorious to those who indulge in it, and do
not be always bringing up your own chastity. "[19]

With precepts like these to follow, it is easy to see
why Rome, despite its introduction of the term and office of
censorship, was not a place where censorship, as we understand it today, flourished.

INTERLUDE

PORTRAIT OF A CENSOR:

2. SAVONAROLA (1492-1534)

"As the intensity of his feelings and purposes increased they wrote themselves upon his features in the fur-
rowed and frowning forehead, the thick lips tight with determination, the immense nose curving out as if to encompass
the world, a countenance somber and severe, expressing an
infinite capacity for love and hate; a small frame racked and
haunted with visions, frustrated aspirations, and introverted
storms.... He fasted and flogged himself to tame what
seemed to him the inherent corruption of human nature....
To aid in the enforcement of ... reforms Savonarola organized the boys of his congregation.... During the week
of Carnival--preceding Lent--these boys and girls went about
the cities in bands, knocked at doors, and asked for--some-
times demanded--the surrender of what they called 'vanities'
or carnal objects ... --pictures considered immoral, love
songs, musical instruments, cosmetics, wicked books....
On the final day of Carnival, February 7, the more ardent
supporters of Savonarola, singing hymns, marched in solemn
procession ... to the Piazza della Signoria. There a great
pyramid of combustible material had been raised, 60 feet
high and 240 feet in circumference at the base. Upon the
seven stages of the pyramid the 'vanities' collected during
the week, or not brought to the sacrifice, were arranged or
thrown, including precious manuscripts and works of art.
Fire was set to the pyre at four points, and the bells of the
Palozzo Vecchio were rung to declaim this first Savonarolan
'burning of the vanities'. "

> --Will Durant, "Savonarola and the Republic, " in:
> The Renaissance, 1953.

"The plain and undeniable fact is that Savonarola lived
his life among strictly medieval thoughts and feelings, and

that ... he tried to revitalize them in an age, into the altered conditions of which they could no longer be fitted. ...
Like the uncompromising heir of the Middle Ages he was,
Savonarola preached that nothing mattered but the life beyond
the grave and that the only proper concern of the sinful son
of Adam during his mundane sojourn was salvation. "

> --Ferdinand Schevill, <u>History of Florence</u>, 1936.

'It is true that some of his strictness and severity
is displeasing, as also the little allowance he makes for human frailty. ...   Any man who insulted Fra Girolamo was
punished promptly and not without a certain factious severity. ... "

> --Roberto Ridolfi, <u>The Life of Girolamo Savonarola</u>,
> 1959.

"Why do our Christian rulers make no sign?   Why do
they dissemble these ills?   Why do they not pass a law ban-
ishing from the city not these false poets only, but even
their works, and those of the ancient writers treating of
vicious subjects, and in praise of false gods?   It would be
an excellent thing were such books destroyed, and only those
inciting to virtue preserved. "

> --Girolamo Savonarola, <u>In Apology of the Art of
> Poetry</u>, 1542.

5. THE JUDEO-CHRISTIAN INFLUENCE

"The different religions have never overlooked the part played by the sense of guilt in civilization.   What is more, they came forward with a claim ... to save mankind from this sense of guilt, which they call sin. "

--Sigmund Freud,
Civilization and Its Discontents, 1930

Chapter 5

THE JUDEO-CHRISTIAN INFLUENCE

Most modern religious obloquy cast upon sex and, in consequence, upon writings about sex, is a logical extension of the widely held orthodox Christian view of the Fall of Man and of Original Sin. A critical examination of these two fundamental concepts in Christianity and their history and significance should help in better understanding the arguments from theological bases for censorship of writings about sexual activity, especially those which correlate pleasure with sexual action.

F. R. Tennant, a Cambridge Lecturer in Theology, and one of the greatest scholars of modern times on the subject of the Fall of Man and Original Sin, made a careful examination of the Old and New Testaments, as well as of similar documents in other religions (Phoenician, Babylonian, Egyptian, Greek), and presents a quite persuasive theory. The Old Testament story of Adam and Eve and the Garden of Eden, told in the third chapter of the Book of Genesis, dates back to about 900-700 B.C. Tennant's exegesis of this narrative is heavily documented and logical, although opposed to the traditional Christian exegesis, which sees all mankind, symbolized by Adam and Eve, doomed to a life of sin and labor because of Adam and Eve's disobeying God's injunction to stay away from the fruit of the tree of knowledge. As Tennant puts it, "...the story is primarily an account of a fall of the human race in its first parents; it is not merely an account of the historical entrance of sin into the world but also an explanation of the origin and universality of sinfulness throughout mankind."[1]

There can be no question that the actual words of Genesis say nothing at all of the state of morality of Adam, either before or after the actual act of eating the fruit. Tennant points out that there is not even any implication to the average reader that Adam's basic nature was corrupted

43

or perverted by his disobeying the Deity. Indeed, "the idea that his sin was the source of the sinfulness of succeeding generations, or in any way an explanation of it, is altogether absent from the narrative," says Tennant. [2]

Perhaps the critical question in all this is: what was the Original Sin? The Old Testament says, very simply, absolutely nothing on this topic. The wording of Genesis, chapter 3, is unambiguous. God told Adam and Eve not to eat of, or to touch, "the fruit of the tree which is in the midst of the garden...." They disobeyed him, and God explains that "...the man is become as one of us, to know good and evil," so we are then made aware of the results of the sin. But still, what was the sin--eating, or disobeying, the knowledge of good and evil, or what, exactly?

Surely Adam and Eve could not have been punished simply for having acquired knowledge of what was moral. Was not their crime basically that they disobeyed their Creator? Whatever their state of primal innocence, the implication is clear that they must at least have been able to know the difference between obeying and disobeying--or God would not have been able to reprimand and punish them for such disobedience. It happens that the basic meaning of the Hebrew words which we translate as "good" and "evil" in this particular section of the Bible is really "beneficial" and "hurtful";[3] so what man can now distinguish, after the expulsion from Eden, is between what is "good," in the sense of "helping," and "evil," in the sense of "not helping" or actually causing something untoward.

Psychoanalyst Theodor Reik has devoted a 432-page volume to his attempt to disprove what he calls a belief "common to the moralists, theologians, and philosophers who regard sexuality as a result of man's criminality and sinfulness, as well as to the educators and psychologists (including psychoanalysts) who hope that freedom from sexual suppression will change man and remove the greatest obstacle in our civilization." He states that "religion, particularly Christianity, traces the guilt feeling of man back to an 'original sin,' which is conceived as sexual transgression, to the 'weakness of the flesh,' or to sexual desire."[4] Reik goes so far as to claim that our entire civilization, including even our education, suffers from this belief. He differs, not about there being a widespread guilt feeling, but about its cause; for Reik "the guilt feelings of mankind have their roots in aggression and violence." Surely the long, sad record of

man's inhumanity to man--in peace and in war--would argue
for Reik's point. There is no record of vast, widespread
"sinfulness"--if that is the correct term to use for sexual
activity--to compare with the iniquity of mass murders,
common to all civilizations, but dignified by the term "war,"
for example.

The quotation which heads this chapter is from the
writings of Sigmund Freud, but its point is just possibly the
key to all post-Pauline censorship. The Jews did not censor; read the Old Testament and try to see what could possibly have been left out, with its detailed recital of practically every crime and sexual act known to man. Jesus did not
put anything like the emphasis on sex-life and sexuality
which Paul did, if the Gospels and the Pauline epistles are
evidence.

The New Testament includes relatively little on what
Tennant calls "...the origin and mode of propagation of human sinfulness...,"[5] except in the Pauline epistles. In
fact, only St. Paul, among the apostolic followers of Jesus,
makes statements connecting the presumed universal sinfulness with the Original Sin. In Romans, V:12-21, Paul says,
that "...by one man sin entered into the world" and "...by
one man's disobedience many were made sinners." Jesus
said absolutely nothing about either original sin or the Fall;
not one of the four Gospels quotes any statement by Jesus
Christ on these topics. Nowhere in the words of Jesus can
there be found any statement that the physical side of sexual
life is evil, or that sexual asceticism, virginity, or chastity
are positive goals.[6]

A liberal theology professor of the early part of this
century, Shailer Matthews, emphasizes that "while Jesus ...
recognizes the physical basis of marriage, he never regards
it as in any way sinful or ignoble; so far is he removed from
the perversions that an ascetic faith has so frequently forced
upon humanity."[7] The implicit position of Jesus was that
either marriage or celibacy could be demanded of a man.
He believed in the possibility of celibacy as a good life, but
He never preached or followed the ascetic standard Himself,
except to the extent that any Nazarite did in those days.
There is no statement in the purely Christ-uttered parts of
the New Testament concerning what proportion of all men
are sinful; in fact, He never said anything at all about all
men being sinners.

This is not to say that Jesus preached anything like looseness in sexual matters. Indeed, He insisted on marriage as being an indissoluble bond, and that sexual intercourse was permissible only to those who were married. Further than that, as German ethical historian Ernst Troeltsch tells us, "Jesus reminds His hearers that sex will not exist at all in the Kingdom of Heaven; that situations may arise in which it may be necessary to renounce the joys of family life in response to some imperious spiritual demand, and that the missionary vocation may require men to 'have made themselves eunuchs for the Kingdom of Heaven's sake'. "[8]

It is Pauline Christianity, particularly as voiced in the Epistles, which said, as reworded 1700 years later in The New England Primer:

> In Adam's fall
> We sinned all.

Actually, Paul never referred to the Fall of Adam or of man as a whole. This particular notion came with some of the early Christian Fathers, in the fourth century A.D.

Paul's ideas of original sin, however, were evinced, and often, directly and by inference in the sections of the New Testament attributed to him. The influences on Paul of both Hellenism and of Jewish rabbinical theology are quite evident. As W. D. Davies has pointed out, in the Hebrew tradition as already made evident in the Old Testament, Apocrypha, and Pseudepigrapha--all readily available to Paul--" ... the appetites and passions are an essential element in the constitution of human nature and necessary to the perpetuation of the race and to the existence of civilization. In this aspect they are, therefore, not to be eradicated or suppressed, but directed and controlled. "[9] In the long run, this kind of thinking certainly contributed to church-directed censorship.

The Jewish equivalent (to a limited extent) of the Christian Original Sin concept is called "yetzer ha-ra, " which means "evil impulse. " This impulse, located in the human heart, was considered to be in large measure connected with sexual sins, sexual passion, or lust. But nowhere in the Old Testament or in other Jewish writings is there a claim that this "evil impulse" is universal or inherent in man. The origin of sinfulness is really not explained

in the Old Testament. [10]   Isaiah's words, "Though your sins
be as scarlet, they shall be as white as snow," illustrate
how Judaism lacked the basic idea of unremediable original
sin. [11]

   But Paul, a close student of the Old Testament, and
of the New insofar as it was available to him, still voiced
an "original sin" concept. Why? The best scholarly evidence and opinion would seem to indicate that the doctrines
of Paul (who was born a Jew and trained in Jewish tradition), relating to the Fall and Original Sin, were based
neither on the Old Testament nor the New, but rather on the
various speculations and the uncanonical literature of the
age between the Old and the New Testaments.

   Any reference to St. Paul and his influence on Christianity must take into account the fact that from his early
boyhood he was strongly affected by the Greco-Roman world
and its ideas. As a man who had been educated in Tarsus,
a city with a university which was, even in his day, "...a
centre of Hellenistic philosophy," he undoubtedly was greatly
affected by both the Stoic philosophy and the mystery cults
so popular at that time. The Stoic philosopher, Athenodorus,
who was a teacher of Seneca, lived in Tarsus just before
Paul's time, and his teaching was still influential in the
University of Tarsus in Paul's day. [12]

   There is a vast literature on Paul, but most authorities agree that, as Rabbi Samuel Sandmel says, "...the attitudes and approaches of Paul to the human predicament
were inherently Hellenistic....   The goal of Greek religion
... was that of escape; escape from the inevitable end,
death, escape from bondage to the body." Within the individual there was a struggle between his enlightened mind and
his sensual desires.   Inevitably, if he followed his senses
and passions, he would behave irrationally. [13]

   Since Paul, although a Roman citizen and educated in
Tarsus, was still a Jew, Westermarck has questioned where
Paul "...had learnt to have such a moral contempt and horror of the flesh and to identify it with sin. This is not a
Jewish conception."[14] Westermarck believed this was because Paul was basically a Greek Jew, and that the Judaism
of the Diaspora was strongly affected by its Graeco-Oriental
environment.

   For Paul, the worst of all of the sins of the flesh was

sexual indulgence. Westermarck quotes the famous passage
from Second Corinthians, "...it is better to marry than to
burn, " as indicating that "even marriage is permitted only
as a means of restraining the sinful licentiousness of the
sexual impulse.... " This idea was absolutely different from
any Jewish religious ideas; the purpose of marriage as expressed throughout the Old Testament and in rabbinical literature is propagative, not palliative. Paul, of course, felt
and said that celibacy was far better for man than marriage.
Westermarck considers Paul as basically an ascetic. [15]

Westermarck's explanation for the rather wide success of the ascetic attitude toward sex, both in early Christian times and later, is a quite realistic one. He associates
asceticism, which looks upon "sexual intercourse ... as unclean and defiling, " with the worldwide notion that "...the
mere discharge of sexual matter, even when quite involuntary
and unaccompanied with any sexual desire, is held to be pol-
luting.... " He ascribes this to "...the veil of mystery
which surrounds the whole sexual nature of man. " It is
"the secrecy drawn over the sexual functions, and the feeling of sexual shame, which gives them the appearance of
something illicit and sinful. " It is also true that the so-
called "defiling" effects which Paul and his followers have
attributed to sexual relations are, in some measure, connected with the idea that woman, as a menstruating and
child-bearing being, is considered unclean--at least, during
her outwardly sexual-functioning periods. [16]

Why is this important? Because the Pauline interpretation, in the long run, was what won out with Christianity as a whole. The early Christian theologians, beginning
with Irenaeus and Origen in the East and especially featured
by the opinions of Tertullian in the West (it was he who first
voiced the theory that man is conceived and born in "uncleanness, " and who described Eve as being "the single
womb of all sin, pouring down from her spring the various
streams of crime"), [17] were the precursors of St. Augustine,
who took the Pauline doctrine and concretized it for practically all Christians to follow from then on.

The important thing to remember about Paul's view
of sexuality is that he thought of it--as he did everything
else--from the apocalyptic point of view, from the point of
view that the world was definitely coming to an end, in the
not-too-distant future. As Robert M. Hawkins has stated,
for Paul "the fashion of this world is passing away; the time

of distress is upon us; those in the flesh shall have great
tribulation ... the effect of the imminence of the end of the
world is the negation of all values. "[18] After all, if the
world is about to come to an end, surely there must be better things to do than to worry about the flesh!

Since, for Paul, the time from his life to the end of
all things was very short and getting shorter, it was far better if those who lived in such times did not get married or
think of sex at all. His grudging concession that "it is better to marry than to burn ... " did not show that he felt that
most people would really "burn" if they ignored their sexual
nature and drive.

Paul's "marry, don't burn" doctrine not only was the
justification given for the excesses of the Desert Fathers
and other ascetic Christians in the years to come; it also
proved to be the basis for St. Augustine's "terrible" doctrine, as Will Durant terms it,[19] that the original sin was
lust, concupiscence.

Augustine came by this theory through a curious com-
pound of pure Pauline thought, blended with Neoplatonism
and Patristic philosophy. Man, for Augustine, was a free
creature, who--in the person of Adam--" chose to disobey
God and ... corrupted the entire human race. "[20]

St. Augustine defined concupiscence as "the tendency
which impels men to turn from the supreme and immutable
good, which is God, in order to find his satisfaction and
comfort in that which is mutable and less than God, that is,
in creatures. "[21] The basic flaw in human nature, which
men inherit from Adam, according to St. Augustine, is "in
the unbridled and inordinate tyranny of concupiscence over
the rest of man's interior microcosm. "[22] Man is born in
sin, according to this philosophy, because the sexual act
which begets him is intrinsically sinful; and this holds good
for both Augustine and his followers. Since there is no way
--except for God--to continue the human race except by acts
of generation which are fundamentally foul, sinful, and wrong,
the very existence of mankind is based on sin. And, logically, anything connected with sexuality is, in various degrees,
ipso facto sinful.

There is a psychological reason for the bitterly anti-
sex feelings of St. Augustine. Augustine's early life, by his
own admission, was a dissolute and wild one; once he

converted to Christianity in his maturity, his own background made him so hostile to sex that he denounced it.
His influence, exerted directly during the latter part of the
fourth and early part of the fifth centuries, was very strong.
Harry Elmer Barnes offers the opinion that "these morbid
eccentricities [by which term Barnes is referring to Augustine's sexual doctrines] of Augustinian thought, growing out
of his own erratic personal experience, were able to pervert
human thinking on sexual matters for a thousand years, and
their influence is still strong with millions. Thus Augustine's personal sex neurosis was elevated to a dominant position in western European ethical theory."23

     In the centuries which followed--the so-called "Dark
Ages"--the Church was dominant, both spiritually and tem-
porally. As Durant puts it, "the new morality exaggerated
chastity into an obsession, and subordinated marriage and
pregnancy to a lifelong virginity or celibacy as an ideal...."24
Durant reminds us that it took the Church fathers "some
time" to come to what seems to be the obvious logical de-
duction that if all followed the ascetic ideal, the society
could not survive. Biology finally caught up with theology,
it seems.

     Another concept which came out of the idea of man's
original sin being the sin of the flesh was that the status of
women was affected by the fairly generally accepted doctrine
that, as Durant phrases the idea, "woman was the origin of
sin and the instrument of Satan."25 Naturally (since men
wrote the doctrine), Adam's Fall must be the result of
temptation by Eve, and she had to bear the brunt of the
blame for it all. Barnes' summary of all this is brief but
encompassing:

          Christianity came to look upon sex as the worst
          form of evil, and the greatest temptation to which
          man is heir. This belief ... was a product of
          orthodox Judaism, pre-Christian asceticism, the
          purification trends in the mystery cults, the gener-
          al supernatural orientation of Christianity, and the
          abnormal personal experiences of Paul and Augus-
          tine. 26

Quite an indictment, but there is strong evidence for all
parts of it.

     Alvin Boyd Kuhn goes even further than Barnes in

criticizing Christianity's historical attitude toward sex. Kuhn
says, "The ascetic Christian attitude toward the body stands
as one of the supreme cultural afflictions and miscarriages
of all time." He criticizes the Christian doctrine of sin because "it has killed the natural instinct of the human part of
man to exult in the boundless gift of life itself."[27] It is not
primitive, Christ-following Christianity which he blames for
this, but rather "the shadow of the Third Century"--that century (plus actually the fourth) when asceticism began to
flourish--the age of Origen who, paying literal heed to Matthew XIX:12, emasculated himself; Methodius, who ranked
"unstained virginity ... high above the married state";[28] St.
John Chrysostom (who once described woman as "nothing
else but phlegm and blood and humor and bile, and the fluid
of masticated food.... If you consider what is stored up
inside ..., you will affirm the well-shaped body is nothing
else than a whited sepulchre..."); and St. Jerome, who admitted that his "mind was burning with the cravings of desire, and the fires of lust flared up from [his] flesh...,"
and who consented to praise marriage "...merely because it
produced virgins."[29] Indeed, St. Jerome went so far as to
say, "He who too ardently loves his own wife is an adulter-
er."[30]

Tertullian called woman "...the gate of hell, the un-
sealer of that forbidden tree, the first director of the divine
law,"[31] and told his wife, in a long letter concerning their
marriage and what she should do if she were widowed, that
"widowhood was God's call to sexual abstinence."[32] Since
God preferred celibacy to marriage as a fit state for man
and woman, said this leader of the Third Century Christian
Church, "a widow is really getting a chance to please God"
in this respect! He questioned Paul's dictum about marriage and burning, writing that "it is far better neither to
marry nor to burn,"[33] since the celibate life was the best
way out of the dilemma. A council of bishops held in Milan
in 390 A.D. excommunicated a monk because he would not
agree that "virginity is more meritorious than marriage...."
And as late as 1560 the Council of Trent condemned any one
who did not consider the unmarried state to be better than
being married.[34]

Of course, St. Augustine, in some ways, went even
further. He once said, "Through a woman we were sent to
destruction; through a woman salvation was restored to us."[35]
As a recent biographer says, Augustine thought that "if ever
the pressures of society were relaxed, the reins placed on

human licence would be loosened and thrown off: all sins
would go unpunished. Take away the barriers created by
the laws! Men's brazen capacity to do harm, the urge to
self-indulgence would rage to the full. " When was ever so
clear a mandate given to the Censor? Even the sympathetic
biographer refers to Augustine as having an "oppressive
sense of the need for restraint. "36

During the Dark Ages and the Middle Ages monasticism, featured by asceticism and celibacy, was the ideal set
by the Church for mankind. From 532 A. D. on, there had
been, says the great Cantabrigian historian of monasticism,
G. C. Coulton, "imperial legislation providing that the monk
must choose, once for all, between his cloister and the
world. "37   The Code of Justinian enacted orthodox Christianity into rigid, strongly-enforced law, 38 and for a thousand
years, until Henry VIII's dissolution of the English convents
and monasteries, the monachal ideal was a reality for thousands and thousands of monks and nuns.

With St. Benedict and his Rule came the foundation
of Western monachism.   This late fifth century and early
sixth-century leader imposed what Coulton terms a "quasi-
military Christ Discipline"39 in his 73-chapter Rule, which
still controls Benedictine monks--and many others--to this
day.   Of greatest interest, as it relates to censorship and
its theological causes, is the fact that one of the requirements, number 11, was "to chasten the body. "40 Chastity,
indeed, says Coulton, "is not so much enforced in the Rule
as taken for granted. " After all, these men were warned
in Canon Law "that every human being who is conceived by
the coition of a man with a woman is born with original sin,
subject to impiety and wrath, and therefore a child of
wrath. "41 With all that against you to begin with, why risk
God's future punishment by committing unchastity? As
Coulton puts it, "Nature was cursed since the Fall; the infant was a 'mass of perdition'; celibacy was the holiest of
human states. "42

This is not to say that all monasteries and nunneries
during medieval times, or later, were composed of saints.
Indeed, St. Benedict, in his Rule number 61, required
the monks "not to desire to be called a saint ... but to be
one. "   As Will Durant says, this was one of his "general
counsels of Christian perfection, " an ideal rather than a
working rule. 43

Among the consequences of the monastic movement,
it is important to note that it set apart these "living saints"
in the cloisters as people to be revered and admired for
many reasons, but perhaps most strongly for their attempt
at chastity. If, as Durant tells us, Gregory the Great,
founder of the Gregorian order during the sixth century, felt
and preached that "left to himself, man would heap sin upon
sin, and richly deserve lasting damnation, "[44] then man had
better not be left to himself. So the censor has authoritative theological and doctrinal support. Gregory was not the
only religious leader of his day--or of other days!--to favor
censorship, of course.

The next really significant major leader in Christian
theology and doctrine, St. Thomas Aquinas, graced the thir-
teenth century. For Thomas, who adopted and promulgated
the Pauline-Augustine theory of the Original Sin and Adam's
Fall, "The shamefulness of concupiscence that always ac-
companies the marriage is ... a punishment inflicted for the
first sin.... "[45] He stresses, "if the motive for the marriage act be a virtue, whether of justice ... or of religion ..., it is meritorious. But if the motive be lust, it is
a sin. " Indeed, this philosophy has lasted to this day, with
the Anglican (Episcopal in the United States) marriage service saying that marriage was set up as an institution as
"a remedy against sin, and to avoid fornication; that such
persons as have not the gift of continency might marry, and
keep themselves undefiled members of Christ's body.... "
As the Whiteleys put it, "The rather disgusting practice of
mating is rendered respectable and even meritorious when
it is used for a worthy purpose. "[46]

Censorship was not really a problem for Aquinas, or,
for that matter, for the whole medieval church. Books were
just too few, and the ability to read them too wide-scattered,
to demand an imposed orthodoxy in reading. When even the
Bible was rare outside of monasteries, obviously the thought
and power of the Church did not have to be wasted on censorship. But the invention and wide promulgation of printing
in the Western world in the late fifteenth century changed
priorities.

It is no coincidence that the sixteenth-century Council
of Trent (which codified the rules of the Catholic Church,
and which has prevailed with really very minor modifications,
to this day) was responsible for dealing, among other things,
both with the doctrines of the Fall of Man and with the

details of literary censorship (printing had just begun to be significant at that time, midway in the sixteenth-century). It was perfectly logical for the same body, intent upon setting up "an uncompromising response to the challenge of Protestantism, rationalism, and private judgment,"[47] to announce both that the Fall of Man "caused loss of original righteousness, infection of body and soul ... [and] sin ... transmitted from generation to generation"[48] and that "lascivious and obscene books" were to be censored. As one consequence, the writing or publication of obscene works was made subject to capital punishment, a penalty actually put in force at least once during the next few years by Pope Pius V.[49]

Just before the Council of Trent there was one influential figure who deserves mention in any discussion of censorship, particularly in relation to theology. Girolamo Savonarola, a Dominican monk and religious reformer who influenced the life of Florence for two decades (1478-1498) and has affected the life of repression for centuries, has been called an extreme puritan, "more a fanatic than a saint." The Prior of San Marco characterized himself as "the sword of the Lord, swift over the earth and sudden."[50]

In 1496 he enlisted the boys of the city of Florence into a semi-military organization which was dedicated to these activities: "...to attend church regularly, to avoid public spectacles, such as races, fireworks, pageants, and acrobatic performances, to dress simply, to shun loose company, lewd poets, obscene books, dancing, fencing, and music schools, and to wear their hair short."[51] During the Carnival of 1497 he initiated the famous Burning of the Vanities. The literally thousands of children who followed him collected "lewd pictures and books, lutes, cards, mirrors, and trinkets ... " and piled them for burning in the great Piazza della Signoria of Florence.[52] The Bonfire of the Vanities has been described as "a great pyramid ... 60 feet high and 240 feet in circumference at the base."[53]

After strong differences of opinion with Pope Alexander VI, mainly over political rather than ecclesiastical issues, Savonarola was excommunicated, tried, and hanged, and his body burnt at the stake, in 1498. His influence, as stated earlier, is by no means dead. The Hitlers and the Stalins and the small-town American police-tyrants who burn books are, consciously or unconsciously, in the Savonarola tradition.

George Haven Putnam has devoted two long volumes[54]
to The Censorship of the Church of Rome, the rest of whose
title bears repetition: "...and Its Influence upon the Production and Distribution of Literature: a Study of the History
of the Prohibitory and Expurgatory Indexes, together with
Some Consideration of the Effects of Protestant Censorship
and of Censorship by the State." He tells the fascinating
tale from the first Index (1546) through 1900. (By that time
the Index, as such, had less than a century to go, since it
was abolished, to all intents and purposes, by Pope John
XXIII at the Second Ecumenical Council in the Vatican in
1967.)

According to Putnam, the vast majority of all books
completely censored or permitted publication in expurgated
form were those considered heretical. The Council of Trent,
in 1564, prepared a set of Ten Rules, "...as a guide and
instruction for all ecclesiastics or other authorities who
might thereafter be charged with the duty of literary censorship." Most germane to the topic of sex censorship was
rule number seven, which stated that "books professedly
treating of lascivious or obscene subjects, or narrating or
teaching these, are utterly prohibited, since not only faith
but morals, which are readily corrupted by the perusal of
them, are to be considered; and those who possess them
shall be severely punished by the bishop. But the works of
antiquity, written by the heathen, are permitted to be read,
because of the elegance and propriety of the language; though
on no account shall they be suffered to be read by young
persons."[55]

There are notable in this "rule seven" several of the
principles which have pervaded censorship, theological and
temporal, Catholic and Protestant, ever since. Firstly, the
claim is made--not proven, but simply stated--that "morals
... are readily corrupted by the perusal of them ..."--that
is, meaning by "them," those "books professedly treating of
lascivious or obscene subjects, or narrating or teaching
these...." Next, there is definite latitude given to "the
works of antiquity," but only so far as they are "written by
the heathen...." If written by believers, no matter how
long ago, they must bear the censorship, it seems. The
justification for the special dispensation given to works of
antiquity is that the Greeks and Romans, to whom the Council was supposedly referring, used elegant and proper, rather than crude and improper, language. In other words, it
was not the topic but rather the language that was important,

so far as works of antiquity were concerned. Finally, even
such works were forbidden to "young persons," with no exact
age-limits given.   These guidelines for the Index have had a
definite effect on the work of the censor to this day.

The complete story of the Index's four centuries of
effort at pre-censorship, censorship, and expurgation need
not be retold here; Putnam tells it all very well, and Father
Redmond Burke has brought in a more modern view, in his
abbreviated work on the same topic, to good effect. [56] It is
of interest to note that the 1564 Index called only for elimination from Boccacio's Decameron of "obnoxious references
to ecclesiastics," but left in the text a number of episodes
contra bonos mores which had to do only with laymen. [57]
As Putnam says, speaking of the Decameron, "the record
presents a curious example of a book the vitality of which,
persisting through the centuries, defied all efforts for its
suppression."[58]

Although no less than thirteen popes edited indexes,
assisted by the entire apparatus of the Inquisition through the
early years of the Index's existence, and by kings and arch-
bishops and emperors later on, the conclusive results of the
Index have really been minimal.   Putnam adduces considerable evidence that the Index brought prohibited books to the
attention of many who otherwise would probably never have
known they even existed.   The banning of "opera omnia" (the
entire works) of such well-known writers as Voltaire, Zola,
Balzac, Dumas (father and son) and Stendhal, of the essays
of Montaigne, of the Pensées of Pascal, of Richardson's
Pamela, of Sterne's A Sentimental Journey has hardly affected their fame and dissemination, among Catholics and
non-Catholics alike.   The Index was far from a success, except, perhaps, in giving the censors busy work throughout
the centuries of its existence.

With the onset of the Reformation, the tendency to
control thought was reaffirmed.   As Putnam says, "There
can ... be no question that from the outset, the leaders of
the Protestant Reformation believed as thoroughly in the necessity and in the rightfulness of the censorship of literature
as did the ecclesiastics of Rome or of Spain."[59] The major
difference between the Protestants and the Catholics was that
the Protestants had no such weapons to enforce their policies
on censorship as did the Catholics, who had the Inquisition
as well as excommunication--two strong and often-used pieces
of moral armament.   The Protestants had to work through

the various civil governments, except in such unusual circumstances as Calvin's Geneva, where Protestant theocratic
government set up stronger censorship than in any Catholic
country in history. There is indeed ample evidence that
Protestant censorship laid much more emphasis on anti-ec-
clesiastical (heretical) and "revolutionary" political works
than did Catholic censorship. [60] The Protestant censors, it
seems, were not so sex-obsessed.

With the Reformation, indeed, came the first really
massive attack on celibacy, as far as Christianity was concerned. Martin Luther believed in enjoying life. He once
said, "Thou sayest enjoy every pleasure in the world that is
not sinful: that thy God forbids thee not, but rather wills
it. "[61] In 1521 he wrote a treatise, On Monastic Vows,
wherein he "accepted the sexual instinct as natural and irrepressible, and declared that monastic vows were lures of
Satan, multiplying sins. "[62] He went even further, finding,
as Durant says, ". . . a good word to say for sin itself. " If
the Devil offers persistent temptation, Luther advises man,
"Seek out the society of your boon companions, drink, play,
talk bawdy, and amuse yourself. "[63] Luther is reputed to
have told Melancthon, his fellow theologian in Wittenberg, to
"Sin powerfully; God can forgive only a hearty sinner. "[64]
Hardly the advice of an ascetic!

Luther, like all great religious leaders, had his in-
consistencies. Among them, perhaps, was his exuberant
personality, as contrasted to some of his more formal writings. He was certainly not a puritan. Quite typical of his
hearty, cheerful outlook on how to live are such authenticated
sayings as: 'I seek and accept joy wherever I find it. We
now know, thank God, that we can be happy with a good conscience"; or "Christians must not altogether shun plays because there are sometimes coarseness and adulteries therein; for such reasons they would have to give up the Bible,
too. "[65] Unfortunately, in his later years, Luther became,
increasingly intolerant, but, as Durant says, ". . . his words
were harsher than his deeds. "[66]

But it is still true that, whether Catholic or Protestant, the general Christian theological position held that it
was "the right and duty of the Church, and of the State, under the influence of the Church, to supervise and to control
the productions of the printing-press and the reading of the
people. "[67] The censor, throughout modern history, has
flourished with the active support and encouragement of the

Christian church, Catholic and Protestant, and only in the consistency and endurability of specific policies have the two groups differed.   The intent was the same with both, but the results varied because of the difference in power held and exhibited between the schismatically divided Protestants and the comparatively unified Roman Catholics.

6. THE PURITAN AND THE CENSOR

"There is clearly much resistance among ordinary human beings to any widespread attempt to achieve in practice a rigorous moral order of the kind we must call, imprecisely but clearly, puritanical. It would seem from the record that a degree of moral looseness is far more common than a corresponding degree of strictness. "

--Crane Brinton, <u>A History of Western Morals</u>, 1959.

Chapter 6

THE PURITAN AND THE CENSOR

Suppose you are living in Geneva, Switzerland in the year 1553. You can expect a minister and an elder to visit you and your family once a year, and these men will question you about the most intimate details of your way of living. You are forbidden to gamble or to use profane language or to be drunk. You may not frequent taverns or dance or sing "indecent or irreligious" songs. You are cautioned against excesses in entertainment, extravagance in living, and immodesty in dress. [1]

The law even specifies how many different items can be served at one meal, and which colors and what quality of clothing you may wear. If you are a woman and wear jewelry or lace or frilly hats, you will certainly be admonished by the ruling clergy; you know that a neighbor was put in jail just for "arranging her hair to an immoral height."[2] Books which are considered wrong in religious tenets or tending toward immorality are not available to you. You may not attend any theatrical performances; as a matter of fact, none is to be found in Geneva at this time. You cannot write anything considered disrespectful of John Calvin or any of the ministers in charge of the state, on penalty of reprimand, fines or, if done persistently, jail or even exile.

If you own a copy of such a romantic tale as Amadis de Gaula or a collection of saints' lives, such as The Golden Legend, you will be disciplined. Your children must have names to be found in the Bible. If you write books disagreeing with Calvin, you will not only have to retract your opinions, but will have to throw all available copies of your writings into the fire with your own hands. [3]

You may feel that your child is disrespectful--but you don't dare report this to the authorities, even if he happens to hit you; the child next door was actually beheaded for

striking his parents. [4] If you serve more than three courses
at any meal, even at a wedding or other banquet or feast
occasion, watch out for the ecclesiastical police.   When it
is sermon time on Sunday, you cannot "play or run idly in
the street.... "[5]

If you visit a Geneva inn, you will not be permitted
to sit up after nine o'clock at night, unless you are known
to be a spy by profession! [6]   And, if you become known as a
person who lives in Geneva but regularly "frequents" inns,
the host at the inn is under orders not to make you welcome.

All in all, you may come to agree with a later com-
mentator who said about Calvin that "there was never such a
busy-body in a position of high authority before nor since"--
but you had better not tell that to John Calvin or anyone who
will tell him what you said.   You just might, at the very
least, as one individual was reported to do, be required to
fall on your knees before John Calvin in public and ask his
pardon. [7]

The ruler of Geneva during the mid-decades of the
sixteenth century, John Calvin, is probably the epitome of
all censors.   As a young college student, he already was
known as a censor of the morals of his fellow pupils, [8] so
much so that his nickname was "the accusative case," since
he was so constantly finding fault with the "loose" morals of
his fellow students--whom others found just about normal for
their age and times. [9]   By the time he was 27, when he
wrote the first edition of his major life-work, the Institutes
of the Christian Religion, he had gone far beyond his immediate companions to a censorial view of all mankind.

His was a cast of mind to be preoccupied with the
paltriness of man and the immense power of God. [10]   For
Calvin, "The mind of man is so completely alienated from
the righteousness of God that it conceives, desires, and un-
dertakes everything that is impious, perverse, base, impure,
and flagitious.   His heart is so thoroughly infected by the
poison of sin that it cannot produce anything but what is corrupt; and if any time men do anything apparently good, yet
the mind always remains involved in hypocrisy and deceit,
and the heart enslaved by its inward perversity. "[11]   The
way John Calvin looked at original sin has been described
and characterized in these terms: "The sin of Adam, which
is the sin of mankind, is regarded as a perennial fountain of
filth and uncleanness which is perpetually bubbling up in

black streams of perverted and degraded impulse...." If
one accepted the Calvinist doctrine in toto, "it would seem
to be criminal in the sight of Heaven to be a human being
at all."[12]

When Calvin set up a theocracy in Geneva, Switzerland (1541-1564), it naturally included a very strong censorship, perhaps the strongest religiously-motivated censorship
of all time, even stronger than that of the Roman Catholic
Inquisition. Books which conflicted with Calvinist religious
doctrines, or which were considered even to have a tendency
to immorality, were barred. With Geneva of that time having a total population of less than 20,000, in one year (1558-
59) there were no less than 414 prosecutions for "moral" offences. In one five-year period during the theocratic rule,
76 individuals were banished and 58 were executed for such
"crimes." Indeed, men were severely punished for what today would not be considered any kind of legal misdoings.[13]

A description of him, physically and psychologically
considered, sounds like a portrait of the stereotype of the
Censor. Will Durant, for example, sees him as "severe
and sombre...; dark but bloodless complexion, ... high
forehead, penetrating, ruthless eyes ... a firm, indomitable
will, perhaps a will to power ... his humility before God
became at times a commanding arrogance before men."
Like all censors, Calvin was painfully sensitive to criticism
and could not accept opposition with the patience of one who
conceives the possibility that he may be wrong. Unfortunately, says the historian, "his virtues did not include humor
... nor a sense of beauty...."[14]

It was John Calvin, not Martin Luther, who brought
the Puritan strain to the Reformation. When some Protestant ministers wanted to prohibit playgoing, Luther said,
"Christians must not altogether shun plays because there are
sometimes coarseness and adulteries therein; for such reasons they would have to give up the Bible too."[15]

The Protestant Ethic is primarily a way of getting
done the work of its followers' world. Martin Luther brought
to the Reformation, among other ideas, his conception of
"the calling." For him "the only way of living acceptable to
God was not to surpass worldly morality in monastic asceticism, but solely through the fulfillment of the obligations
imposed upon the individual by his position in the world.
That was his calling."[16] Max Weber points out that this

idea of "the calling" of man's duty to spend his time in work
as a religious obligation leads to an "inner-worldly rational
asceticism, " which "...must reject every sophistication of
the sexual into eroticism as idolatry of the worst kind. "[17]
Under such circumstances, the censorship of literature about
sex--as happened in Calvin's Geneva theocracy and in Puritan New England--was inevitable; how else, how better defend against ungodly eroticism, which, if left unbridled, could
rot the nation from within?

It was the Calvinists, "petty tyrants and universal
busybodies, denying the individual much of his privacy,
pleasure, and individualism, " as they have been described
in modern times,[18] who really emphasized asceticism.   The
Calvinist was not trying to live without, or to blot out completely, the life of the senses.   What he was after was "to
select among his worldly desires those that would further
his salvation, and to curb or to suppress those that would
not. "

As for sex, "although the Calvinist did not hold that
all sexual intercourse was sinful, he believed firmly that the
purpose God had in mind in providing sexual intercourse was
the continuation of the race, and not the sensuous pleasures
of the participants. "[19]   As Crane Brinton puts it, the idea
of "a higher part of human consciousness that can and should
suppress the promptings of a lower part has left a firm imprint on the West, an imprint especially strong where Calvinism has set the dominant tone. "[20]   (Parenthetically, in
which Western nation, after all, did a leader named Calvin
Coolidge appoint a perennial head of federal investigation
who stayed in office and claimed pornography-reading was a
principal cause of crime for over two generations--and did
President Warren G. Harding, Coolidge's predecessor, in
1923, while indulging in some private peccadilloes, accept
the Honorary Chairmanship of the New York Society for the
Suppression of Vice at the time of its fiftieth anniversary?)[21]

There is probably no parallel in history to the strictness of the virtue required of Genevans in Calvin's day.   But
what results did this "holier-than-thou" set of requirements
have?   Since the Genevans of the mid-sixteenth century were
flesh and blood human beings, not bodiless saints, Geneva,
as one might expect, did not come up to what was required
of it.   The official records of the Geneva Council show a
rather high percentage of forced marriages, bastard children,
abandoned children, and death sentences for violations of the

Calvin-formulated rules.   Even Calvin's own son-in-law and
his stepdaughter were found guilty of adultery.[22]

Perhaps the outstanding case of dissidence in the
Geneva theocracy was that of the Spanish physician and theologian, Michael Servetus, who, after escaping from the Inquisition in France on charges of heresy for denial of the
truth of the Trinity and other differences with accepted
Catholic doctrine, came to Protestant Geneva and was tried
by this court of the Reformation, again on heresy charges.
After a two-month trial, with John Calvin as his principal
accuser and prosecutor, Servetus was found guilty of Unitar-
ianism and the rejection of infant baptism, was condemned
to burning, and died within half an hour under the flames.[23]

Servetus, of course, was not the only victim of the
Geneva version of the Inquisition.   A man named Jacques
Cruet was accused of having left a placard on Calvin's pulpit
which began by calling the Reformer (as Calvin was known)
a "gross hypocrite" and threatened his life if he did not
leave Geneva.   After being tortured on the rack twice a day
for an entire month, Cruet was "proven" only to have written the words "all rubbish" in one of Calvin's tracts, but he
was still sentenced to death for blasphemy and beheaded.

Justice with torture is tyranny, says the great American historian of this period, Preserved Smith.[24]   A capsule
description of this unique experiment in theocratic government is "minute regulation accompanied by extreme severity
in the enforcement of morals...."[25]   The government was
one which was based on the Bible as an absolutely immutable
set of moral laws which had to be obeyed and followed to the
letter.   Calvinism should not, however, be judged by what
was accomplished in the lifetimes of Calvin or John Knox
(who had set up his own version of Calvinistic theocracy in
Edinburgh, from 1557 to 1560), the best-known theocratic
censors and reformers, but rather by the eventual results of
their preachings and writings.[26]   For Calvin and Knox exercised direct control over only a small part of the European
population.

Out of Calvinism did come Puritanism, the English
Reform movement which had a crucial moral and religious
influence on the subsequent character of both the Englishman
and the American.[27]   The Puritans, following Calvin, saw
art as a real threat to faith, a focal point where the world,
the flesh, and the devil combined to lure mankind into

forgetfulness of their religious obligations and tempted them
into pleasure-filled vice.

During the two periods when Puritans were in power
in English-speaking countries--the period of the Commonwealth in England, from 1649-1660, and of the New England
colonies in the seventeenth century--censorship was practiced
in just about every conceivable way.   Winston Churchill--not
particularly noted for writing objective history, especially of
those with whose opinions he differed strongly--has described
the Puritan as generally possessing "sour looks, upturned
eyes, nasal twang, speech garnished with Old Testament
texts.... "28

Whether this is an absolutely accurate picture of the
typical Puritan or not, certainly it is the picture which
comes to the minds of most people when "Puritan" is mentioned.   Like most stereotypes, the generally accepted image
of the Puritan is not really a fair one.   But again, like most
stereotypes, that image does have many elements of truth.
The Puritan was not sexless, but he certainly made a big
fuss about sex.   He did not try to keep everybody from reading about sex, but he wasn't exactly anxious to make such
reading widely available.

Was?   The tense is wrong.   The Puritan is--and,
from every evidence we have, will be.   But the Puritan of
today is, generally speaking, at least in the vocal minority.

In Cromwell's time, when the Puritan was in his hey-
day, the state's attempt to legislate morality was nearly at
its height in all history.   Certainly, to make adultery a
crime punishable by death went pretty far; it is interesting
to note that after two or three executions, no more convictions for adultery occurred in England as long as the Puritan
law remained in force.   For blasphemy, individuals were
fined in relation to position in the class-structure.   A duke,
for instance, was forced to pay a fine ten times as large as
a commoner did, three times what the squire paid, and twice
as much as a baron.   And blasphemy was a great deal more
loosely construed than now.   In one case a man was fined
for saying "God is my witness, " and in another for saying,
"upon my life. "29

The period of the Commonwealth was a time when
"beauty was suspect, " says Durant.   After all, if men really
lived only to be sure to escape going to Hell, it really didn't

do to risk hell-fire by reading or writing or listening to the
wrong kinds of things. To the Puritan, singing hymns--
pretty solemn ones--was the only proper use of music, and
graphic art was intolerable.

The Puritans in America were as narrowly orthodox
as those who stayed in England--and perhaps even more so,
because those who could not live with the wide-open times
of the Restoration emigrated in great numbers to America,
after 1660. The climactic severity the Puritans found in
New England was, unfortunately, matched by a moral severity and frigidity which still, too often, attempts to chill
American life as a whole. Literary historian Percy Boynton
sees the origins of American Puritanism as a combination of
the more exacting and tradition-bound influences of the Old
Testament and what he calls "a somber consciousness that
is one aspect of Platonism...." The American Puritan of
the seventeenth century was nearly as severe as his English
prototype in the kinds of punishments he imposed on those
considered to be wrongdoers. As Boynton says, "He was a
cruel man, living in a cruel age in the fear of a cruel God.
He had no qualms about subjecting other men to the rigors
of the bilboes or the whipping post, to the tortures of brand-
ing and maiming, to treating women of unruly tongue to a
swing on the ducking stool or a taste of the gag or the cleft
stick, and to humiliating both men and women in the stocks
or the pillory, with public rebuke in church or the stigma
of the scarlet letter."[30] After decreeing and carrying out
rigorous punishments and forbidding dissenting opinion, the
supermoralist American Puritan leaders still could not hold
their community in line.

The Puritan had more than a wish to censor; he felt
a deeply religious obligation to do so. After all, what he did
to fight the Devil's temptations--and to force others to do
so--was strongly backed by the Deity, to whom he felt he
had somewhat of a direct line of communications. The Old
Testament God of Wrath and Vengeance was behind his censoring. Boynton sees in the Puritan "the will to power, the
desire to dictate, and the fighting spirit...."[31]

There is a fairly new trend in American historiography
which attempts to re-paint the Puritan portrait, eliminating
the "blue-nose" and censor aspects, and accenting the supposedly newly-discovered "facts" about the essential humanity
of the supposedly ascetic and dour Puritan. Yale History
Professor Edmund S. Morgan has presented the thesis that it

is not "the Puritans, those bogeymen of the modern intellectual" who are responsible for what he refers to as American
squeamishness toward the facts of life.   He claims that "the
Puritan attitude toward sex, though directed by a belief in
absolute, God-given moral values [author's italics], never
neglected human nature. "   He also claims that in their effort
to enforce God's laws, "they treated offenders with patience
and understanding, and concentrated their efforts on prevention more than on punishment. "[32]

There is a curious logic here, which in essence seems
to applaud the censor.   After all, what else does the censor
do but prevent?   And as for the "patience and understanding"
Morgan talks about, it is true, by seventeenth century European standards, that at a time when the death penalty was
given frequently for what we today would consider comparaa-
tive trivialities, the Puritans of New England were not too
harsh.   But they did whip, fine, and brand--by Morgan's
own statement--for adultery and fornication.   There is ample
evidence of use of the stocks and imprisonment for various
other sex-associated misdeeds, far short of rape or sodomy.
The Morgan whitewash and even his claim that "in matters
of sex the Puritans showed none of the blind zeal or narrow-
minded bigotry which is too often supposed to have been
characteristic of them, "[33] seems unlikely to make most students of American history willing to alter the traditional,
but still recognizable, sad and somber conception of the Puritan.

This really seems to be a fruitless effort.   To claim,
as Carl Degler does, on the "evidence" of the Morgan article, that "after reading the Morgan article it is no longer
possible to see whatever asceticism or fear of sexuality
there is in America as stemming from the seventeenth-cen-
tury Puritans, "[34] is not necessarily to prove the point.
Degler offers the theory that if any group in the past is to
be blamed as the originators of the so-called "Puritan"
American attitude toward sex, it is the early nineteenth-cen-
tury Victorians.   But there is too much evidence to the contrary to give the dubious honors to Bowdler and Queen Victoria; they were the inheritors, not the founders, of a tradition.

The Morgan-Degler theory has not quite permeated to
the popular lexicographers.   A recent very popular semi-
abridged dictionary gives a definition of "Puritan" (with a
small p) as "one who lives in accordance with Protestant

precepts; especially, one who regards luxury or pleasure as sinful. " It goes on to define "Puritanism" (again, with a small p) as "scrupulous moral rigor; especially, hostility to social pleasures and indulgences. "[35] A modern unabridged American dictionary defines "puritan" (lower case) as "a person who is strict in moral or religious matters, often excessively so, " and "Puritanism" as "extreme strictness in moral or religious matters, often to excess; rigid auster-ity. "[36]

Probably the most puritanical community since John Calvin's Geneva in the sixteenth century, at least as far as controlling reading is concerned, is the Republic of Eire, which is, of course, mostly Catholic, not Protestant.   Irish censorship, especially since the establishment of the Irish Republic in 1949, has been extreme by any measure.   One more or less objective history of censorship in Ireland says that the official Register of Prohibited Publications, including as it did, at various times, works by Proust, Hemingway, Thomas Mann, Aldous Huxley, Kazantzakis, Sartre, Dylan Thomas, Sinclair Lewis, and other luminaries, was charac-terized by one Irish Senator as "Everyman's Guide to Mod-ern Classics. "[37]

The official state censorship in Ireland was established by a Censorship of Publications Bill in 1929, which was the result of an obviously impartial and unbiased Committee of Enquiry on Evil Literature, set up by the Minister of Justice of the then Free State in 1926.   Catholic public opinion caused the setting up of this Committee, and so it is hardly unexpected that its five-man membership included three Catholics and two Protestants (two university professors, two ministers, and a teachers' union leader).   They were supposed to consider whether it was necessary or advisable in the interest of public morality to grant to the state added powers to prohibit or restrict the sale and circulation of printed matter. [38]

After almost a year's study, which they spent listen-ing to publishers, booksellers, the police, postal and customs officials, various Catholic groups (such as the Catholic Truth Society of Ireland, The Irish Vigilance Association, and the Catholic Headmasters' Association), and one Protestant group (the Dublin Christian Citizenship Council), as well as review-ing related statutes then in force the world over, the Com-mittee's Report was published in the spring of 1927.   Their recommendations included, among other suggestions, that

material relating to "the unnatural prevention of conception"
should be made illegal "except to authorized persons"; that
the definition of indecency and obscenity in existing laws be
broadened to include "matter intended to excite sensual passion"; that a 9-12 member censorship board be established;
and that the office of customs be authorized to bar items on
the board's "prohibited list. "39

In 1929 the Censorship of Publications Bill was passed.
In general, it followed the Committee's recommendation.
However, there were a few changes: the Censorship of Publications Board was to include only five, not twelve, members; the word "indecent" was defined as "...including items
calculated to suggest or incite to sexual immorality or unnatural vice or in any other like way to corrupt and deprave. "
On the first point, an interesting argument was presented by
the Minister for Justice, a Mr. Fitzgerald-Keaney, who ar-
gued against trying to make the proposed Censorship Board
"representative of all shades of opinion, " since "...it simply will not work.... It is a Bill upon which there is no
room for difference of opinion, except on one ground: 'Is
this book decent or indecent?...' Everybody knows when a
book is indecent. " (This latter statement is cited as "probably the most naive remark made by the Minister in debate. ")40

The Bill, and the Censorship Board set up under it,
were in force for sixteen years before a Bill "to make further and better provision for the censorship of books and
periodical publications" was introduced into the Irish Dail
Eireann. The principal changes were to empower the Censorship Board itself to order items prohibited (rather than
so recommending to the Ministry of Justice) and to establish
an Appeals Board. The nearly 2,000 books barred between
1929 and 1945 by the Board were, obviously, without any
such right of appeal. A number of minor, clarifying amendments were also approved in the 1946 Bill; one interesting
item prohibited customs officers from keeping out of Ireland
any book on the banned list "which is carried by or forms
part of the personal baggage of an incoming traveler.... "41

In less than two decades after passage of the 1946
act (1946-1964), the Censorship Board examined 11,410 books
and prohibited just about two out of three (a total of 7,622).
During the same period the newly approved Appeals Board
revoked only 154 of the orders for prohibition made by the
Censorship Board. 42

The travail of Irish writers attests to the effectiveness of censorship and explains their exposition to the Board.   In 1956 the Irish Association of Civil Liberty sponsored an open meeting and debate on censorship, with noted Irish littérateur Sean O'Faolain as chairman.   O'Faolain noted that at that time there were no less than seven Irish censorships in existence: censorship by fear, by booksellers, by librarians, by library users, by library committees, by the Censorship Board, and by the public, "especially clergymen...."   His conclusion, as an Irish author, was that "censorship was ... an obstacle race which books have to go through before they reach you."[43]   An interesting sidelight is that in all the history of the official Irish censorship, no book written and published in Gaelic has ever been banned.[44]   Whether this indicates a greater latitude for the indigenous Irish writer, or that no censorable material has ever been written for publication in the Gaelic language, is not clear.

Norman St. John-Stevas, in 1956, claimed that "the Irish censors hold that it is better to lose all the masterpieces of world literature, rather than risk the contamination of a single soul by admitting an impure book."   He said that there was little objection in Ireland to the principle of "some" censorship, but that there was "unanimous opposition among writers to the methods and policy of the present Board."[45]

The judgment that obscene literature is objectionable is generally accepted by the Irish.   There is generally felt to exist a prima facie case for some control of its sale and distribution.   But any conceivable threat to public morality which a book of "marginal" literary merit might have is heavily "outweighed by the constant danger of heavy-handed censorship turning Ireland into a cultural ghetto...."   Michael Adams reflects such ambivalence in stating that Irish children were "being artificially protected, not educated," but that Dublin is "a pleasant place to walk in, where sex is embodied in living persons, not sidewalk hoardings and neonsigns."[46]

Perhaps the most hopeful sign for eventual Irish freedom from censorship is that in 1967 a Censorship of Publications Bill passed in the Dail ("with little or no parliamentary debate...").   This bill limited to only twelve years, instead of permanency, the duration of a prohibition order and permitted appeals at any time, instead of only within twelve months, as previously.[47]   It appears that times do change, albeit slowly.   The Geneva of today--for censors--is still

Ireland, but there is as much hope there as in the United
States for the eventual demise, or at least grave illness, of
Puritanism as a literary force. The bloody internecine
struggles going on these past few years between the Irish
Catholics and Protestants--if they lead, as they well may,
to an eventual union of Northern Ireland and Eire--may some
day politically influence future moral and censorial judgments. The death of strict literary censorship in Ireland is
slow in coming--but it seems to be inevitable.

The Puritan tradition reasserted relationships among
religion, sexuality, and censorship. Christianity's relating
of its sexuality-fear and the work-ethic may derive from assumptions that if individuals spend more than a certain
amount of time and physical energy in bodily pleasures they
will find it hard to compete in the struggle for existence.
A common supposition is that Christian sexual ethics were
particularly appropriate for making use of sexual energy in
societally useful ways. John Langdon-Davies writes: "Sexuality was enslaved to the primary needs of society, an increasing population, and the release of as much human energy as possible for the conquest of the natural environment."[48]
Obviously, if burgeoning populations the world over mean
that a high birthrate is no longer needed by Christian society, and if repressing sexual expression produces such readily observable results as a high divorce rate, excessive concern with pornography, a greater tendency to homosexuality,
neuroticism in large quantities, and similar time-and-energy
(let along guilt-causing) consequences, then perhaps it is
high time for at least a good hard look at the modern sexual
ethics of Christianity, their causes, actualities, and probable
consequences.

As for the paradigmatic puritan--Irish, Swiss, English, American, or whatever--the contemporary American
poet, Karl Shapiro, has described him in this verse:[49]

> He is the Puritan under whose tall hat
> Evil is nested like an ugly toad,
> And in his eye he holds the basilisk,
> And in his weathered hand the knotted goad;
> Brimstone is on his tongue, for he will risk
> Hellfire to pleasure; sin is his abode,
> A barn and Bible his best habitat.

The tall-hatted man with "brimstone on his tongue"
still walks American streets; he is represented in the 60-5

vote of the U.S. Senate, in 1970, to reject the anti-censorship report by the Presidential Commission on Obscenity and
Pornography; he speaks in the local "purity" group with its
vigilante methods; he can even be heard in a majority U.S.
Supreme Court decision condemning a man not for what he
published or writes about sex, but for how he advertises it.
He can neither tolerate any pleasure in sex or any sex in
pleasure.   As Macaulay said, long ago, "The Puritan hated
bear-baiting, not because it gave pain to the bear, but because it gave pleasure to the spectator. "[50]

7. TODAY'S RELIGION AND TOMORROW'S CENSORSHIP

"... Faith, fanatic Faith, once wedded fast
To some dear falsehood, keeps it to the last. "

--Thomas Moore, Lalla Rookh, 1817.

Chapter 7

TODAY'S RELIGION AND TOMORROW'S CENSORSHIP

It is an act of foolhardiness, rather than courage, to try to bring some order into the chaos of confused dogmas and shattered icons which is today's religion. But if what is happening now on the freedom-to-read-about-sex front is to be understood, the attempt must be made. Aside from the disparities of view between major faiths, there are to be taken into account the variances within sects and almost between individual divines, even those of basically the same faith and creed. What follows is a representative sampling of opinions, which should at least offer some revelatory glimpses into the shifting scene of the religion of this generation, in relationship to the censorship of today and tomorrow.

Let us begin with Dr. David R. Mace, a perspicacious, basically conservative, and widely influential sociologist and marriage counselor, who reminds us that "if Christianity persists in presenting itself as an anti-sexual religion, it will not get a hearing in this generation." Since, as he points out, the traditional Christian sex ethic "rests upon foundations that have been almost completely discredited, either by modern scientific knowledge or by the conditions of modern life...," there really is no justification for continuing to regard desire shown through sexual activity as inherently sinful (this dates all the way back to Paul and Augustine, of course) or for accepting what Mace describes as "the Hebrew horror of wasting semen..." (the real basis for condemnation of masturbation). [1]

Since the time is long past when the Church (any church) can impose what it believes are appropriate ethical standards on communities by "force and fear," then maybe it is time--and past time--for the Church to reevaluate and reconsider its stance on sexual behavior. Mace suggests two positive actions for the Church and all Christians, particularly

Protestants, to take: first, that "the Church ... reverse its negative and punitive attitudes toward sex, ... to take a much more positive approach, " and second, that the whole topic of human sexual behavior be opened up "for full and continuing discussion. " His point is that "unless we can talk about sex, we cannot think about it.... " He calls for "a great ongoing dialogue about sex, admitting the light of knowledge and truth where the darkness of superstition and ignorance has lingered for too long. "2

This sounds very open and forward-looking indeed. How consistent--and perhaps this is as good a test as any-- is Dr. Mace's view on censorship with its call for "openness" about sex? Happily, quite consistent. Although he describes pornography as the "undesirable element" of the "new openness" about sex, and describes it as "offensive by any standard..., " he does exhort Christians not to become overly emotional about it. It is clear to him that the very act of bringing sex out of its former hidden and secret place in human existence was bound to expose to the light much unsatisfied curiosity which was always there. He sees whatever risk there is in pornography as just one part of the price which has to be paid for free and open dealing with sex, and thinks it a risk well worth taking. 3

A most distinguished British theologian, the Reverend Derrick Sherwin Bailey, after devoting some 231 pages of his comprehensive history of sexual relations in the Christian tradition to telling what has been the tradition, summarizes his survey in these words: "Almost from the beginning, we discern a markedly negative reaction to everything venereal which has profoundly and adversely affected the character and development of Christian sexual ideas--a reaction expressed with every degree of intensity from mild suspicion or apathy to violent hostility or revulsion. " Out of all the characteristics of human life, it seems, sex alone was singled out as always irremediably evil, in a greater or less degree. Bailey admits there are exceptions to this, but points out that "there is ... a vague and almost unformulated notion that the Church [the Church of England, that is] regards sex as a regrettable and unmentionable necessity, and venereal sin as the worst of all transgressions. "4

In contrast to this, Bailey offers what he describes as the truly Christian idea of sex and marriage in a rapidly changing society where the changes are far from over. 5 These changes, he feels, make the traditional Protestant and

Catholic teachings on sexual relations much more than out-
of-date; they are actually detrimental to the life and growth
of religious faith.

Among the events which have brought about current
thinking on matters of sex Bailey lists the following: the
liberation of western woman, the urbanization of much of
western civilization (and the parallel decline of rural-small
town life), changes in the patterns of political government
and ideologies, the growth of state-supported welfare services, the effect of new types of transportation (the auto-
mobile, the jet plane, freeways) and, "more than anything
else, the extensive and manifold effects of two world wars. "6
All of these have affected society's attitude toward sexual
matters--whether towards sexual techniques, sexual frankness, divorce, contraception, or almost any other action
connected with sex. Bailey admits that the traditional Christian concepts concerning sexual relationships and activities
are "in certain aspects ... clearly inconsistent with the
modern understanding of human personality and sexuality.... "7

An Anglican document was issued a few years ago
which is definitely the product of modern, rather than medieval, theology. This publication, The Family in Contemporary Society, a report of the Lambeth Conference, a world
conference of Anglican and Episcopalian leaders held in England in 1958, offered some up-to-date modifications of traditional Protestant thought. They held false the idea that
"there is, in any sexual relationship, an intrinsic evil. "
They admitted that "the fear which has so often dominated
sexual intercourse has largely disappeared, and with it many
of the accustomed disciplines of sexual conduct. "8 These
are quite sweeping and tradition-breaking statements and
policies.

The report criticizes "the low standards of social
morality which are the content of much that meets the eye
and assails the ear today, " but nowhere do they call for censorship, whether by the government, by secular groups, or
even by religious groups. They say that "Home, School,
and Church have to build up a resistant attitude to ... these
corrupting influences..., " but that resistance is nowhere
linked to actual censorship. 9 So not the most liberal of
modern Protestant sects, the Anglican-Episcopalian Church,
has presented its iconoclastic views as a world-wide group--
views which, unfortunately, have not always seemed to filter
down to the individual communicant or minister, if the

continued prevalence of would-be censorship in both the
United States and the United Kingdom, since 1958, are any
witness.

What can be done about this seemingly impassable
gulf between religion and sex today? In 1964 the British
Council of Churches set up a Working Party (British term
for what Americans usually call an Ad Hoc Committee) with
the following purpose: "To prepare a Statement of the Christian case for abstinence from sexual intercourse before marriage and faithfulness within marriage, taking full account of
responsible criticism, and to suggest means whereby the
Christian position may be effectively presented to the various sections of the community. "10   The Rev. Dr. Sherwin
Bailey, whose ideas were discussed earlier in this chapter,
was the consultant to this group, which included, among
others, a journalist, a Methodist deaconness, a gynecologist,
a biologist, and several teachers and professors, along with
two ministers.

Their report, issued in 1966, included, among other
recommendations, the following: more sex education in the
schools (given as part of courses on human relations which
they suggested should become part of the curricula of all
schools); that "the Government should make itself responsible
for continuing and co-ordinating research into the effects of
the mass media on the maturation of young people"; and that
"the law which affects sexual conduct [should be brought] into
line with informed contemporary opinion. "11

One of the most influential and forward-looking statements of a particular Christian faith's attitude on sex today
was issued by the British Society of Friends (Quakers) in
1964. 12   Although introduced as "unofficial, " it still is pretty
well representative of how this liberal (theologically speaking)
group stands on matters relating to sex.

They refer to what they call "a still repressive and
inhibited outlook towards sex" as one which "...has invested
a normal function with guilt, mystery and ignorance ...
[which] has devalued the sexual currency to the levels of
sensation and pornography. " They feel that "sexuality,
looked at dispassionately, is neither good nor evil--it is a
fact of nature and a force of immeasurable power. "13

They give various historical and theological reasons
for rejecting the view "that there is anything necessarily

sinful about sexual activity ... [since] sexual activity is essentially neither good nor evil; it is a normal biological
activity which, like most other human activities, can be in-
dulged in destructively or creatively. " In the light of this
Quaker attitude, it is easy to understand why, although they
do not say so explicitly, they must be held to be against
censorship; as they say they are not "asking for an impossible conformity.... "14

Their code of sexual morals is quite different from
the traditional Christian code.   They define sin as "...those
actions that involve exploitation of the other person. " They
consider "fundamentally immoral any sexual action that is
not, as far as is humanly ascertainable, the result of a
mutual decision. "15

In summation, the Quaker view, as expressed in this
statement, is that "morality should be creative.   God is
primarily Creator, not rulemaker, "--a dictum which is poles
apart from God as Moral Censor!   The booklet is especially
of note for its fundamental attitude of awareness of and willingness to accomodate to what they call "a deeper morality
... concerned with the whole nature of man, " which certainly
includes sexuality, despite the efforts by some other faiths
to deny its very existence.   The Quakers point out that often
religious groups are so idealistic, so unrealistic that their
moral codes are really "an escape from having to face the
darker levels of our own nature. "16

A modern Presbyterian approach to Christian ethics
is offered by Dr. David H. X. Read, minister of the Madison
Avenue Presbyterian Church, whose book is epitomized in his
statement that "the more determined Christians are to create
a Christian society the more certain they are to ... employ
the weapons of force and compulsion. " He cites Europe in
medieval times, today's Spain, the Geneva of Calvin, and
Puritan New England as would-be truly Christian societies
which failed to be so. 17

Read suggests that perhaps the simplest way to describe modern Christian ethics is to say that "our course of
action is bounded by a response to the revelation of God ...
we are responsible for our behavior to a supreme authority.... " Accepting this, the modern Presbyterian--or Protestant, or Christian--must not really want a middle-man, a
censor, to tell him how to think or what to read.   Read
grants that our "period of sweeping change breeds a moral

rigidity...," but he doesn't think that this is a good thing. [18]
He cites the historically proven dynamism of Christian ethics,
and calls on Christians to be Christians, to face our confusing and ever-changing world directly. He will not accept
either the extreme of the rule-bound moralist or of the
hedonist; Read describes the best place for the Christian believer as in the "dynamic middle"--defined by Read as "an
ethical and theological conviction that expresses both a loyalty to the Christian Gospel and a sensitivity to the unique
needs of our age. "[19]

     An Emory University professor of Christian ethics,
E. Clinton Gardner, has attempted to explain the moral
activity of man as he sees it from the standpoint of being a
Christian--a conservative Christian. He differs strongly
with Joseph Fletcher's situation ethics (discussed in detail
in Chapter XII), since he feels that Fletcher is much too
antagonistic to traditional, "legalistic" Christian ethics; or,
rather, that Fletcher is wrong in describing traditional
Christian ethics as being impossibly legalistic and rule-
bound. [20]

     Gardner does, however, agree with Fletcher in a few
respects. He agrees with Fletcher, for example, that faith
is primary in any consideration of morals; he and Fletcher
both feel that Christian ethics is best understood "in terms
of man's responsive love...," or agape. Both try to deal
with what is in the moral life of man, rather than with an
ideal or a law which tries to set the pattern for each moral
situation as it comes up. Both "are opposed to legalism
and to antinomianism," says Gardner. Lastly, according to
Gardner, both agree in judging the values of good and evil
in relation to what is, not in the abstract. [21]

     Well, then, where do they really differ? Gardner
says his view--the modern version of the traditional Christian ethical concept--is based on both the Old and the New
Testaments, whereas Fletcher's ideas are exclusively
grounded on Christology and the New Testament. Gardner
says that to understand Christian faith and ethics one must
see mankind in the kind of historical perspective provided by
both parts of the Bible, which will bring understanding that,
in ultimate terms, the divine will is and must be paramount.
(There are certainly echoes here of Dante's epitome of early
medieval faith, "in sua volente è nostre pace. ") If one
agrees with Gardner, one will accept his theory which only
slightly modifies the traditional original sin and Fall of Man
doctrines.

Gardner claims that "according to the biblical doctrine of creation, man was created free, but he was not given autonomy; ... his essential humanity can be preserved and fulfilled only on the basis of his recognition and acceptance of the ordered pattern of creation...." And this ties in with Gardner's view that "because man is a being who lives in time and in history, his present needs and potentialities cannot be understood apart from his relationships to the past and future."22 Gardner feels that Fletcher's situation ethics are not sufficiently based on traditional history. The Gardner interpretation of Christian ethics certainly offers a strong justification for ultra-conservative judgments on both sexual conduct and the reading of literature about sex; if his really is the prevailing Christian theological view (which does not seem to be the case), then censorship in the 1970's and the years to follow has at least a strong theological base.

Father Robert W. Gleason, a Jesuit theology professor at Fordham University, writing in the same symposium as Gardner, criticizes both situation ethics and the "new morality" as being too subjective and relativist to be truly Christian. He cites the nobility of love as a motivating force for ethical action, but says that "it is not in Christian tradition to present it as the exclusive motive for moral action." For him, situation ethics, besides having been condemned by Papal ukase in 1956, is not acceptable because it "is a morality that does not adequately represent the spirit of the gospel." He describes the new morality as being based on "an ethics of confrontation," which Gleason sees as an ancient heresy, "the principle of immediate illumination," hardly likely to be acceptable to Roman Catholicism.23

Another symposiast, Los Angeles Methodist Bishop Gerald Kennedy, describes Fletcher's situation ethics as simply heresy, which, in his definition, is "false belief which so distorts a man's view of reality that it makes him unhappy and miserable." He condemns Fletcher because, he says, Fletcher "...absolutizes agape and eliminates the place of law." Kennedy finds situation ethics simply unrealistic if it is attempting to provide an ethos for a truly Christian social life. He concludes by saying, "Absolutes are for God alone and only the meek inherit the earth."24 But his views clearly support censorship, hardly what one would expect "the meek" to do!

Fletcher's response to these criticisms (and others included in the book) centers on his explanation of what he sees as the "critical issue posed.... Are there any moral principles, other than to do the most good possible, which oblige us in conscience at all times?" And his answer, as one might expect, is negative. He claims that although the ethics of classic Christian religion have been essentially legalistic, most men of any faith have actually been situationists in practice. (This certainly is borne out by the insistence in America, on a governmental level, on censorship being enforced, at the same time that the actions about which the censored books are written are, by all indices, at their peak.) He also asserts that "situation ethics is a mediating position between ethical absolutism and the unprincipled ethics of existentialism."25

Fletcher admits freely that situation ethics is definitely relativistic, and sees this as a "plus." As he puts it, those who believe in and practice the new morality use principles but are not used by them. He paraphrases Jesus' statement about man and the Sabbath, in these words: "Moral principles were made for men, not men for moral principles," and concludes, "That is situation ethics in a nutshell."26

In 1967 nine members of the faculty of the University of Toronto collaborated on what the editor of the resulting volume, philosophy professor William Dunphy, called an effort to create a contemporary morality.27 As part of this presentation, Michael Sheehan, a professor of ecclesiastical and medieval history, stresses that it is not essential to the Christian to have a negative morality; he calls for training in what he calls "the positive shaping of morality, in the possibilities of exploiting the permissible...." He describes today's world as one "in which it is very likely that man's liberty will be defended less by institutions and customary systems of action than by a constant tension of the mature intellect judging and directing life as it unfolds."28 Surely this is a truly contemporary, even forward-looking view, one which should be respected and followed by Catholic and non-Catholic alike.

Professor of theology Stanley Kutz points out that "the typical Roman Catholic attitude toward moral questions is one which could accurately be described as 'preventive'--in the sense that we seek always to be one step ahead of life." From the early Christian Fathers on, this philosophy has indeed been constant, and Kutz asks for a new Catholic approach, what he calls "an attitude of 'inventiveness,' whereby

we would seek to learn from the events of life, rather than
to anticipate them. "29   His point is that if one bases his
morals on a spirit of constant discovery, rather than pre-
vention--of which censorship must certainly be an outstanding example--then there would be less conflict between what
reason tells us we should do, and what emotion makes us
feel like doing.

Kutz says that legalism is no answer, because its only result, in the light of the body-mind eternal conflict, must
be self-hatred, accompanied by fear of love--in all of its
meanings.   He says that "hatred and fear are but two faces
of the same reality.   We hate that which we fear...,"30 and
certainly, it should be added, the whole history of censorship bears witness to this.

Robert Grimm, a Swiss theologian, has written a
volume31 which its translator has described as being "the
most daringly positive approach to sexuality that any Christian writer ... has yet adopted. "   Well, let's see.

To begin with, he says that "to deny one's sexuality
is to refuse to accept the order of Creation. "   So he is
strongly opposed to asceticism.   He says that "today, the
majority of Catholic and Protestant theologians are in agreement that the original sin of man was not sexual in nature. "32
For Grimm, and those who agree with him, the only reason
sexuality and sin can be equated is that man has not accepted his commandment from God to be human--certainly
quite a different approach from the traditionalist one; indeed,
almost its reverse.

Grimm decries the traditional Christian theology which,
he says, has too frequently looked upon man's physical nature as the basic source of sin, indeed "as an enemy to be
subdued. "   He says further that it is much more than simply
a Christian tenet; that the distrust of sexuality is the outcome of a deep-rooted belief that sex has a kind of demonic
power, "...a power that can take control of the whole personality and bring about its destruction. "   But he sees no
justification for such a belief in the usual source of Christian authority, the Bible. 33

One clarification offered by Grimm is on the term
"the flesh, " which, although very commonly identified with
sexuality or the body, as compared to the spirit, he says,
"designates our human condition, our revolt against our

destiny, our stubborn pride. " This wider vision is helpful
to anyone who sincerely wishes to look at the Christian sexual ethic from a modern point of view. As Grimm states,
"Identifying the flesh with sexual sin represents confusion of
thought which the Church needs to clear up. "[34]

Grimm summarizes our current situation, most succinctly, as follows: "... love puts us in an embarrassing,
if not an impossible, situation. It is nonconformist and
hostile to all attempts at regulation. It raises more controversial issues than any other phenomenon in human society;
issues which we cannot afford to ignore. " He decries what
he describes as the societal response to love, which is to
"socialize and institutionalize. " When society attempts to
control love by rules and regulations, "we all know the price
that has to be paid for this ... conventional and hypocritical
unions, taboos and inhibitions, constant revolts. " He asks
why there has never been a legal system which "dared to set
love free. " He questions why Eros cannot be granted liberty, "why ... its demonic qualities must be held in check by
putting it under institutional control. "[35] Whether this is a
statement for or against censorship is hard to interpret, but
it is certainly a statement which is in disagreement with the
generally accepted view of what happens when sex is put in
chains.

A symposium of conservative French Catholic thought
on sin, in a book by that name published within this decade,
is most revelatory. The American translation was given the
imprimatur by Cardinal Spellman, and is clearly in agreement with current official doctrine, the world over. The
best-known of the contributors to this symposium, Marc
Oraison, says that "the mystery of original sin ... appears
as the really massive and primordial fact of all human history. " He also says that "the guilt complex ... is one of
the most radical realities about man. "[36] He uses St. Paul
as the principal authority for these statements.

In the same volume, Gustav Siewerth explains the
modern Catholic doctrine of original sin as regarding all
sense inclinations as good. He even goes so far as to say
that as long as it is under the control of reason, desire is
an acceptable part of man's nature. He presents the view
that St. Thomas Aquinas (his main authority) differed from
St. Augustine on original sin, in feeling that man's sexual
tendency was the effect of original sin, not of other causes.

Siewerth goes beyond St. Thomas somewhat by re-defining original sin as lust, which he sees as being not sensual desire but rather the pleasure involved in such desire. He says that sense pleasure is definitely not intrinsically bad; it is only bad if not procured as part of normal married life. He puts it this way: "... lust as such [is] ... not sinful or corrupt, but only ... hidden, absolute sex would be."[37]

One can readily see that, if this is the basic Catholic theological doctrine about sex and related matters, it is most unlikely that a believing, tradition-minded Catholic can go along with any kind of reading which gives him sexual pleasure. Indeed, to avoid sin it is really incumbent on him to make sure that no one else has such a "temptation"; in other words, to avoid sin the Catholic who accepts the Aquinas-Siewerth doctrine should either be the censor, or at least assist him.

There are liberal religionists in France, as elsewhere; in the past few decades a neo-Catholic theology has grown up, fostered by believers in "Christian humanism." Their leader, Pierre Teilhard de Chardin, who was a Jesuit priest, said that "original sin ... is the tight collar which strangles our minds and hearts...." Teilhard de Chardin was not reconciled to living in "a universe whose principal business was reparation and expiation..." for this sin. He thundered that "for a variety of reasons, scientific, moral and religious, the classic formulation of the Fall has ceased to be anything more than a yoke and a verbal affirmation...."[38]

A comprehensive French study of sexuality today[39] which included ideas on the subject by liberal theologians, psychoanalysts, philosophers, and psychologists, gives some further insights into this whole point of view and its implications. The editor is concerned with what he sees as the dominant theme in Western religious thought, mainly "hatred of life and anti-sexual resentment...." He sees the chance of current society's breaking away almost entirely from the concept of sexuality as being merely "a social function of procreation..." and instead, suggests it as having the goal of "...the cultivation of pleasure." Once this happens, the erotic, rather than the social, element in the sexual life of man is dominant, he says.[40]

Paul Ricoeur attributes this trend to several factors: the first is sex's fall into relative insignificance because of

increased sexual freedom (which he attributes to all the different things which make sexual encounters easy nowadays),
and next is "the fact that vulgarized sexological literature
had entered the public domain...." What D. H. Lawrence
once called "the dirty little secret" is far from a secret and
is not considered dirty by an increasingly large percentage
of the populace, in France and elsewhere.   Finally, Ricoeur
refers to the "depersonalization and anonymity" of modern
life in Western civilization as a cause of the new trend
toward looking on sexuality as pleasurable.   His conclusion
on all this is that "sexuality remains basically impermeable
to reflection and inaccessible to human mastery. "41 If this
is true, then perhaps Ricoeur's whole theory is self-negat-
ing!

          Orthodox Catholicism today is still opposed to erotic
writing: an authorized spokesman, writing in The Encyclopedia of Sexual Behavior in 1959, whose statement bears the
"nihil obstat" and "imprimatur" of Bishop O'Connell and
Archbishop O'Boyle, says that, "because of the sensitivity
of weakened nature to sexual arousal, dress, movies, literature, television, radio, and similar means of suggestion
and communication should be free of anything of an inciting
nature. " He describes sex as "nature's deepest secret... "
and says, "... secrets must not be easily disclosed, especially if they are associated with a function so important to
the welfare of the race. " In sum, on the need for censorship, the spokesman for Roman Catholicism generalizes that
"because of man's lack of autocratic control over lower nature and his sensitivity to sexual arousal, modesty in dress,
posture, movies, literature, television, etc., is imperative. "42

          Another quite acceptable source for the modern tradi-
tional American Catholic attitude toward censorship and sexuality is a book43 subtitled "A Text on Sex Education for
Christian Parents and for Those Concerned with Helping Parents, " written by a Catholic priest and published in the very
widely sold and distributed paperback Image Books series.
The book bears all the Catholic seals of approval, the im-
primi potest, the nihil obstat, and a bishop's imprimatur.
In the foreword we are told that "Father Sattler bases his
teachings on the rules laid down by the Catholic Church for
the sex training of the young, and particularly on the directions given by the two most recent Popes, Pius XI and Pius
XII. "

He recites the doctrine of original sin just about as did St. Paul, St. Augustine, and St. Thomas Aquinas. As Sattler puts it, "on account of Adam's sin, we, his descendants, came into the world deprived of sanctifying grace, and inherit all his punishments. This sin in us is called original sin." He says that the most difficult of all immoral tendencies to control are the sexual passions, and that "original sin creates more havoc in that realm than in any other."[44]

In his chapter on "Dangers to Purity," Father Sattler stresses the "danger" of personal immodesty, in which he includes "the evil effects of obscene, sexy and pornographic books, magazines, photographs, movies, plays and burlesque shows." He alludes to the requirement for Catholics of "modesty of eyes...."[45] This is because, Father Sattler says, of "our modern pagan surroundings, with the allurements to sexual pleasure painted on all sides...." Shades of Savonarola!

There are several other Sattlerian admonitions which bear reprinting. Speaking of sexual pleasure, he says "...it must not be delighted in with the will; that is, it must not be wished, wanted, caused, approved, or deliberately enjoyed outside of marriage.... Sin lies in willful consent or deliberate delight, not necessarily in the mere experience of bodily pleasure" (Father Sattler's emphasis). Catholics are advised, again with emphatic stress, that "any deliberate thought, imagination, reading, look, touch, or anything else which may arouse sexual feelings is a mortal or venial sin, or no sin at all, depending on the degree of sexual stirring such acts cause in proportion to the reason for acting."[46] Certainly this kind of sex-education, if adhered to, would make any faithful Catholic at least a believer in censorship, if not himself a censor.

A more liberal Catholic cleric, Father John Courtney Murray, agrees with the traditionalists to the extent of stating that "the influence of inordinate and unregulated sexual passion on the life of reason in man is a commonplace of human and historical experience." But he seems to differ in being careful to warn that censorship by civil authorities must be according to due and proper legal process. He also says that although literary obscenity may be "a major social evil, the power of the police against it is severely limited." He claims that the "ordinary father and mother ought to be qualified to act as censors within the family ... " but he approves extralegal censorship, outside of the family, only

under severe restrictions. [47]   Civil rights matter to Father
Murray.

Judaism today has its share of censorship-minded individuals, but Rabbi Robert Gordis has expressed more or
less the "official" Jewish point of view on issues involving
sex and censorship in the following statement: "Judaism
has a healthy-minded, affirmative attitude toward sex, which
it recognizes as an essential and legitimate element of human life.   Since God created man with his entire comple-
ment of impulses, sex is a manifestation of the Divine.   It
is therefore neither to be glorified, as in the exaggerations
of romantic love, nor denigrated, as in classic Christian
theology. "[48]

Rabbi Gordis stresses that the two basic documents of
the Jewish faith, the Old Testament and the Talmud, "are
frank and outspoken in dealing with the sexual component of
human experiences. "   He says proudly, "The pages of our
classic literature are free both from obscenity and false
modesty, from pornography and comstockery.... "   He admits that "... a negative attitude toward sexual relations is
sporadically encountered in Jewish literature ... " but says,
"it is far from representing the romantic view" which is that
husband-wife sex is "... a perfectly legitimate form of pleasure, " self-justifying, even if not aimed at procreation. [49]

The New Standard Jewish Encyclopedia, speaking of
the very few known efforts by the Jewish community to censor particular writings, says: "None of these attempts, was,
however, permanently successful and, on the whole, such
suppression was alien to the Jewish spirit. "[50]

One of the most liberal of today's Jewish theological
leaders, Rabbi Richard L. Rubinstein, has unequivocally expressed himself as opposed to literary censorship, basing
his opinion on his aesthetic judgment that "the value of literature depends upon its capacity to lend insight into some aspect of the human predicament. "   He feels that the almost
certain lack of objectivity by those people who are constantly
involved in the human problem makes the job of the censor
difficult, if not impossible.   As a background for these opinions, he states that "the fundamental Jewish posture is one
of realism before existence rather than of seeking an escape
from the world's necessities. "[51]   He sees Judaism as more
what he calls a "this-worldly" religion than Christianity,
which he sees as basically an "other-worldly" or "next-world-
ly" faith.

Or, as American Jewish novelist Herman Wouk puts it
(referring to sexual intercourse), "What in other cultures has
been a deed of shame, or of comedy, or of orgy, or of physical
necessity, or of high romance, has been in Judaism one of
the main things God wants men to do. If it also turns out
to be the keenest pleasure in life, that is no surprise to a
people eternally sure God is good."[52] Under such circumstances, and with such a belief, how could Jews be censors?

Thousands of years ago Aristophanes wrote of his
times, "Whirl is King, having driven out Zeus." The fer-
ment in religious thinking today, only touched upon in the
preceding section--from the "Death of God" adherents to the
Catholic priests who advocate marriage for themselves instead of celibacy; from the Berrigan brothers and their acti-
vist interpretation of social ethics to the fundamentalist
"Jesus cultists"--is far from nearing any stability. In the
area of sexual ethics and morality it would be hard to state
a clear-cut, generally accepted Judeo-Christian doctrine for
the 1970's.

But some trends and tendencies are beginning to become evident. As psychologist and theologian William Graham Cole has said, "It must be confessed that there is much
not worth defending in the interpretations of sex found in
Augustine and Aquinas, in Luther and Calvin." He indicts
the Church for manifesting what he calls "its typical social
inertia...,"[53] especially in its moralistic teachings.

Today's religion is beginning to see the body as a dis-
cussable part of man, in Cole's phrase, "to be used, not
abused, to be enjoyed, not punished." Asceticism, as such,
is no more moral or "Christian" than sensuality. "Sex,"
Cole says, "can be affirmed as one of God's greatest gifts
to man, the key which unlocks the door to community," so
there must be, for the truly modern religious man, "a glad
and grateful acceptance of sex and of the human body and the
organs that render coitus possible. Anything less than this
is a denial of God's handiwork."[54]

Censorship, in such a religious milieu, is both unnecessary and impractical. When a modern Protestant religious leader can say that "it is perfectly normal to enjoy a
mild erotic stimulation from such activities as dancing, the
reading of novels, or watching movies and plays...,"[55] the
religious rationale for censorship has all but vanished.

Cole's conclusions on this whole matter are pertinent; he finds that the Christian who is true to his basic faith is appreciative of receiving joys of the flesh from God, looking upon sex as "a divine gift." The Christian of today, says Cole, will not have shame or guilt feelings about his or anyone else's body, or <u>any</u> of the body's organs and functions.

Without shame, super-modesty, ultra-respect for asceticism, how can the censor flourish? Unfortunately, there is no real unanimity, in any time-period of human existence, in regards to morals. As Nicolas Berdyaev has put it, "The modern man has, in addition to his civilized mentality, the mind of the man of antiquity, of the child with its infantile instincts, of the madman and the neurasthenic."[56] What is important is that we are aware of our split personalities, of our internal conflicts, and that we not use them as justification for advocating censorship, just in case the civilized portion of our mind is really the part that is in error.

It is certainly a sign of progress toward true civilization when the official statement on this topic by as tradition-following a group as the conservative American Lutheran Church (Missouri Synod) can conclude its lengthy exegesis on <u>Sex and the Church</u> by saying flatly: there is "no room for a false asceticism in the Christian view of sex. Sex is not 'evil' or 'dirty'...."[57] It goes on to say, "Prudery has failed miserably. It made matters of sex secretive and unwholesome for the child, lustful for youth, and then often resorted to face-saving moralisms." If even this ultra-conservative religious sect can argue in this way, there is indeed hope for an eventual general acceptance of the age-old belief that "Ye shall know the truth, and the truth shall make you free."

8. THE PSYCHOLOGY OF REPRESSION: THE MOTIVATIONS OF THE CENSOR

> "... man is condemned to oscillate between a restricted and uneasy gratification of his drives and a regretful and guilt-loaded renunciation."
>
> --Theodor Reik, *Myth and Guilt*, 1957.

Chapter 8

THE PSYCHOLOGY OF REPRESSION:
THE MOTIVATIONS OF THE CENSOR

Viewing the origins of censorship as purely anthropological or historical or religious or linguistic, as we have so far, is to overlook one of the basic reasons for the existence of the censor and of censorship. The psychobiological explanation for censorship, or, to put it another way, the search for the censorious element common to all men, must be derived from a study of what man is like in his basic, psychosexual nature.

Most individuals, as Rollo May phrased it, have "difficulty in accepting the instinctual, sexual side of life."[1] Freud, of course, made no exceptions. He found that "the neurotic is above all inhibited in his actions...."[2] He predicated his whole theory of psychoanalysis on the frustrations of man's psychosexual nature.

In one comparatively little-known article,[3] Freud postulated that all mankind can be divided into three main types, at least in terms of the amount of libido in their psyches. The least common type Freud calls the "erotic," whose "chief interest ... is bestowed upon the love life," who lives primarily "to love and be loved...." The second (and perhaps most prevalent) order of man Freud describes as the "compulsive" type, the kind of man who is "mastered by the fear of conscience instead of by the fear of losing...." This type of man, says the Viennese sage, is the "conservative pillar of civilization." Third in this Freudian gallery is the "narcissistic" type, whose "chief interest is toward self-maintenance...." Narcissistic man either becomes a leader or else attacks his own existing order in society; he is "independent and little intimidated." Actually, there are few people who correspond exactly to these three types, as might be expected. Of the three, it might seem that the compulsive type most nearly corresponds with the censor, as revealed by his works.

Freud says that most people are actually, in various
degrees, mixtures of "erotic-narcissistic"; although there
are both erotic-compulsive and narcissistic-compulsive types.
Freud characterizes the latter as the "most valuable variation for civilization...." The narcissistic-compulsive is
described as one who "combines vigorous activity with outward independence and respect for the dictates of conscience
and reinforces the ego...."

Sigmund Freud was quite precise and definite in saying[4] that "the sexual factor is the essential one in the causation of true neuroses..." and "...all factors which operate
injuriously upon the sexual life and suppress its activity or
distort its aims ... [are] pathological factors in the psycho-
neuroses." He is not critical of what he sees but simply
states the fact, as he sees it, that "our civilization is, generally speaking, founded on the suppression of instincts."
We all give up something--our complete anarchistic freedom,
our unlimited sexual desires, our tendency to dominate, or
our tendency to be vindictive--as part of living in a civilized
society. Through first the family, then the nation, we have
become civilized and cultured. But of all the instincts, it
is the sexual one which is most difficult for us to suppress,
or permit to be suppressed.

We displace our sexual drive by sublimating, according to Freud--that is to say, exchanging our original, wholly
sexual goals for another which is only "psychically related"
to sex. We all need some direct sexual satisfaction, and,
if this minimal amount is frustrated, we become neurotic.

Freud sees a development of the sexual instinct as
each normal individual matures, "from auto-eroticism to ob-
ject-love," and then on to procreation and reproduction. An
analysis of these is discernible in the progress of civilization: "first, the stage in which the sexual impulse may be
freely exercised in regards to aims which do not lead to
procreation; a second stage, in which the whole of the sexual
impulse is suppressed except that portion which seeks procreation; and a third stage, in which only legitimate procreation is allowed as a sexual aim." Freud says that it is
this third level which is our present-day "'civilized' sexual
morality."[5]

Freud deplores the fact that "under the presence of

education and of social demands ... a miscarriage of suppression" occurs. He says that "one of the obvious injustices of social life is that the standard of culture should demand the same behavior in sexual life from everyone.... "6 Surely the work of the censor is aimed at what never has been and never will be: the ideal individual, sexually speaking.

Under the accepted code of Judeo-Christian morality, in Freud's day and ours, the only approved sexual fulfillment can be sexual fulfillment between man and wife. Freud criticizes enforced sexual abstinence as detrimental to the individual and even to the civilization which enforces it, bringing about, or at least encouraging, "the so-called perverse forms of intercourse between the sexes.... " He describes in some detail other consequences of "the insistence upon abstinence, " including limited or no potency in married men, frigid (to some degree) wives--indeed, neurotic families. Putting it very simply, he sees a causal relationship between "civilized" sexual morality and a generally unhappy citizenhood. 7

The censor's role in all this is that of helper, working within the accepted code to help frustrate any indirect manifestations of the sexual drive. Why does the censor exist, psychologically speaking? Or, to put it another way, what is the psychological makeup of the kind of person who wants to censor, to deny, to restrict, to repress or inhibit others? A reasonably acceptable theory is offered by J. C. Flugel in his discussion of what he calls a "fundamental human tendency--the tendency to take pleasure in the exercise of mastery.... "8

This is stated otherwise as "repressive morality. " According to Flugel, "a number of the writers taking this general point of view believe that excessive repression is connected with the child's attitude to the father.... " In other words, the child who grows up under paternal repression, who uses a tyrannical father as a model, is likely to grow up to be himself authoritarian and anxious to tell others what to do, and--in particular--what not to do. Flugel attributes these views mainly to anthropologists who favor the matriarchal theory of the origin of the family. As a psychoanalyst, he simply believes that the process of human development includes going "from a relatively crude moral compulsion to a relatively free and spontaneous play of those natural impulses of men that are compatible with, or

conducive to harmonious social life. "[9] And censorship is
clearly a part of that "relatively crude moral compulsion. "

    One of the real problems in analyzing the sources of
censorship is the vagueness, the indeterminacy of the definition of exactly what the censor is trying to prevent.   In
broad terms, it may be said that the censor is attempting to
suppress two practically universal impulses, sexuality and
curiosity.   From Eve to the astronauts, man has had the
desire to know more--and, for various reasons, the ultimate
knowledge sought is usually not considered quite proper for
any but a very few to learn.

    Ludwig Marcuse, European social historian, whose
work on the changing standards of creative eroticism in literature through the past century or so is quite authoritative,
stresses "how small is the influence of erotic world literature ... beside the psychological and physiological stimuli
of sensuality which are not manufactured. "[10] This seems
almost obvious, but certainly needs to be said, in the light
of the fantastic bugaboos which the censors erect as their
estimates of the quantity and effects of erotic reading.   Surely man, who can not be regarded as anything but fundamentally a sexual animal, really does not need much stimulus
to his natural impulse toward sexual activity.

    Putting it quantitatively, Marcuse reminds us that the
Vatican Library, considered to have perhaps the greatest
collection of erotica in the world, has only about 25,000
books of this type. [11] The British Museum, rated second in
size of its obscenity collection, has around 20,000 such
volumes. [12] Compare this to the total size of libraries the
world over; in the U. S. alone there were (as of 1968) over
60 libraries with over one million books each.   The U. S.
book publishing industry is a nearly $3-billion industry: of
this amount only about 21 per cent--around $600 million--is
in combined sales of adult trade books, paperback books and
book clubs.   And the recent (1970) authoritative Report of the
Commission on Obscenity and Pornography, which contains
among other things the result of a most thorough study on
this topic, estimated that the total sales of sexually-oriented
books in the U. S. is in the range of $45-$55 million. [13]
In other words, less than 10 per cent of all books sold in
the United States are sexually oriented.   This hardly seems
enough to cause the volume of anguished reactions from the
censors and the censorially-minded.

The well-known translator and pupil of Freud, Dr. Ernest Jones, has a theory on the origin of the censor which certainly deserves attention in relation to the matters which we have been discussing. According to Jones, "people who feel themselves secretly attracted to different temptations are eagerly bent on removing these temptations out of other people's ways. " The censors are so afraid of their own inability to resist the allurements of erotica that, Jones says, "they protect themselves on the pretext of protecting others.... "14 From the biographical facts we have about perhaps the best-known of all American censors, Anthony Comstock, we judge that he followed this pattern almost exactly.

Marcuse suggests that "if all the laws and all the discussions concerning the obscene were to disappear today, no doubt innumerable people would lose opportunities for letting off steam....   The only permanent damage done would be to the eternal Mrs. Grundys. "15 There are certainly some rhetorical flourishes in these pronouncements, but his fundamental point, that one of the reasons for the existence of the censor is the existence of the idea that there is reading which should be censored, is too logically sound to ignore.

One of Freud's most renowned pupils, Otto Rank, has described the neurotic, the person whose psyche is not normal, in terms which seem eminently applicable to the description of the censor. Rank describes the neurotic (read, "censor") as "a man whom extreme fear keeps from accepting [death] ... as a basis of life, and who accordingly seeks in his own way to buy himself from his guilt [concerning sexual activity]. He does this through a constant restriction of life (restraint through fear).... "16

In fact, Rank goes on to stress, the sexually repressed person views sexual promiscuity (in which reading about sexual conduct would be included) as his "greatest danger, which he seeks to escape ethically by a definite moral code.... " Naturally, the apparent absolute necessity for such a "definite moral code" would encourage censorship, whether by the authorities or by the individual himself. However, Rank reminds us, "Sexuality ..., as it awakens in the individual about the time of puberty, is an incomparably stronger power than all the external authorities put together. Were it not so, the world would have died out long since. " And furthermore, "...prohibition strengthens the impulse, as we know, just as permission lessens the desire. "17

Rank sees a continuing conflict of the individual against society, a society which "at all times and under all circumstances [is] endeavoring to deprive the individual as far as possible through convention, law, and custom, of the arbitrary practice of sexuality."[18] Yet the individual will, consciously or unconsciously, continue to try to circumvent or escape societal inhibitions and repressions. His most common way of doing so is by substituting language for action in the sexual sphere--in other words, by creating or reading erotic literature, by uttering obscenities, by using the Word instead of the Flesh. If he does not try at all he is no longer really an individual, but a "mass man," practically a robot.

Herbert Marcuse has indeed described modern man as "one-dimensional,"[19] without the freedom to develop many of his basic instincts, including the erotic ones. He sees a vision of a non-repressive culture which "aims at a new relation between instincts and reason."[20] But, sadly, this is only a vision. Modern man has the possibility, says Marcuse (contrary to Freud's thinking), of a non-repressive sublimation of his sexual urges; if this is true, then what happens to the arguments for the urgent necessity of censorship to (in a manner of speaking) save man from himself?

The question, of course, is whether man really wants to be saved. The famous collaborative study of The Authoritarian Personality, while intended to demonstrate the direct connection between certain personality traits and overt prejudice, revealed as one of its significant by-products that there was a definite pattern in many men, in childhood background and adult history, which correlated the authoritarian personality and the censorious personality. The individual who was revealed by questionnaire and interview to be of this type, according to this study, was one who repressed his own "unconscious but strongly active" sexual desires, which were "...suppressed and in danger of getting out of hand," and further, "the authoritarian must condemn the moral laxness he sees in others...."[21]

In his childhood the embryo censor, we are told, usually "has been forced to give up basic pleasures and to live under a system of rigid restraints...." His annoyance, as he matures, at his own deprivation and at other, less rigidly restrained individuals, who are "getting away with something" makes him one who "will have a desire to condemn, reject, and punish..." whoever violates his narrow values and rules, in matters involving the emotions and, in particular, sexual behavior and discussion. [22]

The Authoritarian Personality report showed that the typical individual of this sort diminished his fear of his own tendencies to immorality (and that, of course, was quite formally defined) "by exaggerating and condemning the immorality of others. " And where did he get this way of living? Usually, says the study, "...the parents of prejudiced subjects not only seem to have been rigid disciplinarians ... " but also themselves followed "a set of rigid and externalized rules. "[23] This certainly sounds like the Puritan redivivus.

Perhaps if we want to limit, if not eliminate, censors and censorship in the future, the best place to start is in the family. There is a quite widespread acceptance by psychoanalysts that "the first social relationships to be observed within the family are, to a large extent, formative of attitudes in later life. " The A. P. study found that the type of discipline which the individuals under personality-analysis had received in their childhood was definitely "a source of the basic fear so often exhibited ... --and so often compensated for by sadistic toughness. " They refer to the typical authoritarian's childhood discipline as "a threatening, traumatic, overwhelming discipline, " in marked contrast to the non-authoritarian's childhood discipline, which was "an assimilable, and thus non-destructive, discipline.... "[24]

In sum, the censor is usually a man who has been severely repressed as a child, practices self-repression as an adult, and wants others to suffer as he did and does, rather than to get pleasure out of what the censor has, lifelong, wanted to do but was afraid to do for a multitude of reasons. What Flugel referred to as "repressive morality" the experimental psychologists of our generation feel is less morality than sociology--the sociology of the nuclear family.

An interesting point about the argument whether the conditions which result in censorship are different in different cultures has been made by British psychologist Ian D. Suttie, who sees a real difference, a real separability, between love and the sexual appetite. He exemplifies this by showing that "our culture represses the latter, while Trobriand culture censors the former.... " That is, what we consider morally or socially wrong--sexual intercourse between two young unmarried people--is considered perfectly proper in the South Seas. What we in our culture cannot see

as in any way possibly to be considered wrong behavior--
what Suttie refers to as "the forging of bonds of affection,
e. g. , by mutual services, conversation, caresses, or eating
together ... " is definitely repressed and inhibited by the
Trobriand Islanders.   The point here is that both cultures
are alike in repressing, but differ widely in what they repress. 25

          Suttie, a revisionist Freudian, defines the ideal soci-
ety "as that which gives the maximum socially permissible
freedom of expression and development to human nature (the
minimum restriction and coercion) along with the most effective substitution and suppressions where this is inevitable. "26 Of course, this begs a few questions.   When and
where are "substitutions and suppressions" absolutely inevitable? If there are such times and places, then perhaps the
operative phrase in the above statement is "socially permissible. " Is censorship ever "socially permissible?" Is it
"inevitable?"

          Suttie defines the basic problem of mankind as the
"maturation and the harmonization of his love-needs with his
appetite-needs and the attaining of maximal satisfaction in
both. "27 If this is really man's central goal and problem,
then censorship can readily be seen as more likely to give
"minimal" than "maximal" satisfaction.

          There are modern psychologists who look at this prob-
lem a little differently.   For instance, psychiatrist and social anthropologist Abram Kardiner reacted to the Kinsey reports with a book28 which stands almost alone in its willingness to face up to the facts of sexual life in America in relation to their likely, if not inevitable, consequences for sexual morality and ethics.   Many other writers since 1948 (the
date of the first published Kinsey report) have talked about
sexual morality as it should be, in utter disregard of what
is happening in American sexual life.   A great many people
have written about sexual action without any consideration of
moral reaction.   Kardiner faces up to the interaction of the
now known facts about American sexual life on policy, both
individual and social.

          Professor Kardiner puts great stress on what he calls
"the most obvious thing about sexual activity.... " This is
"that the biological end of perpetuating the species is advanced not by a known, deliberate quest for perpetuation ...
but is mediated through ... the pursuit of a specific form of

pleasure: orgastic pleasure. " This pursuit of pleasure, he says, "is present in every human form of sexuality ... ," while the other main part of the sexual instinct--the desire to procreate-- "... can be by-passed. "29

Reproduction can, of course, take place without any attendant pleasure; as Kardiner puts it, "the pleasure function can be impeded by terrorization and other forms of interference with the development of the whole psychosexual apparatus. " And the pleasure attendant to sexual activity can, equally obviously, and does, take place without any relationship to procreation or reproduction. Observation of what Kardiner calls "pleasurable excitation of the external genitals in both male and female" has been observed even as early as "very shortly after birth. "30

But sexual morality is much more a social than an individual matter. Kardiner says that we cannot discuss our contemporary mores of sex in vacuo; we must assume "they are a part of social change and experimentation over a period of many millenia. "31 He gives the rule of thumb that any custom observed by 75 per cent or more of the group involved has to be considered effective. By these standards our sex morality, which, in broad outline, has been endorsed for thousands of years by many more than three-fourths of our population, has to be considered effective.

Effective, yes. But worth preserving intact? This is quite debatable. Kardiner's detailed listing of what he calls "the price of sex morality"32 is devastating. He calls for keeping what is useful to today's culture in our sex morality and discarding whatever seems likely to bring harm to it. The guilt feelings caused to countless millions of children by our stress on the evils of masturbation, for example, are cited as a prime instance of the deleterious results of enforcing sex morality by what he calls "terrorization. "

Kardiner sees shame, modesty, even prudery as induced, not innate, feelings. In western civilization's culture, there is an unusually long period between birth and maturity. Kardiner says that "the combination of ignorance, fear, shame, the connotation of 'dirty, ' of disapproval, violence and fear of injury ... all conspire to produce an extremely harmful effect on the growing child. " The resulting "confused and distorted ideational and emotional equipment ... " for sexual activity is, of course, the main reason for our plethora of sexually-related neuroses, complexes, and perversions among matured modern men and women. [33]

The point of all this, as it relates to pleasure, is that what is affected by undue parental and societal repression of maturing youth is not the ability to reproduce, but rather the distortion, even incapacitation of "the whole apparatus for sexual pleasure." If sex is associated exclusively with punishment, retribution, and remorse in one's youth and adolescence, it is hardly likely that it will suddenly become a source of pleasure in maturity. Kardiner says categorically that "there is no one living in our culture whose personality does not bear the imprint of sexual difficulties or character distortion from our form of sex morality." Indeed, he claims that it is an indisputable fact that "the sexual unrest and the high incidence of perversion we see in the world today are the product partly of a restrictive upbringing of children. "[34]

In describing the effects of fear on sexual activity, he stresses the "inhibiting agent" nature of fear. Since, for all normal individuals, "sexual pleasure is an urgent, recurrent and irrepressible quest, and the effects of fear cumulative, the individual must contrive devices to circumvent his fear and reach the desired objective of orgastic pleasure." And, of course, neurosis or perversion are the only devices possible to achieve his goals, if normal sexual pleasure is inhibited or forbidden.

Censorship of writings on sexual conduct is clearly an inhibiting factor, part of our several-millenia-old code of sexual morality and ethics. Perhaps, as Kardiner says, "sex morality, with many of its implementations, once served the ends of social survival." But it does not any more, and so "we need a fresh appraisal of sex morality. "[35] Even though we may agree with Kardiner that "the act of repression is one of the innate capacities common to people in all cultures, "[36] this is not to say that the capacity for repression must be exercised by all people in all cultures, perhaps least of all in our own.

Kardiner, as an anthropologist-psychiatrist, has almost a unique perspective on our morality problems. Perhaps his most significant comments are these: "One cannot preach morality at people. It has to be built into them. Preaching and exhortation do not reach the sources of human motivation. They can only reinforce morality; they cannot create it.   Morality is built by constant interaction with parents in early life. "37   Censorship is a peripheral, vain effort at doing by repression and inhibition what parents should have done by example--that is, to have built up a sound, natural, workable set of sexual mores in the family and in our society.

In our media-pressured civilization no child except a neurotic one can be "protected" from the presumably noxious influences of the world outside the family by setting up what will inevitably be leak-filled protective shields.   It accomplishes little to institute, for example, grading systems for viewing movies, or to attempt to enforce Index-type listings of "bad" books, whether in libraries or bookstores.   The neuroses of our time are the result of major cleavages and disproportions in our entire culture.   It will take the combined efforts of the specialists--psychiatrists, psychologists, counselors, and such--and of the schools, the churches, and, particularly, of solid, stable, informed, exemplary family life to seek to undo the evils accumulated by many centuries of unneeded repression and restraint.   The whole of life must be viewed, not just carefully selected portions of it.

9. THE CENSOR, THE CREATIVE ARTIST, AND THE LITERARY CRITIC

"Whatever narrows the boundaries of the material fit to be used in art hems in also the artistic sincerity of the individual artist. It does not give fair play and outlet to his vital interest. It forces his perceptions into channels previously worn into ruts and clips the wings of his imagination."

--John Dewey, Art as Experience, 1934.

Chapter 9

THE CENSOR, THE CREATIVE ARTIST,
AND THE LITERARY CRITIC

Let us go back to the beginnings of man as creative artist: the Upper Paleolithic period, perhaps ten, perhaps thirty thousand years ago. The scene is a cave in the Dordogne valley of what is now France. By the flickering light of a torch made of moss soaked in bison fat, a man is painting on the walls; another is watching. Without being able to vouch for the exact authenticity of the ensuing dialog, here is what may have been said and done (the language, of course, is a little more advanced than their primitive knowledge permitted, but the meaning was probably about the same):

> Artist: I'm tired of painting bison. We've certainly had plenty of reindeer and bison to hunt since I brought good magic to our tribe by painting the bison on the wall. But we don't have enough women in our group. I'm going to paint a woman. Then maybe we'll have enough.
> Onlooker: Good idea--but better not show too much.
> Artist: What do you mean?
> Onlooker: Well, you know we can't show women as they really are.
> Artist: Why not?
> Onlooker: Well, it would be in bad taste. Why don't you cover them up with skins and shadows and keep the wrath of the gods from us?
> Artist: I don't understand your logic, Ug. The gods bring us plenty of game to hunt when I draw their pictures on the wall, and I make those pictures look as much like the particular kinds of game as I can. Now you say if I make pictures of women that look like women, and don't hide their feminine attributes, we'll all be in trouble.

103

Onlooker: Don't talk about logic. Just remember
that if you do paint bad pictures, I'll cover them
up or scratch them out or block the cave entrance.
It's just not right to make sex pictures.

And that dialogue--and the censorial attitude--has
lasted ever since. Every time an artist wants to depict life
as it really is, whether in paint or in words, the censor-
critics come up like summer weeds in an untended garden.

The distinguished French art critic and historian,
René Huyghe, has written, "The prehistoric artist [was] less
concerned with apparent results than with the act that generates the form thus created.... "[1] And the censor--of countless millenia ago and of today alike--always seems to be
much more concerned with the act of creation than with what
is created. And, of all representations, those dealing with
sex are the most likely to be censored.

The difference between censorship and legitimate criticism is often misunderstood. When the creative artist has
converted the stuff of reality into the artistic object, then he
must, of course, be willing to accept the evaluation of the
critic and audience. This he expects. But he is not usually
willing to submit to actual repression of his artistic effort.

So the clear line of demarcation between criticism
and censorship is not hard to draw. Let the product of the
artistic imagination and creation take its chances in the market-place, and only the most sensitive of artists will com-
plain about criticism. The aims of literary criticism and
of literary censorship are far, far apart, although often the
censor attempts to rationalize his intent, really for legalistic,
moralistic, theological, or psychological reasons, by citing
aesthetic--or at least pseudo-aesthetic--justifications. Perhaps this is the point in the argument being developed here:
to urge the reader to remember that the literary critic is,
and must be, concerned with literary criteria, such as form,
style, diction, while the censor is basically concerned with
but one criterion: is what is written "good" or "bad"?

A strong argument for censorship (this one voiced by
a sociologist) could be this: "If we indulge pornography, and
do not allow censorship to restrict it, our society at best
will become ever more coarse, brutal, anxious, indifferent,
de-individualized, hedonistic; at worst its ethos will disinte-
grate altogether. "[2] So the argument for censorship here

hinges on the possible effects of the "pernicious" item, which (to quote a dictionary definition of "ethos") will dissolve "the fundamental spiritual characteristics" of our culture.   This is pretty strong language, but rather difficult to document. Those societies which have had the least censorship are not necessarily the ones which have lost their "fundamental spiritual characteristics. " In fact, their most salient, their most important cultural characteristic may well have been that very freedom of speech and communication which Ernest Van den Haag wants to eliminate.   Putting up bogey-men is only useful as long as whoever is being frightened or intimidated is not aware of the falsity of the bogey.   And lack of censorship as being synonymous with lack of spirituality hardly jibes with the facts of history.   Surely the history of Periclean Greece alone is sufficient evidence of this.

As Will Durant says (referring to Plato's advocacy of literary censorship on a moral basis in his Laws), "When Athens' most famous philosopher could find so little to say for freedom Greece was ripe for a king"[3]--and for the rapid diminution of its cultural power and influence, as well. Plato threw the artists, the creators, right out of his model Republic, his hoped-for Utopia.   Rather than being driven into censorship as a practice, the Platonic counsel was to eliminate entirely the poets, the makers, the creators.   Then the censor would have nothing to censor.

The only thing the artist does, said Plato, is to bring in new ideas likely to upset the status quo, to stimulate man to more emotion and feeling, and less discipline.   In short, the artist is not good for the State--so keep him out.   This advice is about as efficacious as King Canute's attempted stemming of the tides.   Somehow, no matter how Establishments through the centuries restrict and restrain, bar and inhibit, creativeness creeps in.   As modern philosopher Horace Kallen says, "The maker or 'creative artist' goes his own way, independent and incoercible, not to be tamed to society's uses, not to be harnessed in social rule. "[4] Maybe not, but society certainly tries!

Kallen has given us what he calls "the Ciceronian formula" (the way the Roman Empire looked at the arts), as it might have been expressed by Marcus Tullius Cicero, who was a classical Stoic: "Let ... the slave and the tradesman and the artisan and the artists obey and conform.   Let them not join in the rebellious brotherhoods of their crafts.   Let them keep their stations, reverence their owners and

masters, worship the gods, consult the auspices, obey the
judgment of the censors. Mistaken, harsh and cruel as any
of these sometimes may be, they are also the work of the
divine providence which is universal reason and eternal justice. The sage is he who has learned it, and by submitting
to its authority wins the good life. The arts envisage it,
and beauty accrues to that which imitates and represents it.
Obviously, freedom can have no part here, save as freedom
is held to mean this conformation to necessary and ineluctable
law...."[5]

This was the Establishment view of the proper place
of the artist in Roman society. Cicero and Quintilian and
Longinus were the arbiters, the dominant aesthetic critics
who preached order and decorum (as opposed to disorder and
passion), who backed the actions of the censors, and applauded discipline, strict formalism, and regimentation in the
arts. Certainly Rome, as elsewhere, had its share of free
spirits among its artistic creators, but the creators who opposed the will of the Roman Establishment suffered the consequences of their daring. Ovid and Martial and Catullus,
who wrote boldly and openly about sex, were all the object
of some censorship; the works of Ovid, for instance, were
banned from the Roman public libraries, by edict of August-
us, and the poet himself was banished to a little island on
the Black Sea, where he died after nine years of sad exile.[6]
And certainly what was true of the Roman Establishment is,
unhappily, the historical fact in almost all (certainly all major) Western societies.

This book does not concern itself with political censorship, but, in many ways, all censorship is basically political, or at least ideological. The aim may be to restrict
or deny writing and reading with sexual content; but the
method used is customarily through the laws, the courts, the
whole system of justice. As Iredell Jenkins puts it, "for
many years in the United States ... the courts [were] en-
visaged as the necessary protectors of the established order
of things, and hence as dedicated to the preservation of the
established institutions of the family and the state; to fill this
function, they must protect the young and the weak from any
possible immoral or anti-social influences; and to guarantee
this end, art must be denied circulation if it contains any
potentialities of contamination."[7]

This has certainly changed of late years, particularly
in the light of some recent U.S. Supreme Court decisions

(discussed later in this volume). But the argument between those who, like Oscar Wilde, set art and morals far apart, and those who, like Jacques Maritain, intertwine them inextricably is an exemplification of a fundamental conflict of views which is probably eternal. The same John Milton who compared the killing of a good book to the killing of a good man was himself an exponent of marked moral intolerance when it came to books written by and espousing the beliefs of people with whom he vigorously disagreed.

Those who believe in art for art's sake are, of course, anti-censorship. One of the strongest arguments for official or state censorship is that the only way to look at a piece of art is in terms of its presumed consequences on the reader, viewer, or listener. So far, there is really no acceptable proof of a direct relationship between reading and action, except on the "Stop" and "Go" sign level.

As early twentieth-century American literary critic, W. P. Trent, wrote, "we must all learn to read precisely as we learn to live--applying to the problem all the experience and all the conscientiousness we can." Trent says, "There is no royal road to learning or to reading or to conduct...." And Trent stresses that the effects of books on particular people are as unpredictable as the people themselves. So, he says, why censor? Trent goes even further on censorship, describing the censor in quite strong terms: "He who does not trust literature to do its noble part in the salvation of the race, who would shackle men's thoughts and kill their books, the children of their brains and hearts ... is not to be listened to without danger...."[8]

What has developed in much of the history of American literary criticism until quite recently is almost a sellout to the censor. Instead of an evaluation of literary works in terms of that which "breathes the full abundance of humanity," the so-called "genteel tradition," in both American literary criticism and literature, has triumphed. As Ludwig Lewisohn has said, "[American] literature [from the eighteenth century through the early twentieth century] was graceful, imitative, superficial and sought not life and reality, but an escape from these." Lewisohn defined "the genteel tradition in American literature" as "the tradition ... of the Puritan gentry who excepted themselves ... from the corruption of human nature and concentrated that corruption in the lower classes and in the present...."[9] So, in that tradition, all the way through American literature until Walt Whitman,

sex was conspicuous by its absence.   The polite poetizing on
such topics as "The Culprit Fay" and "The Death of Absa-
lom, " the fictional romances of James Fenimore Cooper and
William Gilmore Simms, were a long way from realistic,
honest representations of the world as it really was when
those works were written.   Yet they triumphed, in both critical and reading audience popularity (at least, during their
lifetimes), over the Hawthornes, the Melvilles, and the
Whitmans.

As Lewisohn says of the "genteel mind, " "it is a
mind often nimble but always afraid and ashamed.   The
world is too rough for it, thought too athletic; man too human. "[10] This kind of creator found critics only too ready
to receive and accept favorably his creations.   Those few
mavericks who dared to do more than suggest the existence
of a world in which the genitals existed and functioned were
cast into outer darkness as--oh, awful word of opprobrium!--
"vulgar. " Walt Whitman was certainly typical of this kind
of literary outcast.

Back in 1902, Establishment literary critic Bliss Per-
ry said proudly, "Although American fiction may not be national and may not be great, it will have at least the negative virtue of being clean. "[11] The American novelists of his
day--the F. Marion Crawfords, the F. Hopkinson Smiths, the
Margaret Delands--were well-described by Lewisohn as authors who "were determined that men should be angels, and
at the same time choked uneasily over the secret of a dark
conviction that men were mammals. "[12]

When the work of the political or unofficial censor
was being so well taken care of by the writers themselves,
it was really hardly necessary for the censor to perform.
The Anthony Comstocks and the John S. Sumners were sometimes hard put to it to find worthy targets; a well-known
cartoon by Art Young, in one memorable issue of The
Masses, satirically showed a policeman who was hauling a
drab-looking woman into court, claiming, "Your honor, this
woman just gave birth to a naked child! " Very few of the
reputable, accepted authors of American literary tradition--
all the way up until Stephen Crane, Theodore Dreiser, Frank
Norris, and the other new realists of the early twentieth
century--gave literary birth to any but clothed children!

If, as Norman O. Brown has stated, "the function of
art ... is to help us find our way back to sources of

pleasure that have been rendered inaccessible by the capitu-
lation to the reality-principle which we call education or
maturity ..., "[13] then surely the function of the criticism of
art is to show how well artistic creation fulfills that function.
The kind of creative literature which glorifies concealment,
even obfuscation, of sexual reality will be sure to disguise,
rather than reveal, the basic sources of human pleasure.

The critic, as compared to the censor, usually sees
the relationship between art and life as a two-way one. Art
affects life, and life affects art. But the censor, harking
back to the old, primitive faith in the magic of the word,
fears the effect of art on life, disregarding the obverse of
the picture. If there is to be a choice, somehow the logic
still remains with life as the source, and art as the product.
For most of us, the critic, who recognizes this fact, is more
realistic than the censor, who ignores it.

The act of censoring is based on certain judgments.
Although usually these are presumed to be legal in nature,
they are, in fact, more commonly moral, aesthetic, social
and, particularly, personal in their sources. The policeman
who picks up a "girlie" magazine and says, "This is obscene," or, "This is dirty," is not expressing as cleancut
and nearly precise a judgment as when he sees a citizen
walk out of a store without paying for something the policeman saw him pick up from a display counter and goes over
to him and arrests him on a charge of being guilty of theft.
The judgment of theft can be, and practically always is, quite
easy and certain; the judgment of "dirtiness," or obscenity
or pornography is a highly subjective one. The literary
critic who is called upon to testify in support of the presumed "literary quality" of a book on trial is all too often
reduced to near incoherence or double-talk in his valiant effort to express an aesthetic judgment which will bear on social importance.

It is only recently that some serious effort has been
made to express the aesthetic quality of pornography in modern, understandable terms. University of Michigan philosophy
professor Abraham Kaplan's brief but cogent and perceptive
"Obscenity As an Aesthetic Category"[14] was one of the first
statements of this type. He has presented an aesthetic view
of obscenity which puts the whole problem of judging sexually
controversial writing in a useful perspective. He stressed
that "beauty and obscenity alike are in the eye of the beholder." But he does not stop there. He asks why, if this

is true, we are willing to accept critical, evaluative, aesthetic judgments of what is considered beautiful, but not willing to accept similar judgments of what is considered ugly-- the realistic or fantastic (take your choice!) side of sex.

Kaplan discards altogether the idea that obscenity should not be considered as "an objective property of a work of art.... " External motivation of the author, the immediate purpose of his work, the intent of the work itself--all are examined and found wanting as justifications for not accepting obscenity as a separate aesthetic category.

More likely than these as an appropriate alternative in this quandary is to consider what effect the work which is presumed to include obscenity has on its audience. Kaplan finds what he calls "the test of effect" completely irrelevant. What must be considered is the aesthetic effect; Kaplan says that "the aesthetic experience requires a kind of disinterest or detachment, a 'psychic distance'.... " He quotes George Santayana, who once wrote that "there is a high breathlessness about beauty that cancels lust.... "[15] The same principle obtains here as in the classical tale of the prostitute Phryne who, when on trial in Athens, denuded herself before the court as the best possible argument for her innocence. He sees "the moral content of art ... [as] nothing less than the affirmation of life, a great yeasaying to the human condition. " Note that he is referring to the whole of life, not just a portion selected for its aesthetic qualities. Indeed, Kaplan says, speaking of human life, that "art insists on seeing it whole, for only thus can it understand and rationalize it. "[16]

If truth and beauty are identical, in Keats' famous dictum, then the "facts of life"--writings about sexual conduct--must be beautiful, no matter how "obscene. " Unfortunately, as Kaplan admits, "when art uncovers what men wish to keep hidden, it is despised and condemned. "[17] To find an aesthetic quality in writings about sex, these writings, it seems, must be on a sentimental, euphemistic, fact-finding level.

Kaplan's conclusion is that "a proper judgment of obscenity in the arts can only be made by an informed and sensitive reader. " So it is ultimately the reader, the critic-at-large who determines the aesthetic values of a work of art; "beauty and obscenity alike are in the eye of the beholder. "[18]

This is more or less in agreement with classical German critic Friedrich Schlegel's declaration that "it is impossible to offend a man if he will not be offended." Schlegel, commenting on the relationship between art and morality in literature, said, "The morality of a book lies not in its theme or in the relation of the writer to his public, but in the spirit of the treatment. If this breathes the full abundance of humanity, it is moral. If it is merely the work of an isolated power and art it is not moral."[19]

The philosopher proceeds to a classification of obscenity into various sub-types: the "conventional," which he describes as "the quality of any work which attacks established sexual patterns and practices"; the "Dionysian," "... an expression of an exuberant delight in life"; "the obscenity of the perverse," described as "the obscenity of the leer and innuendo"; "romantic" obscenity, categorized as that "which preserves the sense of sin yet celebrates sexuality in spite of it"; and, finally, "the pornography of violence," where "sexual desires find symbolic release only as transformed into acts of aggression...."[20]

By so analyzing the obscene in art, Kaplan has pretty well proven his point; obscenity is and must be an aesthetic category, and deserves consideration as such. But, curiously, after claiming that art must see all life whole, including "what men wish to keep hidden," he still stigmatizes pornography as being "in the service of death, not of life,"[21] without clarifying this seeming paradox. (Perhaps Kaplan's basic sympathy with orthodox, Establishment-related Judaism is herein revealed!)

Susan Sontag, a very "with it" modern literary and social critic, agrees with Kaplan that pornography is a branch of literature. Those who argue to the contrary, she says, rest their case on the following arguments: that the aim of pornography, to arouse the reader sexually, "is antithetical to the complex function of literature"; that pornographic works lack appropriate literary forms and conventions; that pornographic writing is not concerned with the verbal, but really with nonverbal fantasies "in which language plays a debased, merely instrumental role"; and, finally, that pornography is concerned only with "the motiveless tireless transactions of depersonalized organs," and not with the relationships of human beings with each other.[22]

Sontag answers these criticisms by instancing several

current works, such as Story of O, which fulfill none of
these criteria and yet are clearly pornographic. Unfortunately, as she points out, some of the same criticism which
seeks to remove pornographic works from literature would
also eliminate much else in contemporary fiction which is in
no way pornographic according to the accepted canon. Her main
argument is that fictive literature includes, or should include, a much wider spectrum than the conservative, traditional critics will accept, what she calls "an infinitely varied
register of forms and tonalities for transposing the human
voice into prose narrative."23   What she is doing is transforming a discussion of the admissibility of pornography to
accepted literary genres into a discussion of what all literature is.

         In so doing, she refers to the natural inclusiveness of
art, and to the duty of the artist to be "a free-lance explor-
er of spiritual dangers...."24   Once the function of the artist is broadened, then whatever he produces cannot be dismissed as "fantastic" or even "masturbating." She concludes, on this topic, that "the materials of the pornographic
books that count as literature are ... one of the extreme
forms of human consciousness." If this is so, then it should
not be the police, or the U.S. post office, or the U.S. Customs officers who judge whether a particular written work is
or is not the kind of pornographic work that does not count
as literature. The literary critic--and a perceptive, modern, wide-ranging one at that!--is the only fair judge, and
he will, if he operates on the Sontag principle, be extremely
catholic (with a small "c") in his judgments.

         In the concluding sections of her important study,
Miss Sontag is clearly trying to be of assistance to future
critics, by defining and analyzing this branch of literature
which does exist in our society and must be reckoned
with, and not only by the censor or the critic, but also by
the general reading public. She says that "one of the primary intellectual tasks of future thought ..." is "to try to
make a fresh way of talking at the most serious, ardent, and
enthusiastic level...." And what she calls "the pornographic
imagination" has an opportunity to be at least one of these
"fresh" ways. She grants that some find pornographic writing can be "a crutch for the psychologically deformed and a
brutalization of the morally innocent." But her answer to
this charge is that "there's a sense in which all knowledge is
dangerous, the reason being that not everyone is in the same
condition as knowers or potential knowers." And if we agree

to censorship of pornography, we are certainly opening the door to what she calls a "censorship much more radical than the indignant foes of pornography ever envisage.... "25

A more recent critic, Peter Michelson, differs with both Sontag and Kaplan. In fact, the very title of his book on this topic, The Aesthetics of Pornography, is an immediate challenge to the "yes, but" Kaplan aesthetic; not a conscious one, however, for no reference to Kaplan or his ideas is specifically or even indirectly included in the Michelson book. Like Susan Sontag (to whom he also does not refer), Michelson is very much concerned with the feeling that due importance--not too much, not too little--should be given to pornography as what he calls a "poetic" rather than a literary genre. He sees pornography as "neither more or less damnable than any other partial mythology, religious revivalism for example." Again like Sontag, he grants the dangers of knowledge, but points out that "they are balanced and calculated--with the reasonable expectation that knowledge itself will help us deal with its own dangers." After all, he reminds us, "ignorance has no options." Accepting this reasoning, then what is important is not whether we find in pornography what is agreeable or useful, but rather that what we find in any particular pornographic work "gives us knowledge, however partial, of the truth of human being.... "26

In an otherwise fair and perspicacious review of Michelson's book, Peter S. Prescott offers the interesting opinion that "the essence of pornography is mendacity..., "27 as if this were a distinguishing characteristic only of this particular type of fiction. Distinguishing between "mendacity" as the act of lying, and "fiction" as the act of imagining or making up something, is really a distinction without a difference. If one permits the Truman Capote In Cold Blood kind of thing to be considered as fictional rather than documentary, one loses the whole point of imaginative prose literature.

Virginia Woolf has stated that "the problem before the novelist at present, as we suppose it to have been in the past, is to continue means of being free to set down what he chooses." If the pornographic novelist chooses to exaggerate some feat of sexual prowess rather than to "lie" about a war-hero's abilities at killing (see almost any popular war-novel of the Green Berets genre), what makes that an act of "mendacity" rather than "fiction?" One novelist chooses the

bedroom, the other the battleground: does the setting or the
topic decide which is more "truthful" (whatever that means!)?

        Michelson delimits his book as being an attempt "to
demonstrate that obscenity is not simply a cultural aberration but that it is a complex expression of human imagination, humanistically vital enough to have its own poetics. "
He bases this on the modern recognition that goodness, truth
and beauty are not by any means a "holy trinity, " and that
"there is no necessary or constant equation between them. "28
If what is beautiful is not necessarily good; if what is true
is not necessarily beautiful; if what is good need not be
either true or beautiful, then why not consider obscenity--
pornography--as a literary genre?   It is clearly not what
pornography is, but how one looks at it which makes all the
difference.

        Michelson goes on to say that the basic principle of
"hard-core" pornography is "to tap into the mythos of animality and derive its energy and appeal therefrom.   Its audience directs its imaginative energies, and the function of
this pornographic mode is to provide the vehicle for surfac-
ing the animal dimension of its audience's mythic sensibil-
ity. " [my italics - EMO].   This serves several purposes.
In the first place, the fact that man is a sexual animal is
acknowledged and accepted, rather than repressed and hidden
and inhibited.   Secondly, it keeps the animality which does
unquestionably exist in man from exercising what Michelson
calls "its subliminal power over the psyche...."29

        It goes further than this.   If it is true that civiliza-
tion, as Freud says, can only exist by suppressing man's
uncivilized, animalistic instincts, then reading what the censor would deny us gives us, as Michelson says, "a psychic
joy that transcends the bounds of its imagistic physicality,
the joy of acknowledging our own lust, and of being figura-
tively assured that it is not necessarily destructive of our
humanity. "30   In other words, it serves something of the
same function to individuals that the Oktoberfest does to German society, the New Orleans Mardi Gras and nationwide
New Year's Eve celebrations to American society, the Bra-
zilian Carnival to its culture, the Feast of the Lupercal to
the Roman Empire, and similar "explosions, " periods of
license, to practically every known society.

        Harvey Cox, a modern Harvard Christian theologian
of note, has recently discussed the significance of such feasts

at some length.   He is concerned about what he calls "an
unnecessary gap in today's world between the world-changers
and the life-celebraters. "[31]   (It is significant to note that
he leaves out entirely those who would leave the world as
it is, as well as those who are anti-life--which would be a
fair description of the censors!)

        Cox expresses regret for the real lack of festival and
true fun in our gray days, when "our celebrations do not relate us, as they once did, to the parade of cosmic history
or to the great stories of man's spiritual quest, " and "our
fantasies tend to be cautious, eccentric, and secretive ...
appreciated only by an elite. "   But he sees hope in the beginnings of "a rebirth of the spirit of festivity and fantasy. "[32]

        Surely the current wide interest in pornography is
exemplary of this.   Cox sees "festivity, like play, contemplation, and making love ... [as] an end in itself. "   He finds
fantasy to be a useful instrument for social criticism and
reform.   Both together, he says, presage "a renaissance of
the spirit"[33]--and the wide reading of pornography, now as
in Renaissance times, may be part of the needed spiritual
rebirth of our day.

        To clarify this idea, let us look at Cox's further de-
finition of his terms.   He sees festivity as 'the capacity for
genuine revelry and joyous celebration...." He regards fantasy as 'the faculty for envisioning radically alternative life
situations. "   These are "uniquely human, " he says, but, unfortunately have badly deteriorated nowadays.   We have elevated Luther and Marx (who glorified work) and Aquinas and
Descartes (who applauded thought), and, in Cox's words,
"man's celebrative and imaginative faculties have atrophied. "

        More than that, it would seem that we have deliber-
ately, by the use of censorship--legal and illegal, formal
and informal--done everything we could to keep man's nose
to the grindstone.   Cox says that 'this worker-thinker emphasis, enforced by industrialization, ratified by philosophy,
and sanctified by Christianity, " certainly was of assistance
in producing our present-day Western scientific and industrial technology.   But, in addition to a few other rather sad
by-products (exemplified by the exploitation of underdeveloped
nations and the existing air-water-earth worldwide pollution)
"we have also terribly damaged the inner experience of Western man. "[34]

Where is it then, "the apple-tree, the singing, and
the gold" of which Euripides wrote? Is it possible for modern man to recover this joie de vivre of his ancestors? We
live such cramped, contained, confined, restricted, inhibited,
repressed, and routinized lives that the very idea of some
release, some open expression of life--the Woodstock festi-
val, for example--turns off most of us, at least, most of
those over thirty! Cox characterizes the loss of our capacity for festivity and fantasy as "calamitous" and gives these
reasons for so believing: "(1) it deforms man by depriving
him of an essential ingredient in human existence, (2) it en-
dangers his very survival as a species by rendering him
provincial and less adaptive, and (3) it robs him of a crucial
means of sensing his important place in fulfilling the destiny
of the cosmos."35

Michelson admits that both "hard-core" pornography
and its source, the mythos of animality, are "threatening at
once to personality and society. Consequently it is frightening." We are afraid to "let go," to go "right on," to say
the words and do--even read about--the actions which make
us aware of our inmost, most intimate core of being. We
have been told to hide our feelings since infancy--almost
since the infancy of our civilization--and in maturity most
of us feel fear, shame, prudery to some degree when con-
fronted with "the primal act," in word or deed.

When the "crazies" invaded Washington, D.C. in the
late spring of 1971, there was as much disapprobation for
the lack of inhibition exhibited by many of the young as for
the sentiments they expressed in their words, posters, and
actions. When Time magazine--surely a representative
spokesman for America's middle-class--wanted to epitomize
in a prominently-placed photograph what was going on in our
Nation's Capital that week, they used a photography of a nude
young couple embraced in broad daylight in their "camp" in
a Washington park. Public copulation--or, at least, em-
bracing in the nude--had the shock-value the magazine's editors wanted, to symbolize the attack the protesters (who, of
course, were where they were to attack the ever-on-going
war in Indochina) were making on American conventionalities.

Michelson's aesthetic of pornography is perhaps best
summarized in his statement: "In the modern recording of
Truth, obscenity has become the flipside of Beauty.... Many
are now persuaded ... that obscene rhetoric is a necessary
probe in the search for true understanding." The point is,

says Michelson, "not that existence is obscene, merely that
obscenity has existence. " He admits that "to assert an obscene truth is necessarily to deny the universal authority of
a beautiful truth. "[36]

An author who has been "accused of employing obscene language more freely and abundantly than any other
living writer in the English language ... , " Henry Miller,
has voiced the almost-Freudian view that "what man dreads
most is to be faced with the manifestation, in word or deed,
of that which he has refused to live out.... " He sees as
the truly obscene that which is repressed, hidden, censored.
Unfortunately, Miller goes off into a fantasia of the unconscious, seeing obscenity as compounded of the magic, the
mystical, "...vast as the Unconscious itself, and as amor-
phous and blind as the very stuff of the Unconscious. "[37]
This is lovely rhetoric, but hardly enlightening as to the
aesthetic qualities of the obscene or the pornographic. Yet
it does give us an insight into what a truly creative mind
sees as the place of obscenity in the workings and creations
of the artist's mind.

Steven Marcus, young American literary critic, concludes his notable study of mid-Victorian pornography with a
view of the aesthetics of pornography which is quite opposed
to Michelson's. He asserts that pornography is simply not
literature, whether in respect to form (no beginning, middle,
or end), language ("...clichés, dead and dying phrases ...
stereotypical formulas; ... also heavily adjectival ... [and]
the forbidden tabooed words ... "), its use of metaphor, and
in being "not interested in persons but in organs. " But
Marcus makes clear where he stands on censorship by saying "that I would indeed be troubled if I came across my
small son studiously conning Justine. " Yet he terms the
present era when pornography, perhaps for the first time in
history, "is now being openly and legally published ... " as
a period when a development has come which "was inevitable
and necessary, and, on the whole, so far as we are able to
see, benign. "[38]

One of the most ambitious attempts to formulate an
aesthetic for or of pornography is Morse Peckham's recent
work, [39] whose subtitle, "An Experiment in Explanation, " indicates its tentative, groping nature. Dr. Peckham's volume
is included in the series of "Studies in Sex and Society, "
sponsored by the group which Dr. Alfred Kinsey began, the
Institute for Sex Research at Indiana University. (The series

already includes the Marcus volume on Victorian pornography and Studies in Erotic Art, as well as other volumes.)

Dr. Peckham admits he feels a "sense of intellectual contradiction and incoherence" on this topic, which is only reasonable and logical, in light of the fact that his major work on humanistic aesthetics (published just before this one) was on the topic of Man's Rage for Chaos. But considering that his preface also refers to his subject as a "messy and scandalous"[40] one, one must be prepared for some "contradiction and incoherence," even, perhaps, for a plea for censorship. His index, however, does not even include the term "censorship," to indicate that it is in any way referred to in 301 pages of text.

However, he certainly does refer to censorship cases, to "sexual and pornographic policing," to "legal control," to "censorship boards," to "censorship laws," and to "censorship and police control." Indeed, he uses the term "policing" throughout his book as a synonym for "censorship"--but there is no reference to "policing" in the index, either. (Incidentally, as a matter of actual count, the word censor or its derivatives are used on no less than seven different pages, and on one page twice.)

The point is that Peckham's attempt to show the relationship between pornography and art, between aesthetics and imaginative writing about sex, really ends up in being a book about his theory of aesthetics, with pornography and its significance coming out a poor second. As for censorship, Peckham turns out to be in favor of it. He says, for example, that "any artist is bound by the values of his culture; it is difficult to believe that the mere spelling out of some of these binding values in the form of laws and edicts makes it impossible for him to create what his culture will call great art." He also points out that "the dreadful reactionary ... is committed to the proposition that what holds a society together is its stable belief in unquestioned truths, and that holding a society together is the highest human value."[41] Obviously, Peckham does not really think being a reactionary is dreadful!

Peckham disagrees with the Marcus theory of the relationship of pornography and aesthetics. Since he feels that "there is available no definition of pornography which would make it possible to investigate the relation between the category 'pornography' and the category 'art,'" he proffers a forthright definition of pornography: "pornography is the presentation in verbal or visual signs of human sexual organs in a condition of stimulation. "[42] Most authorities on the subject might not accept this wording, but it does have its interesting sideviews.

After such a definition, one would reasonably expect a little more frankness in discussion of his topic than he uses, for example, in describing the cause of an orgasm which occurs to a character in D. H. Lawrence's The Plumed Serpent. This may be almost unbelievable, but here is the Peckham formulation: "a psychic condition in which the cognitive model which is responsible for the perceptual and interpretive organization of the experience is not corrected by any sensory data not consonant with that experience. "[43] (My rough translation of this "pedagoguese" goes like this: "a condition of the mind where the one who is having the orgasm is not distracted by any non-relevant feelings. ")

Peckham's aesthetics differs from Peter Michelson's, basically, in Peckham's belief that pornography, in a sense, is only a branch of generally "low cultural level" literature, rather than a separate and distinct major genre. He says that "it is by no means difficult to find pornography of both the nineteenth and twentieth century which displays the same beginning-middle-end structure as the ordinary novel. " Here, of course, Peckham is questioning the Marcus definition of pornography. Peckham claims that "the confusion is between literature at a low cultural level and pornography. "[44]

Perhaps it is sufficient to summarize the quite lengthy and jargonized Art and Pornography as "much ado about nothing. " It is really far from a notable contribution to the discussion of a most important matter, except in the sense that it does indicate where a conservative littérateur, philosopher, and critic stands on this question today.

Of course, there is a devil's advocate argument for the censor. One of our most distinguished liberal literary critics, Malcolm Cowley, has said, "Instead of trying to end the conflict between artists and censors, let us regard it as normal and even desirable. Let us say that both sides are right, not in any particular skirmish but in the battle as a whole. " For Cowley, "the censors are right in attacking books and pictures which they regard as immoral or subversive. The artists are right in counter-attacking the censors and in fighting not only to save but widen their own freedom

of expression.   There is no final decision to be reached,
but there is a temporary stability to be`reached as the re-
sult of struggle. "45

    The Cowley doctrine on censorship seems more like
a counsel of despair than a practical suggestion to end what
looks like an interminable artist vs. censor war.   The element which has been left out is--and this may seem rhetorical, even hyperbolic, but is nevertheless worth considering--
the cause of Truth.   Censors have never been known to set
up or even to obey any fair rules of conduct, if such there
be.   The artist always loses, except when his work becomes
shielded by the most effective defense in facing up to the
Establishment--the passage of time.

    Works which seem vile and dangerous one year or
one decade or even one century are widely accepted if dubbed
"classic. " They are then considered not even possible targets for the censor.   Make a list of some of the now generally accepted books which were censored in their own times:
The Odyssey, Lysistrata, The Praise of Folly, Gargantua
and Pantagruel, Gulliver's Travels, Leaves of Grass, Ma-
dame Bovary, Tess of the D'Urbervilles, Sister Carrie,
Jurgen, Ulysses; surely the verdict of time can be seen usually to be pro-artist, anti-censor.

    What will ultimately come of the supposedly unending
and inevitable conflict between the censor and the artist is,
one may safely predict, "no surrender" on either side.   The
strong impulse to see life steadily and see it whole surely
predates Sophocles; the equally strong impulse to see life
through a morality-tinted lens is equally universal.   No censor has ever admitted fallibility; no creative artist has ever
admitted that either critic or censor was justified in unfavorable criticism or in attempted banning or expurgation of his
work.   Somewhere on the battlefield the general public must
make its own decisions, preferably on an objective and realistic basis.

    The good, the true, and the beautiful have always been
a sort of nonreligious trinity, a linked, associated group of
values which were more or less accepted as (a) universal
and (b) universally comprehensible.   "Everyone" knew the
true from the false, the good from the bad, and the beautiful
from the ugly.   But nowadays these values have become what
Erich Kahler calls "open concepts. "46

In our ever-and-quickly-changing world, there are very few, if any, of what Kahler calls the "comfortably stable absolutes." But, fortunately for man, there is "a certain constancy of basic values," what Kahler calls "relative absolutes"; and the true, the good, and the beautiful are all values of this type. In describing them Kahler stresses that the three values are actually one, divided as a means of description, of analysis. They are also one in their attempt at being genuine absolutes; indeed, the Greek philosophers generally "identified the good with being, pure and simple ...," says Kahler. He quotes Plato's Republic: the Idea of the Good is "what endows the things known with their truth"; it is "the source of knowledge and truth."47

The main point of all of this is that the true, the good, and the beautiful are interrelated, are linked so clearly that they finally do become one. All are important, but the primary one is still truth; Kahler calls it "the arch-value, the mainstay of all values." If there is really no goodness and no beauty without truth, then the censor is aiming at evil and ugliness when he represses, inhibits, changes the true to suit his preconceived bias. Kahler refers to "the Protestant residue of Christianism in moralistic enlightment, the fossil conventionality of the nineteenth century middle class, and finally the melting away of values in the wars and crises of the twentieth century ..."48 as engendering our present situation in the aesthetic realm.

Kahler cites Baudelaire as being the original artist "to break through the barriers of classical aesthetics by drawing the ugly and even the decaying into the compass of form, thereby submitting it to beauty."49 Without Baudelaire's courageous attempt to acclaim the sensual, "qui chantent les transports de l'esprit et des sens,"50 the admittedly tentative attempts at an aesthetic of the pornographic by such people as Michelson and Peckham would not even have existed, or had any pretensions at viability or likelihood of being accepted generally.

Goodness, truth, and beauty are all important life-binding concepts, more important than ever today in our chaotic, iconoclastic times. To deny the artist his audience on the ground that his work must be limited by outdated standards and moralities, which are neither standard nor moral, is itself immoral. It is certainly an argument for badness, lies and ugliness.

One of the most impassioned defenses of the right of
the artist to choose his material where he will and write
about it as his artistic conscience alone dictates was expressed by Anton Chekhov. In a letter he wrote to a friend
in 1887, Chekhov said, "to think that the task of literature is
to gather the pure grain from the muck heap, is to reject
literature itself. Artistic literature is called so just because it depicts life as it really is. Its aim is truth--un-
conditional and honest." He says of the artist that "no matter how painful it is to him, he is constrained to overcome
his aversion, and soil his imagination with the sordidness of
life." In the same letter Chekhov comments on censorship
as follows: "think what you will, you cannot find a better
police for literature than criticism and the author's own
conscience."[51]

Finally, it is the creative artist who must play the
vatic role in society. He must be the one who looks into
what Shakespeare called "the dark background and abysm of
time," who faces the world as it is now, and who, as Arthur
Rimbaud wrote, "makes himself a seer by a long, prodigious,
and ritual disordering of all the senses [italics in the origi-
nal--EMO]."[52] Unless he is willing to become what Rimbaud
terms "...the great accursed--and the great learned one!--
among men," unless the artist is willing to "...die charging
through those unutterable, unnameable things ..." (as Rimbaud describes the poet's horizons), he cannot fulfill his essential obligation to humanity or his duty to his own talents.

The censor--legal, moral, conventional, and restrictive in all ways--is always trying to keep the artist from
being an artist. Rimbaud calls on the poet to deal with "the
new in ideas and in forms."[53] The literary artist who
knuckles under to the heavy hand of the censor is, by definition, really not an artist. Seer, creator, innovator--the
artist, the maker, the poet is a man of commitment (Sartre
says, "What counts is the total commitment"[54]). Zola felt
that the creative artist, "in order to be able to foresee the
unknown ... must begin by studying the known."[55] And the
known includes all that goes to make up life. Walt Whitman's
critique of Matthew Arnold perhaps sums all this up: "Arnold always gives you the notion that he hates to touch the
dirt--the dirt is so dirty! But everything comes out of the
dirt--everything...."[56]

One of the revealing insights afforded by John Dewey,
who is still very much unappreciated as a philosopher of

aesthetics, is that most of us resolutely separate sensation from reason, to a degree that almost denies the importance of such; as Dewey says, "sense and flesh get a bad name." And the censor, as might be expected, is not about to ignore this situation. Dewey reminds us that "the moralist knows that sense is allied with emotion, impulse and appetition. So he denounces the lust of the eye as part of the surrender of spirit to flesh. "[57]

Dewey questions the polarization of the body and the spirit; he says that "oppositions of mind and body, soul and matter, spirit and flesh all have their origin, fundamentally, in fear of what life may bring forth." To recognize man's animal origins, for Dewey, is by no means "a necessary reduction of man to the level of the brutes." Instead it makes us better able to recognize man's uniqueness, complexity, and "the continuity of the organs, needs and basic impulses of the human creature with his animal forbears...." When we are looking at man's artistic achievements, we cannot do as Dewey says the moralist (read "censor") does: "He identifies the sensuous with the sensual and the sensual with the lewd. "[58] This is a rather cheap and illogical confusion, which, unfortunately, has influenced not only public taste but even judicial decisions.

Perhaps George Santayana clarifies this point in his statement that "the relation between aesthetic and moral judgments, between the spheres of the beautiful and the good, is close." He cites, as one factor of this close, but existent, distinction that although aesthetic judgments are mostly positive ones, of the good, moral judgments are basically negative ones, "perceptions of evil. "[59]

Another portion of this important distinction adduced by Santayana is that moral judgments are generally utilitarian, "based, when they are positive ... upon the consciousness of benefits probably involved" and, of course, when they are negative, upon evils or detriments which the material being considered may bring about. On the other hand, aesthetic judgments are "necessarily intrinsic and based on the character of the immediate experience...." It is this latter distinction which makes it so difficult to speak of the "aesthetics" of pornography; moral judgments on this topic, of course, are easy and prevalent.

Santayana has another statement on all this which is also pertinent: "The moment ... that society emerges from

the early pressure of the environment and is tolerably secure
against primary evils, morality grows lax. " And then (italics not in the original), he says, "The forms that life will
farther assume are not to be imposed by moral authority,
but are determined by the genius of the race, the opportunities of the moment, and the tastes and resources of individual minds. The reign of duty gives place to the reign of
freedom, and the law and the covenant to the dispensation of
grace. "60

John Dewey is concerned with what happens to the artist when he confronts the moralistic approach to art. He
stresses the freedom inherent in creative art, saying that
"impulsion beyond all limits that are externally set inheres
in the very nature of the artist's work.... Refusal to acknowledge the boundaries set by convention is the source of
frequent denunciations of objects of art as immoral. " But
this is only to be expected, since "one of the functions of
art is precisely to sap the moralistic timidity that causes
the mind to shy away from some materials and refuse to admit them into the clear and purifying light of perceptive
consciousness. "61

For John Dewey and George Santayana and others who
have upheld the right of art to be considered in its own
right, aesthetically rather than morally, as Dewey says,
"whatever narrows the boundaries of the material fit to be
used in art hems in also the artistic sincerity of the individual artist. "62 The artist cannot be limited by theological
or moral or Marxian or any other pre-fabricated, conditioned boundaries. He must say his say, or he is no artist.
If his say is in poor taste, the reader or viewer or critic
will so judge. But the coming into existence or the death of
the created work should not be decided by moralistic standards. What is beautiful, paradoxically, may be "bad, "
"evil"--even "filthy"--to some; but the artist, if he is really
a creative being, is to be judged by the aesthetic, rather
than the moral, effects of his creation.

Walter Allen, a British novelist and critic, claims
that "there is no aspect of human experience, however seemingly perverse, obscene or private, that is not fit material
for art. " Naturally, he points out, the writer who goes into
the "perverse, obscene or private" realm of life must accept
"full artistic responsibility for what he is attempting. " He
sets high aesthetic standards: "in the absence of falsification
by sensationalism, sentimentality, or vulgarity" and "aesthetic

detachment"--but aesthetic standards do not mean repression
or censorship.   Allen says that "there is no law against the
corruption of public taste";[63] obviously, if there were, much
advertising, most movies, and nearly all of television would
be illegal!   But there are laws against obscenity and pornography.

Almost by definition, the artist is and must be a free
spirit.   If he is not free to follow where his creative spirit
takes him, he can, at best, be an artist in name only.   Yet
the artist is something like the famous paradox of the cannon
fired by remote control on an unpopulated desert isle.   If no
one hears the cannon, is there a sound?   If no one gets to
hear or see the products of the artist's creative imagination,
the soul of the artist is certainly not fulfilled, and, in broad
perspective, probably mankind is generally a little the worse.

As Horace Kallen says, "If art were merely the self-
expression of the artist, it could be passed by and ignored."[64]
But art is not simply the artist's concern; what the artist
creates affects, not to be too rhetorical about it, eternity.
And the censor is mortally afraid of the artist's power.
Whether that power is really quite as great as stated in Shel-
ley's dictum that "poets are the unacknowledged legislators
of the world" is not really the point.   The censor thinks so,
and he will go to almost any length to stifle free expression.

Santayana differs; as indicated earlier, he feels that
the artist's skill transmogrifies what it touches.   Even when
dealing with what some might consider ignoble themes, "the
artist ... renders them innocent and interesting, because he
looks at them from above, composes their attitudes and surroundings harmoniously, and makes them food for the
mind."[65] Santayana goes so far as to say that "lascivious
and pious works [and that is Santayana's coupling--EMO],
when beauty has touched them, cease to give out what is wil-
ful and disquieting in their subject and become altogether intellectual and sublime."   Even if the artist who is dealing
with the "lascivious" doesn't always, or even often, reach the
high levels set by the eminent philosopher, it still is good to
know that the possibility for high art does exist.   It is important to be aware that the censor's delicate and tender
judgments are seldom discriminating and certainly never conducive to the creative atmosphere.

But the censor doesn't really have to be a literary
critic.   There is a rather widespread feeling among the

general populace that all of human life, one way or the other, must and should be regulated by law. It makes living
so easy when life-decisions are not individual choices. The
literally thousands of laws--federal, state, and city--and of
regulations imposed under authority of these laws, under
which we all must live, become such an accepted burden
that we sometimes forget that not every part of life is--nor
should be--subject to legal control.

There is much of life, particularly on the creative
side, which must not be under actual or threatened control
and coercion if mankind is to have any chance for change or
growth. It is the artist who has the perceptive insight, the
ability to express what needs to be expressed, and his domain is one which the law often enters upon, usually with
heavy, clumsy, non-discriminating efforts to make the artist
conform to the non-creative, the standard, the accepted.

Just as long as the law remains flexible, amenable to
change, and in line with the true desires of the society it is
attempting to regulate, the law will be accepted. But when
the law is not in line with what the society (of which it
should be a servant rather than a master) really wants, then
the law will be eroded, altered in execution and, ultimately,
ignored completely. Without the power of the people behind
it, ultimately any law is only a hollow shell of reality.

The creative artist is the one who is willing to take
risks to interpret life as he sees it. If to do so risks suf-
fering the censor's wrath--or, what is possibly worse for
the artist, the critic's distaste or the general reader's
scorn--then so it must be. Anyone who writes to please any
God but Truth (as he sees it), whether that God be Mammon
or Christ or Yahweh or whoever, can hardly be creative in
the truest sense. And if he writes with two pencils--one
blue and held forever poised for obliteration of what might
worry the censor--he deserves whatever variety of oblivion
his work will probably get.

When the writer is more concerned with what Mrs.
Grundy will say than with what should be said, he is not going to be more than a literary hack, a seeker of popularity
at the expense of self-respect.

One of the leading authorities on Grundyism was Victorian novelist, moralist, and satirist Samuel Butler, who
may be known to literature students as a "one novel" writer,

but his satire Erewhon is perhaps better worth remembering, particularly for those interested in censorship, for its "Mrs. Grundy" references.   Butler was concerned with what was really going on in his day, below the facade of the middle of the nineteenth century in Victorian England.   The whole book is really a picture of Victorian England through his rather astringent and acerb vision.

He describes the inhabitants of "Erewhon" (mid-Victorian England) as worshipping the goddess "Ydgrun" (Grundy).   Butler describes her as "not an elevated conception, and ... sometimes both cruel and absurd."   "Even her most devoted worshippers," Butler writes, "were a little ashamed of her, and served her more with heart and in deed than with their tongues....   Take her all in all, ... she was a beneficent and useful deity, who did not care how much she was denied as long as she was obeyed and feared, and who kept hundreds of thousands in those paths which make life tolerably happy...."   He speaks of the "high Ydgrundites," who "would never run contrary to her dictates without ample reason for doing so...."   Butler goes on, "in such cases they would override her with due self-reliance, and the goddess seldom punished them; for they are brave and Ydgrun is not."66

"They are brave, and Ydgrun is not."   Butler's insight into the nature of the censor and of censorship is penetrating.   Cowardice and censorship go hand in hand; who looks on beauty--or ugliness--bare must have courage.   The equivocations and concealments of the censors are well-known enough not to need exemplification.   Equally obvious is the forthrightness of those with the courage to face up to truth. "They are brave, and Ydgrun is not."

Butler reminds us that the practice of conformity until it becomes "absolutely intolerable" is an immutable law of "Ydgrun."   The land of Mrs. Grundy does not exist only in satire.   Sadly, Mrs. Grundy speaks in many tongues, in many lands.   But the true artist will never submit to conformity, even though it be "a law of Ydgrun," wherever and whenever Mrs. Grundy is both chief literary critic and censor.   She certainly has outlasted Victorian England, and still lives in permissive modern America.

INTERLUDE

PORTRAIT OF A CENSOR:

3.   ANTHONY COMSTOCK (1844-1915)

"Anthony Comstock was adapted to the folkways of his time and place. Often in the fight against obscenity he stood alone. Always he was in the van. But somewhere behind him an army of Puritans was solidly massed. For this reason, he was feared and hated--because he was so strong. Had his crusade run counter to the mores of his people, he would have been a pitiful figure, a martyr to his lonely ideal. But in him people cursed the spirit of enforced righteousness made palpable--fleshly and menacing, with ginger-colored whiskers and a warrant and a Post Office badge. He was the apotheosis, the fine flower of Puritanism. "

> --Heywood Broun & Margaret Leech, Anthony
> Comstock: Roundsman of the Lord, 1927.

"Comstock had things pretty much his way. He was-- or at least so he believed--public conscience incarnate; he could bully officials and judges. "

> --Morris L. Ernst and Alexander Lindey,
> The Censor Marches On, 1940.

10. THE COMMUNITY AS CENSOR

"The peeping Tom has always been an object of
loathing and abomination. But a group of peeping
Toms is invested with the sacramental holiness of
democracy. "

>   --William Seagle, "The Paradox of American
>   Censorship" in: S. D. Schmalhausen, Behold
>   America!, 1931.

Chapter 10

THE COMMUNITY AS CENSOR

Extra-legal censorship is a technique which, although quite common throughout history, has had wide variation in public support. Censorship validated by law has back of it all the paraphernalia of the law and order system of the particular place and time, but the censorship which begins with an awareness that it has no legal base, and no police powers to enforce its wishes, must rely on extra-legal--and occasional illegal--enforcement methods.

On occasion the censorship is really spontaneous, begun perhaps by a well-meaning parent or other local citizen in disagreement with the library or bookstore or newsstand making available the allegedly censorable material; there soon clusters around the enraged or aroused individual a group which is determined to bar the purchase, or sale, or distribution of the item or items concerned.

More commonly there is a statewide or even national group, such as the well-known Boston Watch and Ward Society, the Citizens for Decent Literature (which began in Cincinnati and managed to get its leader, Charles Keating, Jr., on the Presidential Commission on Obscenity and Pornography as a Nixon appointee), or the New York Society for the Suppression of Vice. Usually these groups are supported by such organizations as the American Legion, the Daughters of the American Revolution, local Parent-Teachers' organizations, and the Women's Christian Temperance Union.

Between 1888 and 1893 one of the more interesting (at least in title) regional anti-vice organizations flourished in England. Its title was "The Birmingham and Midland Counties Vigilance Association for the Repression of Criminal Vice and Public Immorality." Its goals went beyond simply censorship: we are told that "beside the subjugation of child prostitution, it also tried to suppress houses of ill fame,

130

indecent performances in concert halls, the exposure of indecent pictures on the doors of theaters, music halls, and
on walls, quack advertisements, and the circulation of 'impure' literature. " The group only lasted for five years, but
it did manage to produce a junior branch, which bore the
obviously appropriate title of "The Snowdrop Band. "[1]

The most usual weapon used by the group--local or
otherwise--attempting to cause particular reading matter to
be suppressed is an economic one. The threat or the actual
use of boycotting--asking sympathizers not to shop in a particular store or asking advertisers not to advertise a particular publication--has happened often. The fact that boycott, if proven, is often against the laws of city, county, or
state, hardly seems to worry the already extra-legal censor.

What does affect them is that in most large cities the
boycott is even less effective than picketing. The Great
American Consumer hardly ever seems to notice such attempts to limit his free use of his shopping dollar--unless,
of course, he happens to be as fanatic as the group running
the censorship attempt and therefore conscientiously insists
on following their edicts. The big city dweller is usually
too preoccupied with other urban-related problems to be of
much help in boycott-censorship.

As might be expected, the picture is quite different
in small towns. For one thing, the lower level of sophistication and education likely to be found there will often mean
that particular retailers are all too ready and willing to co-
operate. If for no better reason, they may have felt their
own individual qualms about certain publications, and the ex-
cuse offered by threats of boycott is a very welcome one.
If the retailer, for whatever reason, does not indicate his
compliance with the censoring group's wishes or commands,
the word-of-mouth method, plus letters to the editor of the
local newspaper decrying the immorality of some of the city's
businessmen, is usually sufficient. Indeed, the very threat
of bad publicity often intimidates the book or magazine seller.

More prevalent than the extra-legal community group
technique is the activity of the local public official, practicing
what is at best a quasi-legal technique. Again--although a
few large cities, such as Boston, Chicago, and Detroit are
notorious exceptions--this is most common in the less-popu-
lous areas. As William Hempl and Patrick Wall, who have

done considerable study on this matter, say, "The number of
people whose reading material has been or is being controlled to some extent by police application of an obscenity
standard which is at variance with the constitutional guar-
antees of free speech is quite large. "[2] And this "police application" is done, more or less unofficially, purely by
threat of possible persecution, followed by a "raid" to remove the actual books or magazines considered "obscene. "

It is a good political ploy, in many rural or small-
town areas of America, to this day, for the sheriff or state's
attorney or city attorney to dramatize his moral rectitude
just before election day by well-publicized efforts to burn
books. No one ever seems to notice that actual charges
are rarely, if ever, brought against the presumed culprits,
but the spotlight usually pays off, in terms of re-election.

Hempl and Wall describe how, between 1949 and 1957,
paperback editions of many hundreds of books--many by quite
well-known and generally accepted writers--were picked up
by the Detroit police and referred to an assistant prosecutor
for a one-man judgment. They quote this official as offering the following as his standard: "If I feel I wouldn't want
my 13-year-old daughter reading it, I decide it's illegal. "
Once he had so objectively and informedly decided the matter, if the book was what he deemed to be "illegal, " the
distributors of the books so termed were asked to take back
those volumes from their customer-dealers. Usually, they
did so. [3]

So, without a vestige of true legal process, the citizens of Detroit were, in effect, denied particular reading for
nearly a decade--and no one even complained. In 1957,
when John O'Hara's popular novel, Ten North Frederick, was
so proscribed, the publishers did get an injunction, prohibiting the Detroit police commissioner from continued practice
of extra-legal censorship, at least so far as this one book
was concerned. Although he tried to circumvent the injunction, when threatened with being cited for contempt of court
he finally agreed that in Detroit, at least, there would no
longer be what was in essence illegal censorship by the police.

In 1956 the Prosecuting Attorney of St. Clair County
(Port Huron), Michigan notified local paperbound book distributors that by a specific date all publications on the proscribed list of the National Organization for Decent Literature

(a national Catholic censorship group founded in 1938) were
no longer to be sold in Port Huron. As Hempl and Wall
say, "...In Port Huron official sanction was given to a list
compiled by a private organization which itself admits that
many works which it cites as objectionable are not legally
obscene. " After a number of the publishing houses involved
obtained a Federal district court injunction against this prosecution, for going beyond legal authority, "pre-distribution
censorship by local officials then ceased. "4

These are recitals of a few--a very few--victories
over self-chosen censors; the list of defeats, mostly for lack
of any community or even publisher reaction, is a great
deal longer. It seems to be a pretty well accepted American philosophy that until some particular grievance affects
the vast majority, the rest simply grumble, and comply with
the powers that be. Police censorship is still a commonly
threatened, if not often used, weapon of the censor, especially in smaller communities.

One student of censorship has posited that only legal
restraint on allegedly obscene literature should be called
"censorship. " "Control" is what he defines as "all extra-
legal influence and pressure applied by private citizens to
restrict the sale and distribution ... " of allegedly obscene
writings. Actually "control" has often been as efficacious
as censorship, if not more so. This "control" has been
used by educational, religious, professional and veterans'
groups. 5 Of all of these groups, Haney considers the religious groups most potent and active. Even though such
groups as the National Organization for Decent Literature
tell their members and followers that their lists of "non-ac-
ceptable" publications should not be used for the purposes of
coercing or boycotting merchants and libraries, there is ample evidence that these and similar lists are frequently used
for such purposes. The neighborhood censor, armed only
with a set of general principles, is surely at a disadvantage;
pinning objectionableness down to titles such as The Wapshot
Chronicle, Bonjour Tristesse, Catcher in the Rye, Forever
Amber, Room at the Top, Slaughterhouse Five, and similarly
popular fiction of our time makes the would-be censor's job
much easier.

Religious groups can, of course, use the coercions of
their individual faiths when trying to influence people who are
members of that particular faith. When trying to get non-
members to follow their points-of-view, the best weapon for

any group is indisputable evidence of a strong, even united, public opinion behind their arguments. The pro-censorship adherents often <u>assume</u> a unified following which really does not exist.

An interesting theory about this is voiced by sociologist Kai Erikson, who presents a definition of deviance which in many ways accounts for the widespread tendency toward community group censorship. According to Erikson, "the term 'deviance' refers to conduct which the people of a group consider so dangerous or embarrassing or irritating that they bring special sanctions to bear against the persons who exhibit it."[6] Note that it is <u>not</u> a question of whether such deviances--say, the selling of reading material some call "obscene"--are in fact potentially or actually "dangerous or embarrassing or irritating"; it is sufficient that the ones who set themselves up as community guardians "consider" the activity a deviant one.

As Erikson explains, "Deviance is not a property <u>inherent</u> in any particular kind of behavior; it is a property <u>conferred</u> upon that behavior by the people who came into direct or indirect contact with it."[7] Furthermore, it is not possible for deviance to be ascribed to a particular behavior-pattern unless one is aware of the life-patterns or standards of the community under consideration. In a nudist colony, for example, a clothed person is obviously a deviant, regardless of the general opinion outside of the colony.

A significant portion of the Erikson theory of deviance is that it indicates a real plus-benefit to those involved in judging or controlling deviance. Erikson says, "The deviant act ... creates a sense of mutuality among the people of a community by supplying a focus for group feeling...."[8] More than this, Erikson feels that by alerting the community's "collective conscience," by showing the individuals they have a joint interest, action against deviance benefits whatever social organization there is. Putting it another way, "occasional moments" of behavior which appear contrary to the generally accepted standards of a community are good, according to Erikson, because they act as unifying elements for the community or group.

This looks like a rather weak straw for censorship proponents to hold on to, if they are looking for an acceptable raison d'être. Indeed, the relationship between censorship and the availability of sexually-oriented materials may even be symbiotic. Erikson claims that "deviant forms of conduct often seem to derive nourishment from the very agencies devised to inhibit them. " In England, for instance, it has been said that the trial and conviction of Oscar Wilde for practicing homosexuality was a real stimulus to wider general acceptance of this deviance from generally accepted heterosexuality. It just might be that eliminating the censor might eliminate any need for one!

The current lay-Catholic view on the relationship between public action and morality is evidenced by a recent advertisement inserted in nationally distributed publications by the lay-Catholic organization, the Knights of Columbus. Their advertisement, headed "Who's Responsible for Public Morals?"[10] says, "We have no right to set moral standards for the man next door. " But, referring directly to a claim that "obscenity flourishes in the name of freedom of speech, " they say that "moral depravity thrives on public indifference. "

They postulate that "there is a border area of morality which is everybody's business, " and claim there is a "public conscience, " which they define, somewhat nebulously, as "a reflection of the individual conscience of all people who are concerned in preserving a high standard of moral order. " It is also characterized as "the watchdog over the God-given rights of the individual to freedom of conscience, and to the security of his person and property. " Some might think that "freedom of conscience" would also include the freedom to read--but obviously the Knights of Columbus do not feel that way. It is certainly not necessarily true that the Knights of Columbus, or any other self-constituted group, can speak for either a majority of, or the entire, public in matters of conscience or freedom.

Their declaration states that "preserving a high standard of moral order ... is not an obligation to be delegated to the police and the courts. Nor to the church, the school or civic societies. " This seems to leave the implication that, given the right circumstances, the Knights of Columbus might well back vigilantism or something like it. If it were really true, as they say, that "public morality is everybody's business, " then what happens to individual morality--or to the rule of law? When everyone is in charge, it is hardly likely that the individual will retain such a personal right as that of choosing his own reading matter.

The basic dispute between the extra-legal censor and the civil-libertarian comes down to the theory, voiced by the foremost proponent of censorship for morality's sake, Jesuit priest Father Harold C. Gardiner, that there is nothing illegal about the methods of the NODL or other, similar groups. All they are doing, he claims, is persuading, convincing, arguing; and, if they are successful, then all that happens is that citizens are denied their manifest right to the freedom to read anything not found illegal. Says Father Gardiner, rather surprisingly, "a good citizen, if alerted by morally aroused public opinion, would be willing to waive this legal right for the common good"--a premise which even Father Gardiner admits is "idealistic."[11] One wonders just how far Father Gardiner and his followers would be willing to go in "waiving legal rights for the common good!"

The Roman Catholic Church, with its long tradition of attempted and actual book censorship, is not alone in its efforts to stifle sexually-oriented reading. For example, the Lutheran Church (Missouri Synod), in its officially-issued manual on Sex and the Church, stated, "There are times when the church needs to join forces with social and law-enforcement agencies to clean up a situation which is threatening the moral welfare of a whole community ... the Christian church ... can and should co-operate in well-conceived programs of community action together with statesmen, teachers, and editors in molding public opinion...." Yet the same publication paradoxically affirms, "Prudery has failed miserably. It made matters of sex secretive and unwholesome for the child, lustful for youth, and then often resorted to face-saving moralisms."[12]

One of the best-known sociological authorities on censorship, University of Illinois Professor William Albig, has constructed a closely-reasoned definition of censorship which pretty well covers most of the ways in which it operates: "Censorship is the process of restraint on freedom of thought and communication imposed by the minds of individuals, by climates of opinion, or by the process of deleting or limiting the content of any of the media of communication."[13] The author of this definition says that his definition implies a censorship process best understood by looking at the chart he has prepared [see below] entitled Levels of Censorship in the United States.

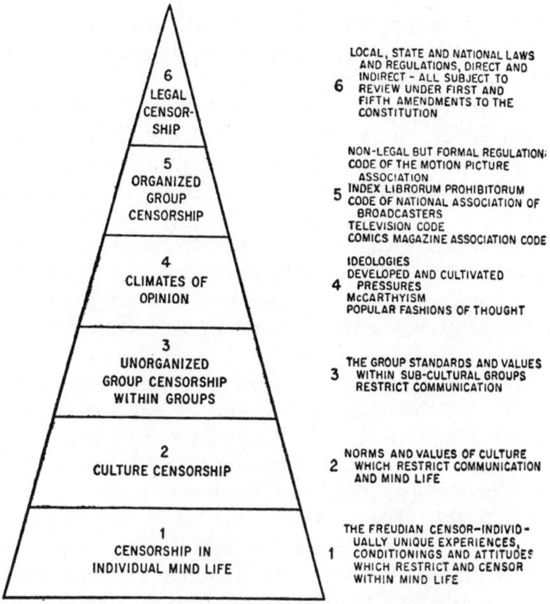
6
LEGAL
CENSOR-
SHIP
5
ORGANIZED
GROUP
CENSORSHIP
4
CLIMATES OF
OPINION
3
UNORGANIZED
GROUP CENSORSHIP
WITHIN GROUPS
2
CULTURE CENSORSHIP
1
CENSORSHIP IN
INDIVIDUAL MIND LIFE
6 LOCAL, STATE AND NATIONAL LAWS AND REGULATIONS, DIRECT AND INDIRECT - ALL SUBJECT TO REVIEW UNDER FIRST AND FIFTH AMENDMENTS TO THE CONSTITUTION
5 NON-LEGAL BUT FORMAL REGULATION: CODE OF THE MOTION PICTURE ASSOCIATION
INDEX LIBRORUM PROHIBITORUM
CODE OF NATIONAL ASSOCIATION OF BROADCASTERS
TELEVISION CODE
COMICS MAGAZINE ASSOCIATION CODE
4 IDEOLOGIES
DEVELOPED AND CULTIVATED PRESSURES
McCARTHYISM
POPULAR FASHIONS OF THOUGHT
3 THE GROUP STANDARDS AND VALUES WITHIN SUB-CULTURAL GROUPS RESTRICT COMMUNICATION
2 NORMS AND VALUES OF CULTURE WHICH RESTRICT COMMUNICATION AND MIND LIFE
1 THE FREUDIAN CENSOR—INDIVIDUALLY UNIQUE EXPERIENCES, CONDITIONINGS AND ATTITUDES WHICH RESTRICT AND CENSOR WITHIN MIND LIFE
Levels of censorship in the United States.

From Modern Public Opinion by William Albig. Copyright 1956 by McGraw-Hill Book Co., Inc. Used with permission of McGraw-Hill Book Company.

First, Albig lists what he calls "censorship in the individual mind-life." Essentially, he accepts the Freudian idea of the so-called "dominant consciousness," keeping out of each individual's active thoughts and feelings those items which it feels are likely to be contrary to what the "dominant consciousness" has set up as its life-standards. Such "censorship" is rarely self-perceived, but it is present in all of us, with the censored ideas emerging, on occasion, from the unconscious mind.

Next in Albig's scale is "culture censorship," still on the informal level, which would include what William Sumner has called "the mores," what Sir James Frazer and others have called "taboos"--in short, the basic values of the culture in which the individual lives. Albig calls this type of censorship "pervasive and insidious."[14]

The two middle levels of Albig's six-layered picture of censorship, "unorganized group censorship within groups"

and "climates of opinion," are again self-imposed, but powerful.   The differences between the language a man will use
at a P. T. A. meeting and what he might say at a stag poker-
game, exemplify level three; level four, which is on the
ideological level, may be illustrated by the way in which an
Orange County, California resident might restrict himself in
reading, as compared to someone from Berkeley, California.

        The other two levels--"organized group censorship"
and "legal censorship"--have been discussed earlier or are
left for a later chapter.   They are the ones which we most
usually think of when discussing censorship.

        The famous case of Tolstoy's unwillingness to write
what he feared the Czarist censor might forbid bears repetition at this point.   Tolstoy once wrote: "You would not believe how, from the very commencement of my activity, that
horrible Censor question has tormented me.   I wanted to
write what I felt; but at the same time it occurred to me
that what I wrote would not be permitted, and involuntarily
I had to abandon the work.   I abandoned, and went on aban-
doning, and meanwhile the years passed away."15   Who knows
what riches for the human spirit have been lost to society
through fear of the censor?

        Pressure groups which in some way affect authorship
are as American as the proverbial apple-pie, but this does
not mean that they are the best means to accomplish a presumably good end, or that their goals are always really
good.   The Carry Nation technique toward the Demon Rum,
the Ku Klux Klan technique in keeping the nation's minorities
from aiming at equality, and the John Birch Society program
and procedures are, each in its own way, also representa-
tively American--but not necessarily defensible.

        Actually, the community censors in other ways than
those listed by Albig.   There is certainly a kind of <u>family</u>
censorship which operates in some degree in perhaps every
family.   The reading permitted to mother and father is not,
in most families, identical with the reading acceptable for
the children, at least under the family roof.   The common
memories, shared by most of us, of unwillingness to be seen
reading what might be considered "wrong" or "bad," or even
trivial, by parents or older siblings demonstrate a form of
self-censorship.

        There is no great likelihood that the kind of reading

available in the so-called "porno shops" of the big cities will
be found at every book-outlet, even in the big cities. The
men who distribute such items wholesale and who sell retail
know where and what their market is, and, even without
group pressure, are unlikely to sell what won't be bought.
After all, these men--particularly the local retailers--are
part of the local culture scene, and for them to try to sell
to the mass audience the tasteless, the vulgar, the extreme
(no matter how "legal" such publications may be) is as unlikely as that national television chains would present drama-
tizations of the works of De Sade in place of the activities
of Doris Day and Carol Burnett.

But this kind of "censorship, " if the word can be
stretched that far, is not what is usually meant by that term.
Censorship has been denied by most public libraries, for
example, though it is difficult to find even a few examples
of circulation of clearly erotic ("hard-core") literature in
the public libraries of America. The librarian--very much
like the author, the publisher, the distributor, and the retailer of books--is very conscious of his market and his support. The always limited funds of any American public library pretty well delimit the librarian in what he purchases
to those things which are generally accepted or are likely to
be.

Albig says, "An informal, extralegal censorship of
books is always operative. As a rule the prevailing standards of a culture limit the expression of an author in so far
as they are incorporated in his own standards, in his hopes
for large sales and wide circulation, and in the standards
set up by his publisher. "[16] The words of Tolstoy, quoted
above, referred to the restraints which fear of censorship
placed on his creativity. Yet Tolstoy managed to write and
get published and widely read such sexually significant works
as The Kreutzer Sonata and Father Sergius. These would
certainly have fallen under the censor's blue pencil if they
had been written in so-called "indecent" language--but they
stayed inviolate because they were not.

Very often, indeed, it must be admitted, the pressure
of the community as censor has been ineffective, even to the
extent of giving publicity to, stirring up curiosity about, and
eventually resulting in an increased readership for books
which otherwise might have been little read. After all, the
greatest censorship (in the broadest sense) is the censorship
of silence. The un-noted book, especially in these days of

great competition for the leisure hour, will usually also be the unread one.   To coin a phrase, "better read than dead!"

As psychologist Leon A. Jakobovits has written, "We know ... that individuals tend to expose themselves to information that is consonant with their beliefs and attitudes and tend to avoid information contrary to their beliefs.   Hence, it is likely that the consumers of pornography have a positive attitude toward it, enjoy it, and find it subjectively beneficial."[17]   It is only when the felt needs and wishes and generally accepted civil rights of the majority of the community come into conflict with the law that deep, community-dividing issues come to arise.

11. THE LAW SAYS, "NO!"

"The first instinct of modern man is to get a law passed to forbid or prevent what, in his wisdom, he disapproves. A thing which is inevitable, however, is one which we cannot control. We have to make up our minds to it, adjust ourselves to it, and settle down to live with it. Its inevitableness may be disputed, in which case we must re-examine it; but if our analysis is correct, when we reach what is inevitable, we reach the end, and our regulations must apply to ourselves, not to the social facts."

--William Graham Sumner,
"The Absurd Effort to Make the World Over," 1894.

Chapter 11

THE LAW SAYS, "NO!"

Through the long, steady growth of the Anglo-American system of jurisprudence, from the Magna Carta on, one central theme has predominated. The rights of man are more or less first; then come the laws restricting and punishing invasions of these rights--from the right to private property to the right to one's own life. In dealing with matters relating to sex, the law has always found difficulty. No one questions that killing (except for the soldier and the executioner) is against the law--but there is a great deal of question on the right to create life. And, when it comes to artistic or written representation of life's inception, then the laws have certainly varied widely.

Before 1727 the British Common Law did not take cognizance of obscene literature.[1] Indeed, it was not until 1857, with the passing of the Obscene Publications Act, that specific legislation on this topic went into effect in England. In America, where, as in England, there had been censorship of writings expressing political and religious dissent almost since its beginnings, it was not until 1821, in Massachusetts (and here the seller of Memoirs of a Woman of Pleasure was found guilty of obscene libel) that any book was censored on obscenity charges. The first federal legislation on obscenity, in 1842, was against permitting such books to be imported, and it was 1865 before the first law was passed concerning mailing of obscene items in the United States.

There is little point, for the purposes of this volume, in further reviewing the detailed history of the processes and expressions of U. S. laws directed against the written word dealing with sexual behavior. It has been so detailed in many expert volumes, including Robert Haney's already cited work, Ernst and Lindey's classic The Censor Marches On (1940), and, in particular, Norman St. John-Stevas' thoroughgoing Obscenity and the Law (1956). Many other popular

histories of the legal side of censorship have been published
in recent years.

What is worth analyzing for our purposes are the motives behind legal censorship, as revealed by some of the
judicial language in reported decisions and by Congressional
discussions, both on the floor of Congress and in various
committee hearings. And, sad to relate, although the U. S.
Supreme Court, during the late Fifties and the Sixties, indicated a leaning toward suppression of censorship, there is
really comparatively little progress, at least from the standpoint of freedom, in the words and actions of Congress. A
detailed description of more recent Congressional actions on
censorship is given later in this volume, but some earlier
efforts are related in this chapter.

The very first case of indictment of a reputably pornographic volume (1727) by the civil courts of England involved a book entitled Venus in the Cloister, or The Nun in
Her Smock. The decision was that the publishing of the book
was ''an offence at common law as it tends to corrupt the
morals of the King's subjects and is against the peace of the
King. ''2   The argument on the latter point was that the
King's peace was broken where an act ''is destructive of
morality in general ... [and] if it does or may affect all the
King's subjects. '' Thus we see that the first legal censorship in Anglo-American history pretty well set the standard
for all such future efforts.

The bald statements that the publishing of this book
was ''destructive of morality in general'' and that ''the peace
of the King'' was disturbed or broken by the very existence
of the book were upheld by the judges, who asked for none
of the proof to back these statements up which might be expected in a court of law. How all Englishmen--literate or
illiterate--might be deleteriously affected by a single book is
certainly not clear. How the very framework of British
eighteenth century morality might be torn down by one book
is likewise unclear. But, as St. John-Stevas pointed out,
''thus the misdemeanor of 'obscene libel' entered the law and
has never been seriously challenged. ''3 (Incidentally, the use
of the word ''libel'' in the phrase ''obscene libel'' has nothing
to do with ''libel'' in its generally accepted sense, but derives from ''libellus, '' or ''little book. '' ''Obscene libel''
means merely ''obscenity in writing. '')

With the advent of the nineteenth century came the

great tide of legal censorship efforts.   St. John-Stevas records the following as the reaction of one magistrate, in
1817, to reputedly obscene literature: "The mischief done
to the community by such offenses greatly exceeds that done
by murder, for in the latter case the mischief has some
bounds, but no bounds can be set to the pernicious consequences of a crime which tends to the entire corruption of
morals."[4]   It is interesting to note here the 90-year-old
echo from the 1727 judicial allegation that promulgation of
obscenity is all-pervasive in its effect on morality.

In 1857 the British Parliament approved a new law on
this topic, which came to be known as Lord Campbell's Act,
from the name of its principal sponsor.   Campbell said,
"The measure was intended to apply exclusively to works
written for the single purpose of corrupting the minds of
youth and of a nature calculated to shock the common feelings of decency in a well-regulated mind."[5]   This law gave
British magistrates the authority to have destroyed any book
or print which they deemed obscene.   Many members of
Commons criticized the bill, one of them saying the bill
"was an attempt to make people virtuous by Act of Parliament," but after some discussion and amendments the bill
was finally approved.[6]

A decade later the famous Hicklin Case, on appeal,
came up before Chief Justice Alexander Cockburn, who delivered a verdict which has had a tremendous influence ever
since on all obscenity trials in English-speaking countries.
This is what has come to be known as the Hicklin test for
obscenity: "The test of obscenity is whether the tendency of
the matter charged as obscenity is to deprave and corrupt
those whose minds are open to such immoral influences and
into whose hands a publication of this sort may fall."[7]   So
impressive and persuasive was this judgment that it actually
affected both British and American judicial decisions on obscenity almost to this day.   The Obscene Publications Act,
passed in England in 1959, includes this statement: "For
the purposes of this Act an article shall be deemed to be
obscene if its effect or (where the article comprises two or
more distinct items) the effect of any one of its items is, if
taken as a whole, such as to tend to deprave and corrupt
persons who are likely, having regard to all relevant circumstances, to read, see or hear the matter contained or embodied in it."[8]   As can readily be seen, the 1959 act still
uses Justice Cockburn's phrase, "...to deprave and corrupt,"
but a rather significant change has occurred during the

century since Hicklin.   The obligation to consider the supposedly obscene item as a whole is clearly an advance.

The censor has now obviously lost one of his principal weapons, because it is much more difficult to prove an
entire book obscene than to take episodes, even individual
"dirty" words, out of context as a basis for extirpation of
the complete work.   The recurrent attacks--usually in American small-town high schools--on J. D. Salinger's The Catcher in the Rye, for its inclusion of a generally opprobrious
Anglo-Saxon monosyllable (despite the fact that the protagon-
ist of the novel is himself shocked by its possible viewing
by his younger sister), is an example of the latter technique.

Just as the Hicklin case had served as a rather widely followed precedent for both British and American judges
and law-makers, so the 1959 Obscene Publications Act has
had its influence on Anglo-American justice and law concerning obscenity.   But the 1959 act was not enough of a change
from the 1867 verdict to satisfy the non-censorious.   Another
act was passed in 1964, but it proved of little help in this
regard.

In 1969 the Arts Council of Great Britain (an official
governmental organization) called a conference on the effects
of the British obscenity laws on writers and others.   This
conference set up a "working party," including representatives of thirteen interested organizations: the Arts Council,
the Booksellers Association, the Defence of Literature and
the Arts Society, the English Centre of International PEN,
the Institute of Contemporary Arts, the League of Dramatists, the Library Association, the National Book League,
the National Council for Civil Liberties, the Publishers Association, the Society of Authors, the Society of Young Publishers, and the Writers Guild of Great Britain.   This
"working party"--which included such luminaries as Frank
Kermode, Kathleen Nott, and Benn W. Levy--came up in
July, 1969 with a report which, interestingly enough, in
many ways was paralleled by the 1970 Report of the Commission on Obscenity and Pornography in the United States.

The Arts Council Report proposed to repeal both the
1959 and the 1964 Obscene Publications Act, and to repeal
or amend other relevant laws.   Just as the President and
Vice-President of the United States, and later the U. S. Senate, repudiated the C. O. P. Report in 1970, the British

Home Secretary "made it clear to the House of Commons
that he did not intend taking any action."9   The evidence
was clear (as in the reaction to the American report) that
most, if not quite all, of those who evinced disagreement in
Commons with the Arts Council Report had not actually read
it!

        The Arts Council Report on Obscene Publications gave
twelve main reasons for recommending that there be no
more anti-obscenity laws in England (they may be found in
full in this book's appendix).   In sum, their arguments were
on the reasonable, humanistic side, arguing for the weapons
of "social reprobation" rather than legal punishment to do
any safeguarding which society really finds essential, in relation to literature and art.

        The reasoning of the Arts Council is, of course, di-
rectly contrary to most of what the censor, through the centuries, has given as his justification.   The idea that reading
about sex will "deprave and corrupt" is a deeply-rooted one,
and it will take a long time before it is ever completely out
of the background, if not of the foreground, of censorial
thought and action.

        Unfortunately for the cause of truth-seeking, there is
reason to doubt the efficacy of the most commonly accepted
social science techniques for determining the reliability and
validity of cause-and-effect in the matter of obscenity-pornog-
raphy and their relation to various anti-social activities.
Dr. James Q. Wilson, a Harvard professor of government,
avers that "social science probably cannot answer the questions put to it by those who wish to rest the case for or
against censorship on the proved effects of exposure to obscenity, media violence, scurrilous political literature, or
whatever."   He states that the findings of the Commission on
Obscenity and Pornography on this question "are not nearly
so conclusive as they are made out to be--provided one
adapts a proper measure of 'harm!'"10

        If the American judicial system puts the burden of
proof on the social sciences, and the social sciences cannot--
or, at least, have not yet--been able to prove either that the
reading of obscenity causes or does not cause illegal behavior, then in essence, isn't censorship really dead, logically
and legally speaking?   This would seem to be a reasonable
conclusion, but censorship, like the proverbial cat, has
several lives.

As Wilson asks, "to what mode of inquiry should a reasonable man turn to decide on the issue of censorship...?" He feels that since there is really no "conclusive" social science evidence, "all judgments about the acceptability of restrictions on various media will have to rest on political and philosophical considerations." At the same time, he admits to not being sure "what forms of legal restraint, if any" should be placed on "easily available materials that portray what should be tender and private as base and brutal."[11] (He was speaking particularly of material readily available to children, in this case.)

This is how and why a modern professor of government differs with the Commission on Obscenity and Pornography's methods and conclusions. In essence, he says, "Who knows what to do? I don't like political censorship, but I can understand the need for censorship of materials on sex." In fact, he calls this a moral issue--and one wonders why he doesn't simply call for a revival of the Medieval Church's attitude, techniques, and strictures, since he so clearly agrees with the Church's basic approach toward writing about sex.

Another way of looking at this issue is to see how various judicial decisions, American and British, have analyzed the problem. They vary widely in style and conclusions, but together should make evident one indisputable fact about cases involving reputed obscenity and pornography --there is really no consistency of agreement on such matters among, or even within, courts.

For example, Judge Manton, of the U. S. Court of Appeals, ruling on James Joyce's Ulysses in 1934, said: "Who can doubt the obscenity of this book after a reading of the pages referred to which are too indecent to add as a footnote? Its characterization as obscene should be quite unanimous by all who read it." His bland assumption of unanimity was invalidated before even the verdict was announced; the majority opinion, on the same case, as voiced by Judge Learned Hand, stated: "The net effect even of portions most open to attack, such as the closing monologue of the wife of Leopold Bloom, is pitiful and tragic rather than lustful ... the book as a whole is not pornographic...."[12] And Judge Woolsey's historical and pace-setting verdict was thus upheld.

Another famous ruling was the one by Judge Curtis

Bok concerning, among other books, such now-accepted modern classics as Erskine Caldwell's God's Little Acre, William Faulkner's Sanctuary and The Wild Palms, and James T. Farrell's Studs Lonigan and A World I Never Made. Bok, sitting in judgment in 1949 in Philadelphia, said that the Philadelphia law which was supposed to apply could only be so applied when "(1) the writing was sexually impure and pornographic" and "(2) ... when there is a reasonable and demonstrable cause to believe that a crime or misdemeanor has been committed or is about to be committed, as the perceptible result of the publication and distribution of the writing in question. ... "13 Note that simply to state that a tendency toward this result existed, or that such consequences are "self-evident," is specifically stated by the judge to be "insufficient and irrelevant."

Bok even went further than this. The English precedent which had for so many decades obtained, Regina v. Hicklin, he declared not appropriate. Bok said, "The criminal law is not in my opinion the 'custos morum' of the king's subjects as Regina v. Hicklin states; it is only the custodian of the peace and order that free men and women need for the shaping of their common destiny." The landmark language in this case has since been a basic consideration for the American judicial system. As Bok said, speaking of what was now required as proof in such cases, "It is the effect that counts more than the desire and no indictment can stand unless it can be shown."14

The Bok decision obviously puts the burden of proof on the censor to set up standards of what is "sexually impure and pornographic"--a most difficult task. The censor must also go on to prove that the particular piece of reading matter, taken as a whole, has not just a bad effect, but actually an effect which will cause "a crime or misdemeanor" to result. This is considerably more difficult than the requirements under Hicklin.

There are still, of course, British jurists and law-philosophers who are more or less Hicklin-minded. As Lord Patrick Devlin, a British jurist and legal theoretician (who, as Queen's Bench Justice and a Lord of Appeal, had been actively involved in various obscenity cases), once wrote, "The true principle is that the law exists for the protection of society."15 Michael Keeling, an Englishman writing about the law from the traditional point of view, disagreed somewhat, stating that this was not the law's sole aim and also

"...that the rights of society--except very rarely, in the moments of greatest danger (and even this is arguable)--are greater than the rights of the individual in it. "16

For Keeling, "the highest aim of the law is the protection of the individual. " If, he argues, the basic principle of all moral action is that it is _free_ action, with the right to make and execute even moral choices which are wrong, then how can society be both free and morally restrictive? With rather a grand rhetorical flourish, Keeling trumpets that "the one uniquely valuable thing in the world is an individual human being, and whether or not society is worth preserving depends precisely on how far it recognizes this value even in those who do not conform to its morals. "17 Surely, we have here individualistic John Stuart Mill brought into the third quarter of the twentieth century, and shown to be quite modish and comfortable there!

On sexual freedom Keeling has this enlightening comment: "Many people fear that 'moral freedom' may mean 'moral licence, ' but such a fear suggests rather little trust in the power of the love of God and a curiously faint-hearted estimate of the attractiveness of what is good. "18 And even the God-fearing and God-driven can certainly understand how God is denigrated when the presumed power of evil, or the Devil, is presumed to be so much greater than His.

A perennial problem (referred to briefly above) in dealing with censorship is whether the law is really justified in dealing with morality at all. Some years ago Lord Devlin delivered a series of lectures on the relationship of private morality and the law which has stirred up much controversy. Lord Devlin's main contention is that "it is not possible to set theoretical limits to the power of the State to legislate against immorality. "19 He bases this on the following logical arguments:

1.   Society is entitled to protect itself against dangers, by using its laws to do so;

2.   "There is disintegration when no common morality is observed and history shows that the loosening of moral bonds is often the first stage of disintegration"; and so society must take whatever steps are necessary to preserve its morality, in order to preserve itself.

He claims that really there is no such thing as _private_

morality. Whatever a man who lives in a society does, in
some degree affects that society, since he is a part of it. And
to determine what is the moral judgment of society, he says
that "immorality ..., for the purpose of the law, is what
every right-minded person is presumed to consider to be
immoral. " And the "right-minded man," Devlin says, is
really the man selected for a jury; "the moral judgement of
society must be something about which any twelve men or
women drawn at random might after discussion be expected
to be unanimous. "20

Yet he feels that the individual is entitled to "tolera-
tion of the maximum individual freedom that is consistent
with the integrity of society. "21 Indeed, society must be
willing to put up with a great deal to protect and defend
maximum individual liberty, although Devlin says "no society
can do without intolerance, indignation and disgust; they are
the forces behind the moral law...." If this dictum were
to be taken at its face value, it really sounds as though all
the forces of unreason, of emotion, of mindless passion are
what really should motivate societal judgments on moral issues.

Devlin is aware of the difficulty here. In his preface
he defends this language as reasonable; he feels that there
must really be intense feeling about a particular moral issue
before it should come under legal purview. His clinching
argument on this point is that "the average Englishman ...
is not easily moved to indignation or disgust. "22 There
might be some question, not only of the dispassionate calm
of the average Englishman, but also of whether this judgment
is not a rather frail reed on which to lean in the defense of
private liberties.

To give Devlin his due, he does say that "it may be
that overall tolerance is always increasing. " He admits that
"the pressure of the human mind, always seeking greater
freedom of thought, is outwards against the bonds of society
forcing their gradual relaxation ..., " but he clings to his
feeling that, practically speaking, there will result a society
willing to plan toward what it sees as its own decline. 23

It is John Stuart Mill who has most convincingly ar-
gued the case for civil liberty. And Devlin argues, against
the Mill doctrine (which, briefly stated, is that the only reason for which force could be properly used against any citizen is to prevent his doing harm to other citizens), that

according to English law "the Court of King's Bench was the
custos morum of the people and had the superintendency of
offences contra bonos mores. " Or, to put this point another
way, "for the purposes of the law ... morality in England
means what twelve men and women think it means--in other
words, it is to be ascertained as a question of fact. "[24] All
this may sound a little startling, but surely it is consonant
with the theory of democracy to leave such matters in the
hands of the people.

However, an Oxford professor of jurisprudence, H. L.
A. Hart, has written what is probably the best critique of
Devlin's doctrine and the best modern defense of Mill's point
of view on the function of law vis-à-vis morality, in modern
society.   He answers Devlin's arbitrary claim (which Hart
calls "vague") that history shows that the first stage of societal disintegration is "the loosening of moral bonds, " by saying that "no reputable historian has maintained this thesis,
and there is indeed much evidence against it. " Hart cannot
see why, "even if the conventional morality did ... change,
the society in question would ... [be] destroyed or 'sub-
verted. '"[25] Hart's point is well taken.

As an alternative to legal restrictions on private morality, Hart suggests free and open critical discussion.   Give
men an opportunity to state facts and opinions as they see them,
let their arguments be freely and critically reviewed by the public, then see how long such matters as are related to morality
can stand up to public opinion, if that opinion is adverse.

Hart offers three basic propositions relating to
social morality's value.   He describes as "truths": 1) "...
since all social moralities ... make provision in some degree
for such universal values as individual freedom, safety of
life, and protection from deliberately inflicted harm, there
will always be much in social morality which is worth preserving ... "; 2) "...the spirit or attitude of mind which
characterizes the practice of a social morality is something
of very great value and indeed quite vital for men to foster and
preserve in any society"; and 3) "...the moral attitude to conduct has often survived the criticism, the infringement, and the
ultimate relaxation of specific moral institutions. " This
is quite in dispute with what Hart calls "moral conservatism, "
which holds "that the preservation from change of any existent mode of a social morality, whatever its content, is a
value and justifies its legal enforcement. " Hart says that
this proposition is least defensible as regards sexual morals,

"determined as these so obviously are by variable tastes and conventions."26   Certainly, the evidence of the extremely wide range of sexual prohibitions imposed in the fifty states of the United States backs this up.   If it is right to practice homosexuality between consenting adults in the state of Illinois (as it now is), why is it wrong, by <u>statute</u>, to do so in every other state?

        This is not to say, as Hart puts it, "that in morality we are ... forced to choose between deliberate coercion and indifference."27   Again Hart reminds us of the efficacy and advisability of debate and discussion in a free society.   There is nothing which <u>compels</u> individuals in <u>this</u> type of consideration; certainly <u>legal force</u> is no longer necessary if free discussion and advice and argument are all available to those who would, for instance, wish to dissuade someone from reading a pornographic book.   But Hart feels there is nothing democratic about the majority imposing its will on a minority just because it <u>is</u> a majority.   He sees, finally, the restriction of freedom <u>as</u> too great an evil to risk for the sake of a fancied, unproven threat to a society's existence.

        More or less of a reconciliation between the diametrically opposed positions held by Devlin and Hart has been offered by American legal philosopher Ernest Nagel.   Writing under the same rubric28 as Lord Devlin, <u>The Enforcement of Morals</u>, he emerges with a rather different set of conclusions.   He agrees with Hart on the matter of the degree of danger to society imposed by immorality, stating that "neither logic nor history appear to support the supposition that the violation of any <u>specific</u> moral standards prescribed by public morality may <u>threaten</u> the life of a social order."   After all, it wasn't so <u>very</u> long ago in American history, for example, that it was <u>immoral</u> and a violation of the law to help a runaway slave to escape and become a free man.   It took a civil war to change the laws--but the society became stronger, not weaker; it did <u>not</u> collapse, as a result.   Nagel says that "human societies <u>do</u> not appear to be such fragile systems that they cannot survive a successful challenge to some established norm of conduct, nor are they such rigid structures that they are unable to accommodate their institutions to deviations from customary patterns of behavior and approved moral standards."29

        Nagel questions Devlin's faith in the jury system as an ideal mirror and arbiter of community conventions.   He points out that the law is not simply a reflection, a mirror;

it is also a prism, "...frequently an agency for modifying
accepted moral standards." Perhaps the Volstead Act--the
Prohibition Amendment of 1919-1933--is the best example of
such an attempt to change rather deeply entrenched habits by
legal fiat. It didn't work, but certainly it was legal. And
Nagel sees little justification for concluding, as Devlin does,
that "the unanimous judgment of a dozen individuals drawn at
random to serve in a jury is representative of the moral
standards (for what may be to them an unfamiliar type of
conduct) that are entertained throughout the society."[30]

What Nagel concludes is that "there is no general answer to the question whether certain categories of actions
should be legally controlled and whether certain standards of
conduct should be legally enforced."[31] He agrees with Judge
Learned Hand's view on this, that it is a question of relative
values, of group-interest conflicts--and so the kind of gen-
eralizations on morality which become crystallized and en-
capsulated in a hard and fast law are not helpful.

All law, it is almost a truism to say, is the codify-
ing of generally accepted societal opinion. When law ceases
to reflect that opinion, it is either not enforced by the judicial and prison system (witness capital punishment in the
U. S. during the last decade) or it is not enforced by the police (witness a great deal of juvenile delinquency); or it is
finally voided, as with the infamous Prohibition Amendment.
Laws on censorship have been described as being, generally
speaking, "an arbitrary menace to moral reform, sex education, creative writing, and scholarship...." Further, they
are described as "a ready weapon to the hand of authoritari-
ans and obscurantists" and as offering "a constant temptation
to abuse by ignorant puritans."[32]

Among the most radical of current thinkers on this
topic are the Drs. Kronhausen (of Sweden, and now America), who say, "Social institutions and the law tend to lag behind the rapid change in sexual mores in the community."[33]
Or, to put it another way, the laws on obscenity and pornography will continue on after they are no longer being generally obeyed or enforced. This may not sound like a radical
statement, but any intimation that obscenity laws were not
handed down on stone tablets from the hand of God Himself
seems practically sacrilegious to a great many people.

The rationale behind the Kronhausens' unwillingness to
accept laws against obscenity as being necessary at all is

that they feel that "if any part of the human body is indecent, lewd, or obscene, then the whole body is obscene. If the human body is obscene, then life is obscene and the whole creation in a sorry mess."[34] And writing, as well as pictures, dealing with the natural functions of the human body, they feel, should not be barred by law either.

On the relationship between law and morals Dr. Herbert L. Packer, a Stanford law professor, has presented the view that "immorality clearly should not be viewed as a sufficient or even a principal reason for proscribing conduct as criminal." As he puts it, "Our moral universe is polycentric. The state ... should not seek to impose a spurious unity upon it."[35]

If the USA were a theocracy, rather than an officially secular society, the enforcement of morals would certainly be necessarily a central aim of our system of law and justice. But the USA in the twentieth century is neither Geneva, Switzerland in the sixteenth century, nor Florence, Italy in the fifteenth; it is a free, democratic republic, with no state religion, and with church and state separated by a specific Constitutional limitation.

The relationship between law and morals is quite generally accepted. Morals are primary, basic to society, and laws are--or should be--based on the moral code. This sounds very simple; but just exactly what is the moral code? The early Christian code, as expressed in Jesus' statements? Or as revised by St. Paul? Or as including the Old Testament's codifications of morals? Or, indeed, an atheistic or agnostic or Eastern religion's moral code? Who decides?

It has been said that "the function of law in the modern state is to so order human relationships that friction will be minimized." Surely laws dealing with censorship, perhaps more than any other laws, seem to maximize friction. As Huntington Cairns, the writer of the above-quoted statement, has said, in referring to sex laws in general, "By basing its concepts upon principles entirely unrelated to experience and social facts the law has festered almost as much misery and disorder as it has alleviated."[36]

How did this almost classic demonstration of how not to regulate morals come about? Cairn says that "the attitude of the law today toward sexual morality is an attitude derived in the main from the conception and practices of the

ecclesiastical courts. "[37]   And these, of course, go back to
the pronunciamentos of St. Paul, St. Augustine, Luther, and
Calvin--all pretty much in agreement that fundamentally sex
is an evil.

But as another Cairns and his colleagues assert, in
one of the most widely cited discussions on this topic,
"Whatever the view of earlier times, our government today
is not--cannot be--concerned simply with enforcing widely
held religious precepts which inveigh against portrayal or
contemplation in communication of sex stimuli on the ground
that, purely as an intellectual abstraction, such stimuli are
evil. " Indeed, they stress, "the consequences of obscenity
exposure must entail something more than mere elicitation
of a thought which one is not supposed to think. "[38]

If the function of the law is really "to so order human relationships that friction will be minimized, " then why
the continued and long-lasting insistence that the law be used
as an instrument to preserve chastity and monogamy?   Geoffrey May, British social historian, asks why, since "the difficulties of legal control are so great and the failures so
obvious, ... should the law have sought to maintain the doctrine of chastity?" He, and many others, have wondered
why simple fornication should be outlawed, when it is by
definition a voluntary action which does not in any legal sense
injure the two individuals involved and which, if performed
in normal privacy, could not possibly affect any third person
directly and which certainly, even if it results in a child,
cannot affect the health of the child.   May's hypothesis is
that, even "though no individual may suffer by voluntary non-
marital sex expression, society conceives itself to be suffer-
ing. "[39]

And how exactly does society suffer?   May's rather
curious conclusion, not based on any demographic evidence,
is that societal approval--open or tacit--of fornication would
lead to a smaller population, since, he claims that fornica-
tors bear less children and that those they do have "are less
likely to survive in infancy. "[40]   Forty years after May, in
times when leading sociologists and other scientists cry out
against the population explosion, one might, of course, use
the May argument as a strong case for more fornication!

But May's opinion is certainly both dated and almost
sui generis.   An already cited modern critic and authority
on the appropriate place and responsibility of the law

vis-à-vis sexually-oriented reading, Norman St. John-Stevas, summarizes the proper role of the law as being an arbiter to decide "the value that society derives from freedom of discussion in the sexual sphere together with the value to society of the particular book in question ... weighed against the benefit of protection from a harmful effect on sex conduct which may reasonably be expected to result from reading [such] a book. " He admits that "expert evidence" would have to be admitted to help judges and/or juries in making such difficult decisions. [41]

A brief review of the historical background behind the general Anglo-American laws intended to prohibit or limit human sexual conduct may put all this into focus.   The first recorded English law on sexual conduct was Anglo-Saxon law, and Anglo-Saxon law was, to a great extent, ecclesiastical law.   It was founded on the statement by Pope Gregory, in 600 A. D. , enunciating the doctrine that "while carnal relations might be tolerated for the purpose of procreation-- and that only by way of divine indulgence--when pleasure, not procreation, bears rule in this matter, husbands and wives have cause to lament their embraces. " Pope Gregory felt that to think of sex was "the guilt act of a depraved will. Not enjoyed combination, but the pleasure of it, was sin. "[42]

The laws which the Catholic Church in England enforced, called the Church Penitentials, compiled between 690 and 963 A. D. , were quite rigid.   According to Geoffrey May, these rules put more emphasis on matters relating to sex, "both in quantity of regulation and in minuteness of detail, than has, probably, any other general code of conduct. "   Indeed, "the Penitentials of Theodore, Bede, and Egbert, in so far as they concern sex, are unpublishable in English. "[43]

These rules were certainly far-reaching.   They declared that sex, as such, was unclean.   Naturally, and logically, then, everything in any way related to sex--thought, representation, or action--was also not clean.   The penitential rules carried stiff penalties.   Penance (defined as "an outward expression of contrition" and "an external manifestation of repentance"[44]) was not simply a matter of saying a few prayers.   The penalty for simple fornication, for example, was an enforced diet of bread and water for a year. This penance was subject to increase "according to the frequency of the act and disposition of the parties. "   Even attempts to fornicate--not to rape, but in cases where both parties were clearly willing!--were punished under the

Penitentials.   And any monk who fornicated with a nun received punishment equal to that allotted for murder, including enforced abstention from meat, "perpetual lamentation,"
and a day-in, day-out diet of bread and water--for no less
than ten years!

What is important to point out here is that these
church rules, dating back to before the end of the first mil-
lenium after Christ, still affect our civil laws today.   For
"using any vulgar, profane, or indecent language within the
presence or hearing of women or children," a bill in the
1971 Utah Legislature prescribed a $500 maximum fine or
six months in jail, or both. [45] So even talk involving sex--
"indecent" language--is still unclean, more than a thousand
years after the Penitentials!

In Anglo-Saxon times, there were many church-im-
posed restrictions[46] relating even to normal, married sexual
intercourse.   For a full day after performing the sexual act,
individuals were barred from entering a church.   Immediately after marriage, man and wife were not permitted to go to
church for a month, and then had to live on bread and water,
as a penance, for forty more days.   To be "reconciled with
the Church," the couple had to bring an offering.

On all days or periods with some sacred significance,
the Anglo-Saxons were told to be continent, or else suffer
punishment.   Communion was denied if man and wife had
copulated within three days.   For the first three days after
getting married, Anglo-Saxons could not have sexual connection.   Performing the sexual act on a Sunday was punishable
by a week of penance.   At this time Wednesdays and Fridays
were required fast-days, and also times of required sexual
abstinence.   May says that "most arduous ... were the two
annual forty-day feasts, preceding Easter and ... Christmas."
Not only was there punishment prescribed on earth for violating these rules, but there was considered to be a special
section of Hell, "consisting of a lake of mingled lead, pitch,
and resin ...," for the punishment of those married people
who had had intercourse at the forbidden times.

More significant for the background of modern censorship feeling than even these phenomena was the punishment
allotted for even thinking about sex.   The Penitentials ordered a 40-day fast on bread and water for any laymen
"whose thoughts dwelt on fornication...." Theodore, one of
the authors of this rule, said that "the atonement for the

thought was to be as severe as the atonement for the act;
the more excessive the thought, the more severe the penance. "[47]

On one particular sexual matter, auto-eroticism, the
Penitentials were so excessive that English law shows no effect or echo. "Self-abuse" by laymen was the topic of no
less than 25 paragraphs in the Penitentials, more space by
far than was devoted to any other sexual "offense." The
usual penance prescribed was 40 days of bread and water
fasting. One might leap to the conclusion that rarely indeed
would anyone in Anglo-Saxon times admit to his priest that
he had masturbated. May says that although "Christian theology condemned all forms of sex expression, ... it was
auto-eroticism that was the weakest point of resistance.... "
He points out that later Catholic religious leaders, including
even St. Thomas Aquinas, criticized masturbation as even
worse than fornication. But "English law has never since
the Penitentials attempted to regulate the private sexual expression of a solitary individual. "[48]

The importance of the Penitentials was that before the
Norman Conquest the church courts were really authorities
on all crimes, both secular and ecclesiastical, and during
the Norman period of ascendancy, sex offenders, whether
churchmen or laymen, were liable only to Church control on
matters affecting morals--and most punishable actions seemed
to be of this type. The tradition of the law on sex as being
influenced, if only subconsciously, by ultra-conservative religious beliefs still remains in both English and American law
and practice.

It should not be thought that strong ecclesiastical
pressure kept the people of England from actually violating
the rules on sexual conduct. Incontinence, for example, was
so common that the terminology in church courts for punishment of this act was "the usual penance." May describes
the "usual penance" as follows: "the penitent would appear
barelegged and bareheaded in the cathedral, parish church,
or market-place, clad in a white sheet, and would make con-
fession of his or her crime in a prescribed form of words....
The usual procedure was for the penitent to precede the procession down the church aisle on three or four Sundays, ...
carrying a candle of some two pounds weight and of a desig-
nated price, which he would place before the principal ikon.
The penitent would then confess his sin before the assembled
congregation in words prescribed either by the vicar or

directly by the court before which he had been convicted.
He would declare his crime, ask forgiveness of God and his
neighbors, and might lead the congregation in a prayer for
his soul.   He would then receive a certificate that he had
duly performed his alloted penance. "[49]

The Church was too practical to overlook the possibility of profit in these matters, and sometimes a payment of
money was added to or substituted for the "usual penance. "
As any reader of Chaucer knows, pilgrimages were sometimes required as penance for unchastity.   The most frequent alternative prescribed by the courts in those days for
the "usual penance" was to require the guilty--if neither one
was of the church's hierarchy--to marry.

Even more significant than the manner and frequency
of this type of occurrence is the fact that until as recently
as 1813 Englishmen had to obey what church courts ordained
or suffer both the loss of all civil rights and imprisonment.
The imprisonment lasted until the culprit did what the
church courts had told him to do. [50]

But church jurisdiction was limited in 1558 by the establishment of a Court of High Commission by Queen Elizabeth.   In 1583 it was finally left to civil courts to hold trials
on "all Incests, Fornications, Outrages, Misbehaviors, and
Disorders in Marriage.... "[51]

The story of the Puritan and his effect on sex customs and laws in both England and America, although chron-
ologically appropriate here, has already been told herein,
as have the basic historical facts concerning the relationship
of law and censorship, so they will not be repeated.   But it
still remains to assess the significance of the facts cited
above.   It is certainly true that there is no such thing as a
single law or even recognizably similar laws in force today
in England or America to control sexual conduct and expression.   But it seems quite evident that, no matter how different the laws on this matter are or have been, their basis--
the general feelings of political, ecclesiastical, and social
leaders--has not changed.

In the United States it has been pretty well accepted
in recent years that there are different levels of legal responsibility as regards obscenity and pornography.   In 1969
the U. S. Supreme Court, in the case of Stanley v. Georgia,
held that "whatever may be the justifications for other

statutes regulating obscenity, we do not think they reach into
the privacy of one's own home. If the First Amendment
means anything, it means that a State has no business telling
a man, sitting alone in his house, what books he may read
or what films he may watch. "52   Obviously, judging from the
language used in the Court's decision, if the man is not
alone, then it might be the State's business to regulate what
the two or more people involved read or watch!

Yale Law Professor Alexander Bickel feels that "total
permissiveness about obscenity ... is not the sole option left
to us. " He stresses that laws to regulate obscenity will never achieve their ends "always or precisely. " He feels that
such laws ought to exist only in "aggravated cases, " and
sees such laws as "supportive, tentative, even provisional. "
Indeed, he feels that the Supreme Court "should stay out of
the business of censorship altogether ... " and limit itself to
"exercising procedural oversight.... "53

Dr. Herbert L. Packer, writing in another context,
agreed with Bickel to a great extent. He, too, emphasized
that the Supreme Court "must either function as a Supreme
Board of Censors and read every allegedly dirty book ...
that is attacked before it or give up the unequal struggle. "
Writing in 1968, he predicted that the Supreme Court, under
the stress of dealing with other, more important issues, will
be forced to stop acting as such a "Supreme Board of Censors" and leave this kind of issue to local censorship
boards. 54   The June 21, 1973 majority decisions (detailed in
Chapter 15) verified his prediction.

Such a blank check for the local censor, in the light
of the way laws demonstrably lag behind conduct, would
probably lead to a new wave of undemocratic repression.
Packer's solution for this dilemma was to suggest the use of
a legal doctrine which, he said, "has been in bad odor for
at least 35 years"--the doctrine of "substantive due process.... " Packer explained this as meaning that laws which
are irrational are, ipso facto, unconstitutional. If the Supreme Court were to apply this doctrine, he felt, it would be
almost self-evident that it is irrational to enforce morals
legislation "that attempts to suppress consensual transactions, like the sale of pornography. " In less legal and academic language, this could be stated: let the buyer beware!
Certainly no one is forcing him to buy or read the erotic
work concerned. Just possibly, this might work. There is
little question that the present tangled web of Supreme Court

decisions and local or state interpretations of them cannot
bring rational legal analysis. Packer feels that it is to
courts rather than to legislation that the public must look
for a beginning of reformation of criminal law "to bring our
commitments into balance with our capacities."[55]

Writing in still a different context, Packer had earlier offered a constructive discussion of just how far legal,
rather than social, sanctions should go. He suggested that
"the only valid purpose of obscenity law is to prevent public
nuisance."[56] Since, clearly, no one is under any real compulsion to read a particular book or magazine, to watch a
particular film, or to attend a specific theatrical performance, such a law, he says, should only be to help those
persons who wish to avoid having such items "thrust" upon
them. A large "drive-in" movie-screen, showing "X" movies in clear view of individuals who are intolerant of such,
might be a fair example of this.

If such were to become the operative rule for justice,
then the censor would not have any work to do; as Packer
phrases it, "showing that a particular person or persons had
been subjected to psychic assault" would be what the law
would have to determine, rather than judging "obscenity."
Unfortunately, Packer also suggests that items likely to cause
such "psychic assaults" be marked "like the skull and cross-
bones used on poison."[57] And labeling is clearly a violation
of intellectual freedom. Besides which, isn't it likely that
self-appointed individual censors might claim to be outraged
simply to get rid of something which only the "unco guid"
would find offensive?

In the long run, perhaps Professor Packer's chief
contribution to consideration of the vexing problem of censorship versus freedom is his Groucho Marx-like comment,
"anybody who is sure he knows what obscenity is poses a
threat to freedom of community thought and expression."[58]
This is at least in the same general category as Groucho's
well-known remark that he wouldn't join any club whose
standards were so low that they would let him in!

Now, if it is such a moot, highly debatable and almost
insoluble problem to justify the legal control of private morality, what is left for the law to do in regards to such matters as the writing and distribution of supposedly obscene
and pornographic matter? Norman St. John-Stevas has stated
that "the law makes itself ridiculous by endorsing with legal

sanctions opinions which are essentially contemporary and
ephemeral. "[59] He reminds us that since a clash of opposing rights is involved, about all that can be expected is a
compromise between the two views, which will probably
satisfy no one completely.   But he still feels it is possible
to work out a law concerning obscene publications which will
at least be administratively workable--as most thus far have
not been.

     There will be laws of some sort, some degree of re-
straint on writer and publisher and distributor and librarian,
in most Western societies, for some time to come.   The
most crucial question is whether they will be understandable,
reasonable, enforceable.   If there must be laws (on obscenity), at least they should be neither so vague nor so artificially precise that in the long run they are self-defeating.

     The censor likes to have the law back of him.   If the
law today is not even precisely clear or intelligible to the
top legal authorities on the U. S. Supreme Court, how can
local police and courts be expected to try to enforce it?
How can community or nationwide pressure groups intimidate
the local supermarkets or libraries?   How, indeed, can censorship continue?

     One of the most hopeful signs for those opposing cen-
sorship as a problem which is more deleterious to society
than the presumed evils it purports to prevent or punish may
be that the U. S. Congress has now begun to spin its wheels
toward "simplifying" the confusing series of U. S. Supreme
Court decisions on the subject.   In May, 1971, a House sub-
committee approved the very first Congressional definition of
obscenity, specifying that anything obscene under its standards would automatically be considered to have no redeeming
social importance.   This would apply to anything that "has
its predominant appeal to the prurient interests when considered as a whole by contemporary community standards. "[60]
Predominant?   Prurient?   Contemporary community standards?   All this is presumed by the Congressmen not to be
confusing.   If and when such a law is approved, it remains
to be seen what, if any, difference the Congressional "clarification" will make.

     Even if the censor is backed by the law, it is impor-
tant to remember that the law is neither a seamless web nor,
as Oxford University Law Professor Ronald Dworkin once described it, "a brooding omnipresence in the sky. "[61]   The

law is created by men and is amenable to human change, whether by judicial, legislative, or administrative action or lack of action.

If justice, in the common personification, is a blind goddess, then the censor may well be blind and deaf to the realities of life.   The laws on censorship have been modified throughout history, and will certainly continue to be so.

Unthinking acceptance of any law is bad citizenship. The censor feeds on unthinking acquiescence.   Like another Antaeus, he gains strength each time he finds another piece of familiar argumentative ground on which to fall back.   The censor's tired old argument goes something like this:

> You are doing something.   What you are doing is not good for you and/or society.   I, the Censor, know better than you what is good or bad for you and/or society.   If you persist in reading or selling or offering to be read what is bad for you or for the least intellectually or emotionally qualified member of society, then I must protect you or that individual by limiting, as much as possible, the opportunity of reading what is socially reprehensible or individually morally undermining.

Of all laws, those linked to morality are most modifiable and probably should be thought about the most.   Those who oppose censorship and who understand the motives (conscious and unconscious, apparent and subtle, historical and current) of the censor are in a better position to carry on their opposition than those who base their opposition on emotion.   Censorship laws, in particular, are as likely to be changed (if not more so) as any morality-linked laws, if those who desire and work for the change do so rationally.

Dworkin claims that those who disobey laws which are "uncertain" (and a great many laws fall into this classification) are not in the same class as common criminals.   After all, lawyers (presumably upright, law-abiding citizens!) do disagree; judges, and sometimes even identical courts, modify, even reverse former decisions.   Nothing in the law is so sacrosanct that the idea of taking steps to change it is evil.

The books and magazines and "newspapers" which contain reading material on sex which is offensive to some of

the American people must contain something of which a great
many others do approve. Why, otherwise, are they being
purchased? The censor says, "Anyone who reads such stuff
is evil and is likely to do worse things than reading. " No
generally acceptable reasons, no produceable proof exists of
this obiter dictum; it is no more than a statement.

British journalist Alec Craig has suggested a number
of constructive propositions as "safeguards ... to provide
the minimum protection for serious literature in any future
where the principles of freedom are recognized":

1. The idea that a book can be obscene in esse is
wrong. It is the circumstances of publication that
create the evil, if any. Consequently, statutes like
the Obscene Publications Act of 1959, that provide
for the destruction of books, are bad. The law
should confine itself to punishing irresponsible and
anti-social publications, and any destruction allowed
should be incidental. Any matter should be offered
to the learned libraries before destruction.

2. The law should be restricted to publications of
a public nature; private communications and private
possessions should be outside its scope.

3. The condemnation of a book of scientific, artistic, or educational interest as obscene is not a
matter that concerns only the authorities and the
defendants. Not only should the author or any other interested person be heard, but the Court (as in
divorce cases) should be bound to consider all
questions of public policy involved and to obtain expert evidence on the literary, scientific, and sociological issues involved. Trial of such cases
should always be by jury.

4. Special protection should be afforded to bona
fide books of sex instruction (including those of a
popular character) by responsible authors, books
that have been openly published for a number of
years, classics, works of historical interest, and
books treated as serious in the country of their
origin. Integral pictures of the nude human body
should not be held to be obscene per se.

5. Learned libraries, universities, and other

public bodies should be immune from prosecution
so long as they confine themselves to their recognized functions; and printers should not be penalized in respect of work done for reputable customers in the ordinary way of trade.

6.   Any powers given to the customs, post office,
or other administrative bodies should always be
exercised in pursuance of a court order.

7.   Machinery should be set up to secure uniformity in the administration of the law; and the re-
habilitation of condemned books should be provided
for.

Craig concludes his statement by saying that "Finally,
we must remember that the motivation of sex censorship
goes very deeply into human psychology, having its roots in
man's ambivalent attitude to sex.   Biologically, eroticism is
a passing phenomenon; what loves us today repels us tomorrow.   Consequently we are all tempted to be both readers of
erotic books and censors of literature.   Moral integrity and
clear thinking should enable modern communities to resolve
the tensions between these two sides of human nature without
hurt to the spread of truth, the increase of beauty, and the
furtherance of the good life. "[62]

The millions of American citizens who violated an
amendment to the U. S. Constitution between 1919 and 1933
were sometimes referred to as "scoff-laws. "   It is apparent
that there are some laws--such as the Federal one on prohibition of the sale of spirituous liquor--which get changed,
eventually, by the very weight and number of those who ignore their existence.   Our laws--federal, state, and local--
against obscenity and pornography are thus by no means immune from eventual drastic change, if not complete disappearance.

INTERLUDE

PORTRAIT OF A CENSOR:

4.   CHARLES H. KEATING, JR.

"He's out for this group [Citizens for Decent Litera-
ture].   He wants to remove everything that doesn't meet with
his particular approval.   He's a crusader along this particular line. "

--Judge Meredith Wingrove, Library Journal, 1964.

"...the state cannot legislate virtue, cannot make
moral judgments by merely enacting law; but the state can
and does legislate against vices which publicly jeopardize the
virtue of people who might prefer to remain virtuous.   If it
is not the proper function of law to offer citizens such protection, then what is it?"

"...if the majority of the Commission on Obscenity
and Pornography has its way and the laws against the pornographers are repealed, we will witness complete moral
anarchy in this country that will soon spread to the entire
free world. "

"One can consult all the experts he chooses, can
write reports, make studies, etc., but the fact that obscenity corrupts lies within the common sense, the reason, and
the logic of every man. "

"At a time when the spread of pornography has reached
epidemic proportions in our country and when the moral fiber
of our nation seems to be rapidly unraveling, the desperate
need is for enlightened and intelligent control of the poisons
which threaten us--not the declaration of moral bankruptcy

inherent in the repeal of the laws which have been the defense of decent people against the pornographic for profit. "

"The law is capable of coping with the problem of pornography and obscenity, but it must be law, coupled with the logic that an American is innately capable of determining for himself his standards of public decency and, beyond that, he has a right to make that determination. "

--Charles H. Keating, Jr., "Report of Commissioner Charles H. Keating, Jr.," in: The Report of the Commission on Obscenity and Pornography, 1970.

12. THE NEW MORALITY AND THE OLD LIBRARIAN

"The sex continuum, ranging from 'it's bad and sinful' to 'it's as easy as talking,' is somewhere in the middle range today ... it seems doubtful that motion along the continuum of sexual activity will recede; it is more likely to move forward, unhampered by the Protestant ethic of immorality or by pseudo-realistic doctrines of concerted amorality, both of which can easily detach meaning from all sex."

--J. L. Simmons and Barry Winograd, It's Happening: a Portrait of the Youth Scene Today, 1966.

Chapter 12

THE NEW MORALITY
AND THE OLD LIBRARIAN

What are, or should be, the parameters, the limiting factors in choosing reading materials for the modern American public library? Is it sufficient to post a copy of the Library Bill of Rights somewhere near the circulation desk, have a fine-sounding book selection policy approved by the library board, and then make sure that every book or new periodical subscription added is judged as acceptable in some "approved" list? Just what does, or should, determine whether the public library of X-town (population not quite 50,000; cultural milieu, mostly rural-conservative) circulates My Secret Life or Updike's Couples or Slavitt's The Exhibitionist, or even Catcher in the Rye, Lady Chatterley's Lover, and Tropic of Cancer?

Vague and generalized criteria for book selection are surely not the answer. Appeals to the authority of Library Journal or Saturday Review or the New York Times reviews hardly ever result in broad acceptance. The censor and the prude want a book out of the library if it uses four-letter words or exhibits the nudity available in books and magazines sold in every drug store and supermarket. The "liberal" wants every book considered on its literary and social significance. So, it would seem, does the U.S. Supreme Court.

One possibly helpful viewpoint in this dilemma of the librarian is to consider the so-called "New Morality." Even though its newness is as questionable as its right to be called "morality," in the generally accepted sense, since this term is often applied to it, it is useful as a frame of reference.

The New Morality--renamed "situation ethics" by one of its most popular propagandizers, Dr. Joseph Fletcher-- attempts to resolve moral dilemmas in a realistic, pragmatic

169

way. It does not quite say that "whatever is, is right," but
it does say that it is not sufficient to face "decision-making
situations" (such as whether to buy erotic literature for a
small-town public library) on the basis of the ethical guidelines generally accepted by the community. For Fletcher
and the "new moralists" generally, the criterion for action
is no longer what is good, but what permits love.

Love, in their sense, harks back to the Christian
idea of agape, to Martin Luther's dictum that "therefore,
when the law impels one against love, it ceases and should
no longer be a law; but where no obstacle is in the way, the
keeping of the law is a proof of love, which lies hidden in
the heart. Therefore you have need of the law, that love
may be manifested; but if it cannot be kept without injury to
the neighbor, God wants us to suspend and ignore the law."1

If, says Fletcher, "only love is intrinsically good,
then, of course ... only malice is intrinsically evil. If
good will is the only thing we are always obliged to do, then
ill-will is the only thing we are always forbidden to do."
For Fletcher, censorship would be very difficult to approve.
He says that "situation ethics always suspects prescriptive
law of falsifying life and dwarfing moral stature." (The
Fletcherian view of the primacy of life and morals over the
dead hand of the law, incidentally, is in marked contrast
with the opinions of some of the legal thinkers referred to
in the preceding chapter.)

Fletcher, of course, did not come from a vacuum.
He is not only basing his ideas on what he sees around him
in the world today but on some pretty good authorities on
the subject of ethics. For example, John Dewey and James
Tufts, some sixty years ago, said, "Of one thing we may
be sure. If inquiries are to have any substantial basis, if
they are not wholly up in the air, the theorist must take
his departure from the problems which men actually meet in
their own conduct. He may define and refine these; he may
divide and systematize; he may abstract the problems from
their concrete contexts in individual lives; he may classify
them when he has detached them; but if he gets away from
them he is talking about something which his own brain has
invented, not about moral realities."2

When Fletcher was called upon to give some concrete
examples to counter the argument that he was speaking in
airy abstractions, he proceeded to present more than

sufficient practical examples.   In the preface to his second
book, [3] he said, "Most people think of responsibility ... as
a matter of conforming to established practice and conventional morality, out of respect for or fear of familiar sanctions and reinforcements.   What is smugly assumed in the
establishmentarian's soul is that moral rules and reward-
punishments are all set, and that people should come to heel
and play the game that way. "   But, says Fletcher, "Not so.
Responsibility means a free and critical 'conformity' to the
facts first of all--the shifting patterns of situations--and
then to the unchanging single norm or boss principle of loving concern for persons and the social balance. "

This "loving concern for persons and the social balance" is something to which librarians and library trustees
rarely seem to pay much heed.   Our tendency to put things
down in terms of rigid rules and specifications is probably
the single leading reason why librarians may be the greatest
censors of all.   Certainly, the Fiske study some years ago
offered documentation for this charge.

Fletcher begins his second volume with six propositions which he proclaims as "the fundamentals of Christian
conscience. "   The propositions are as follows:

1.   Only one thing is intrinsically good, namely
love: nothing else.

2.   The ultimate norm of Christian decisions is
love: nothing else.

3.   Love and justice are the same, for justice is
love distributed.

4.   Love wills the neighbor's good whether we like
him or not.

5.   Only the end justifies the means: nothing else.

6.   Decisions ought to be made situationally, not
prescriptively.

These will probably seem shocking, if not in individual parts, then certainly in toto, to the average follower of the
Judeo-Christian ethic.   But Fletcher is not concerned with
whether he is shocking us or not; his concern is to present
the new morality as he sees it.   He says, "Gone is the

former sense of guilt and cheated ideals when we tailor our
ethical cloth to fit the back of each occasion. We are, for
this reason, closing the gap between our overt and covert
cultures. " Surely, he is referring here to the America
which wants sex in every conceivable fashion and then, in
most states, proscribes even the display of the naked human
body in photographic or representational form. The re-
searches of Dr. Albert Ellis and Dr. Kinsey have definitely
shown the wide gap between our laws and our actions, and
libraries somehow have to fit in between.

Fletcher's point of view is expressed in another way
in one section, "The new morality is a form of ethical relativism. " Ethical relativism is not exactly what is understood by the Puritan ethic or even by the ethics of book selection by librarians. The conflict is there and needs to be
resolved somehow. As Fletcher says, 'It is this relativism
which is our era's birthmark. "[4]

This "New Morality, " says Fletcher, "... simply re-
fuses to accept any principle, other than neighbor concern,
as always binding. " He stresses that "it is, therefore, an
ethic of tremendous personal responsibility and initiative--
and an ethic for a social policy which is nondoctrinaire and
elastic. " He says that "people commonly have been inclined
to make sex evil number one, ignoring or minimizing equally
or even more important ethical issues. Since they have
identified ... morality with sex questions and virtue with
obedience to the sexual taboos, " the more basic spiritual
quandaries of our age have been nearly ignored, he feels.
"Such evils as lack of love, ego aggrandizement, emotional
isolation, envy, lust for power--these were treated as less
important than failing to respect the sexual conventions. "

I have a feeling that the superintendents and school
trustees, in Idaho and elsewhere, who refused to permit their
high school students to view the back portion of the body of
a female movie star as pictured on the cover of an issue of
Newsweek not long ago might well be appropriate targets for
this particular criticism.

Fletcher says, "The ethical 'Pharisees' (of whom
there are too many) fail to see that the most evil and destructive traits are not those of the sexual appetite, which
is biologically given and morally neutral in itself, but the
irrational emotional passions, such as hate, fear, greed,
ulcerous struggles for discrete status--all of our self-regard-

ing--and antisocial impulses. " And none of this, he says,
"actually introduced interest in sex; it activated it at a sly
and prurient level of secrecy, behind-the-scenes humor and
debate, and such 'mental maneuvers' as erotic advertising. "
The result, he says, "was that more time and attention were
given to 'ignoring' sex than to anything else! "

   Fletcher does not say that there is no way of regulating the morals of sex.   He calls it "an absurd subversive
idea" ... "that sexual behavior lies outside any kind of ethical code or philosophical meaning whatsoever. "[5] He documents his charge that we are pharisaical by saying, "we
walk in the paths of virtue because there is an expectation
of rewards and punishment in the background; this is true of
some people all of the time, of all people some of the time. "
He stresses that "our ideals of love and sexual expression
are as high as ever but the sanctions behind our loyalty to
the ideals have changed. " He gives as an example of the
old morality the following limerick:[6]

> There was a young lady named Wilde
> Who kept herself quite undefiled
>   By thinking of Jesus
>   And social diseases
> And the fear of having a child.

   He says, "the technology of sex, prophylaxis, and
contraception have removed the triple terrors of conception,
infection, and detection. "[7] So, with sex becoming safe,
"our sex standards in an area of medical technology and urban anonymity depend for their sanction upon devotion rather
than dread. " This makes it most difficult to deal with new
situations with the old ethics.

   In referring to sex offenses, he says that "there is
some evidence, based on one serious, although debatable,
attempt at research into sexual behavior, that if existing
laws were actually enforced, about 95 per cent of the male
population in America would go to jail. " It is much easier,
obviously, to keep unenforced laws on the statute books and
proclaim a morality which does not exist, than to try to
conform to the actual facts of life in 1968.   Fletcher points
out that the main reasons for continued lip service to unenforced sex laws are "fear of appearing indifferent to morality" and "the plain fact that most sexual activities are clandestine, and, therefore, not easily subjected to control by
public policy and judiciary. " About the only obvious sexual

activity is what moralists have until now believed to be evident in the reading of so-called pornographic and obscene literature. Whether it makes sense to punish the overt and not the covert is certainly a debatable question.

Finally, looking at the relation of ethics to law, in general, Fletcher says that he feels that there are four propositions which at least may be asserted if not validated:

> 1. Value (i. e. , moral) considerations enter into lawmaking.
>
> 2. Law should be the means of making social morality effective.
>
> 3. The prelegal, value-finding process lies in the consensus of the community as to the common welfare.
>
> 4. What is held to be private, in the consensus, is not the law's business.

So, he thinks that "as to sex laws in particular, offenses should be restricted to 1) acts with persons under the legal age of consent; 2) acts in situations judged to be a public nuisance or infringement of public decency; and 3) acts involving assault, violence, duress, or fraud. "

Fletcher is well aware of the iconoclastic implications of his writings and thinking. He says, "The 'sexplosion' of the modern era is forcing us to do some thinking about the 'unthinkable' sex epics. If we had to check off a point in modern times when the sex revolution started, first in practice but only slowly and reluctantly in thought, I would set it at the First World War. Since then there has been a phenomenal increase of aphrodisiac literature, visual and verbal, as well as more informational materials. We have seen an unprecedented freedom of expression orally as well as in print, both in ordinary conversation and in the mass media which glamorize sex--the movies, TV, radio, slickpaper magazines. "

Granted this is so, is situation ethics the answer? Should the librarian and library board of trustees do their book selection on the basis of individuals and individual situations? Or is there still some validity to the accepted and conventional ethics?

A very highly respected and conservative Orthodox Rabbi, Abraham Joshua Heschel, has recently stated that "it is our sacred duty to safeguard all those political, social, and intellectual conditions, which enable every man to bring about the concrete actualization of freedom which is the essential prerequisite of creative achievement. " Rabbi Heschel goes on to say that "we have denied our young people the knowledge of the dark side of life. They see a picture of ease, play, and fun. That life includes hardships, illness, grief, even agony; that many hearts are sick with bitterness, resentfulness, envy--are facts of which young people have hardly an awareness. They do not feel morally challenged, they do not feel called upon. " Surely this is a form of documentation of what Dr. Fletcher had to say, from a rather different point of view. Finally, says Heschel, "together with adjustment to society we must cultivate a sense for injustice, impatience with vulgarity, a capacity for moral indignation, a will to readjust society itself when it becomes complacent and corrupt. "8

Rabbi Heschel is certainly not repudiating the Talmud. He is, like Fletcher and others, redefining what is true obscenity. This is nothing new. Aristotle, thousands of years ago, said, "The older dramatists found their fun in obscenities; the moderns in plain innuendo, which makes a great advance in decorum. " To suit modern circumstances, about the only thing that needs to be done is to switch the words "older" and "moderates. " We are long past innuendo and into deliberate obscenity, but whether this is a bad or a good thing is certainly up for grabs.

It is not only the theologians who are attempting to cause us to at least rearrange our prejudices. Literary critic William Phillips, discoursing on "Writing About Sex, " says that "When the Berkeley students shouted dirty words from a public platform, they confirmed the proprieties against which they were protesting. If speech were completely free, no words would bring a blush to a young person's cheek or raise the eyebrows of an older one. As with the language, so with the contents of books. Descriptions of sexual intimacy, if we get used to reading them, ought to provoke no special titillation. We should be able to take them or leave them, depending on whether they carry honest conviction. When everything has been said, we can focus on how it is said. We may still need safeguards for the immature; but for adults so much is already permitted that not much can consistently be excluded. "9

He plumps for a change in perspective, even glories
in the new freedom of the word as an opportunity for the
greater usefulness of his own field, literary criticism.   Indeed, says Phillips, "When writers are allowed to write anything they please and publishers to put it in circulation, then
the great responsibility for discrimination rests with the
reader.   Art in itself may be neither moral nor immoral,
as Oscar Wilde insisted; but, since we are potentially both,
the courts stand ready to correct our overt immorality.
Meanwhile it remains for us to determine the uses of art.
If we abandon censorship, we depend all the more impera-
tively upon criticism.   If we agree that books are neither
dirty nor clean, we must be sure to remember that they are
bad or good and must not be distracted into ignoring that
difference. "

The literary critic is so convinced of the merits (or
powers) of literary criticism, of true discrimination between
what he calls "artistic imagination and autistic fantasy" that
he foresees that "one of the wholesome results of our hard-
won candor is that it could end by driving the pornographers
out of business. "   This conclusion seems based on somewhat
shaky premises, but it is, of course, a possibility.

Perhaps all this has been summarized best by something Henry David Thoreau wrote over a hundred years ago:
"Books, not which afford us a cowering enjoyment, but in
which each thought is of unusual daring; such as an idle man
cannot read, and a timid one would not be entertained by,
which even makes us dangerous to existing institutions--such
call I good books. "[10]   Thoreau was not being consciously a
follower of "situation ethics, " but surely his implied definition of "good" is very different from the narrow legalistic
interpretation given by the typical censor today, and close to
one which Joseph Fletcher might offer.

The old--and the new--librarian cannot afford to ignore the increasingly popular "new morality" when facing up
to one of his most basic professional responsibilities, the
selection of books.   In an epoch when the nude, or might-as-
well-be-nude, is commonplace, and sexual activities are no
longer left to the privacy of the bedroom, the novel, in language and incident, has naturally gone far beyond what had
come to be the accepted norm.   Can the 1972 librarian still
base his judgment on the 1868 views of British Chief Justice
Cockburn:[11]   "the test for obscenity is this: whether the
tendency of the matter charged as obscenity is to deprave

and corrupt those whose minds are open to such immoral influence, and into whose hands a publication of this sort may fall, " or the 1880 opinions of Anthony Comstock:[12] "This cursed business of obscene literature works beneath the surface, and like a canker worm, secretly eats out the moral life and purity of our youth, and they droop and fade before their parent's eyes. "

13. AFTER THE C.O.P. REPORT:
    HAS CENSORSHIP A FUTURE IN AMERICA?

"...the politics of the recent report of the Commission on Obscenity and Pornography are more interesting than the sex in it. For the sexual part of the majority report represents the traditional liberal attitude toward sexual freedom. But the political willingness to organize this attitude as a policy, and thereby to brave all the tumult of political storms is--right or wrong--something new and notable for our time."

> --Max Lerner, "Education is Best Solution to Smut," Salt Lake Tribune, October 17, 1970, p. 6.

Chapter 13

AFTER THE C. O. P. REPORT:
HAS CENSORSHIP A FUTURE IN AMERICA?

In 1970 the American body politic was hit in its most private parts by a presidential commission report which (with twelve of its eighteen members in agreement) recommended "the repeal of existing federal legislation which prohibits or interferes with consensual distribution of 'obscene' materials to adults...." The Commission on Obscenity and Pornography, set up by Congress in 1968, also recommended "the repeal of existing state and local legislation which may similarly prohibit the consensual sale, exhibition, or the distribution of sexual materials to adults."[1]

To say that this was a shock--to President Richard Nixon (who had appointed only one of the eighteen commission members, the rest having been selected by the Johnson Administration), to Congress generally, and to the general public--is understatement. From the days of Anthony Comstock on, for nearly a century the accepted American Way in dealing with reading about sex was to assail it, condemn it, prohibit it, jail authors and publishers and distributors of such material, and even fire librarians who showed any tendency toward approval of its purchase and distribution. Oh, yes--as the Commission report showed--it was, paradoxically, also part of the American Way to read about sex, in rather large quantities. Year after year, the best-seller lists have included such works as Valley of the Dolls, Portnoy's Complaint, and The Sensuous Woman, and conservative estimates (the Commission's) of gross sales--books, periodicals, and underground papers on the subject--came to around $100 million per year (as of 1969-70).[2]

The Commission studies showed that "approximately 85% of adult men and 70% of adult women in the United States have been exposed at some time during their lives to depiction of explicit sexual material in either visual or textual form" and that "most of this exposure has apparently been voluntary.... "[3]   Their studies further told us that between 20 and 25% of all American adult males have what they refer to as "somewhat regular experience" with explicit sexual materials. [4]

One of the most unexpected revelations coming out of the Commission's studies was its almost complete contradiction of the accepted myth that "only bad people buy pornography. "   Rather than the furtive, "dirty old man" stereotype --perpetuated even on national television's "Laugh In"--according to Commission studies, "the profile of the patron of adult bookstores ... in different parts of the United States is white, middle aged, middle class, married, male, dressed in business suit or neat casual attire, shopping alone. " Surely this is a recognizable portrait of Middle American man--even of the "silent majority" which politicos have been telling us about the past few years.   A similar study in Denmark produced quite similar results.

This really gives the censor something to worry and wonder about.   If it is the "average" man who buys sexually explicit reading, then can he (the censor) really count on the "average" man's backing in carrying on future censorship crusades?

One way to judge the possibilities for the future is to see how the government of the United States--the Congress, and the President to whom the report was made on September 30, 1970--reacted to the report.   A plethora of presidential commissions, dealing with almost every conceivable subject, have reported during our republic's history, but none, so far as can be ascertained, received quite the negative response which greeted the Report of the Commission on Obscenity and Pornography.

Shortly after the report was issued--and, as one of its few Senatorial supporters, Senator Walter Mondale of Minnesota, said, when not "one member of the Senate had read the report--issued just one week before and one thousand pages long"[5]--the U.S. Senate, in its solemn majesty, voted, 60-5, to reject the findings and recommendations of the Commission. [6]   The resolution, presented by Senator McClellan of Arkansas, was co-sponsored by 26 Democrats and 24 Republican Senators.   It was perhaps more than coincidence that the vote on the McClellan resolution, taken after practically no real consideration on the floor of the Senate and certainly in violation of its usual procedure of holding hearings, was just a couple of weeks before a national Congressional election.

Even though the report gave rather strong evidence to support one of its most important conclusions, that "a majority of American adults believe that adults should be allowed to read or see any sexual materials they wish, "[7] the Senate, in its resolution, explicitly rejected this finding. McClellan questioned the Commission-backed national survey on this matter; among other reasons, he disputed their findings on the basis that two other national surveys in 1969 (by Louis Harris and George Gallup) seemed to indicate that most Americans were for stricter laws on pornography. [8] If the good Senator had bothered to read the majority-approved report itself (instead of just the minority report, which had similar strictures on the majority report), he might have read the majority's discussion[9] of this significant point, which answers this objection in detail.

It is stated therein that "opinion researchers have become increasingly sensitive to the difficulty of probing beyond 'social rhetoric' in attitude surveys. "[10]   They point out that in giving answers to "questions about morality, especially in the realm of sex, " there is a strong tendency "to elicit stereotyped responses. " In other words, no matter what their real feelings, those Americans who were questioned would, almost to a man, hesitate to show favor to those frightening and ugly immoral monsters, obscenity and pornography.

This is why the basic question asked in the Commission survey was, "Would you please tell me what you think are the two or three most serious problems facing the country today? " Only two per cent mentioned erotic materials. Upon further questioning, "it was found that 51% of the population would be inclined to sanction availability of erotic materials if it were clearly demonstrated that such materials had no harmful effects on the user. " Since the Commission felt its studies and previous similar studies had "found no evidence to date that exposure to explicit sexual materials plays a significant role in the causation of delinquent or criminal behavior among youth or adults, "[11] the conclusion is obvious.   So, if exposure to erotic materials is not proven as "a factor in the causation of sex crime or sex delinquency, " then the 51% figure stands, and Senator McClellan and his 59 fellow-voters are in error on this.   A majority of

Americans, once convinced that erotica does not have the
popularly supposed "harmful effects," did agree with the
Commission recommendation to make the distribution of erotic materials not a subject of law. [12]

Where, then, does the censor stand now? Accept the
findings of the ten massive volumes of "technical reports"
funded and backed by the Commission, accept its conclusions
and recommendations, and the censor--at least in the United
States--would find little to do. The Commission threw out
censorship, and called for so-called "positive approaches"--
sex education, industry self-regulation, and organized citizen
action--to solve the problems which, they admitted, do exist.

On sex education, the Commission suggested that "to
the extent that interest in erotica on the part of young people
is motivated by natural curiosity and the desire to know more
about sex, sex education would appear to be potentially powerful in reducing this interest and thereby decreasing the
possibility of exposure to misinformation. . . . " They concluded that "sex education programs . . . offer the opportunity
for parents, school, and church to cooperate in helping to
form within the individual a set of positive values and attitudes toward sexuality. "[13] This is certainly light-years
away from the desire for negative "values and attitudes toward sexuality" traditionally inculcated by the Judeo-Christian
ethic.

The Commission said that another form of "positive
action" on erotic material lies in the use of "organized
citizen action groups. " Although criticizing these groups as
having the potentiality of seriously interfering with the availability "of legitimate materials in a community by generating
an overly repressive atmosphere and by using harassment in
seeking to implement their goals, " they felt that such groups
"can be effective if they genuinely reflect the opinion of the
community and if they pursue specific, positive, well-defined
constructive goals. " How a self-constituted censorship group
can possibly pursue "positive" or "constructive" aims, in
view of the generally accepted definition of censorship, would
seem very difficult to spell out. But the Commission does
accept the organized "citizen action group" as one "positive"
approach to dealing with obscenity and pornography. They
admit that "research suggests that citizen action groups may
be more successful as symbols than as effective tools, " since
it seems ". . . important to the participants to demonstrate belief in and support for an enduring set of basic values in the

face of threatened change. "[14]   The anti-sex groups may not
be as strong as they were before today's comparatively free
sexuality, but they will certainly continue to exist and to
fight "smut, " as they see it, until the day of <u>complete</u> sexual freedom, if that ever comes.

The last of the Commission's suggested "positive approaches, " self-regulation by industry, is not, it turns out,
very warmly favored.   They suggest that such "self-regulation" may affect "creativity and innovation...." They also
bring up the possibility that such regulation, "...often rein-
forced by pressures from a vigilant minority, not only sets
up rules and internal procedures for deleting or blunting material deemed offensive, but also inhibits experimentation
with new ideas, dampens response to social change, and
limits the source of cultural variety. "[15]   In the long run,
as shown recently by the steadily declining box-office re-
ceipts of "X"-rated movies, and the renewed interest in novels which are something other than erotic compendia, public
taste is still the best determinant of what is produced and
sold in any of the media.

The cause of censorship-abolition is certainly not won.
The laws are still on the books; the small-town prosecuting
attorneys are still busy hectoring booksellers and librarians.
Charles Keating, Jr., author of the Minority Report of the Commission on Obscenity and Pornography, and the only Commission member appointed by President Nixon, wrote the
lead article for a recent issue of the best-read American
general magazine, Reader's Digest, under the title, "The
Report That Shocked the Nation. "[16]   His article refers to the
majority report as "a Magna Charta for pornographers, " as
if this characterization were a sensational discovery.   He
finds the report a "travesty, " criticizes the Commission's
methods as "often bizarre, " and repeats the charges in his
minority report.

For example, he says that "it is ridiculous to imply
that pornography has no effect. "   But this is a straw-man,
because his target did not so imply.   He is in perfect agreement with the Commission report on this.   The Report unequivocally stated that "accumulated research on psychosexual stimulation shows that exposure to erotic photographs,
narratives, and film produces sexual arousal in substantial
proportions of both males and females. "[17]   Indeed, the Commission said that "it is obviously not possible, and never
could be possible, to state that never on any occasion, under

any conditions, did any erotic material ever contribute in
any way to the likelihood of any individual committing a sex
crime.   Indeed, no such statement could be made about any
kind of nonerotic material. "[18]

Widespread misrepresentation of the Commission report and the nearly unanimously negative vote by the U.S.
Senate are not the only indicators of national reaction.   On
the same day that the Senate voted the report down, Congressman John G. Schmitz of California inserted into the
Congressional Record a statement in which, after saying that
"as the father of seven, obviously, I do not regard sex ...
as intrinsically evil, " he charged that "today's pornography
is utter perversion of what man and woman were meant to
be. "[19]   He refers to "the intrinsic evil in such pornography, "
which sounds like an echo of some of the obiter dicta of the
Church Fathers a millenium-and-a-half ago.

Several months later, Representative Thaddeus J. Dulski of New York introduced a resolution into the House of
Representatives asking for another rejection of the Commission report's findings.   Dulski deplored evidence that at least
one U.S. District (in Wisconsin) had already used the Commission's conclusions as a basis for a legal decision.   He
used the interesting argument that "so long as the conclusions of the Commission lack adequate documentation, I believe we must reject them firmly so there is no question
about their lack of stature. "[20]   The term "lack [of] adequate
documentation" is ironic when applied to what is by far the
best-documented and researched study ever made on the subject of obscenity and pornography.   Obviously, the censors
will not buy what the Commission reported and concluded.

Not all the reactions were adverse.   Father Eugene
Kennedy, writing in a liberal Catholic weekly, said, in comment on the Commission report, that "to repress and restrict inquiry into the mystery of man's responsiveness to
pornography on the grounds that this is unfitting or immoral
is the kind of maneuver that invites us all back into the
dark ages. "[21]   A national Jesuit publication stated that "some
voices raised against the report perhaps merit the comment
of G. William Jones, a member of the Commission and the
United Methodist minister and professor at Southern Methodist
University: 'Most critics apparently have tried to maintain
their objectivity by not reading the report. '"[22]   The professional library press and most professional librarians--and
the American Library Association, in particular, speaking

through its voice on these matters, the Office of Intellectual
Freedom, as well as through its Council--vigorously supported the Commission report. 23

But will the American people as a whole really accept the report and, particularly, its wide-ranging, revolutionary conclusions?   Long before the Commission report, a
long series of increasingly "liberal" U.S. Supreme Court decisions dealing in detail with all manner of cases related to
obscenity and pornography stated their feelings about attempting to regulate erotic material.   Whether the court included
liberal or conservative judges, their majority vote throughout
the last several decades has leaned toward the denial or at
least the abridgement of censorship.

But this should not be left purely as a matter of what
the judicial or the legislative or the executive arm of the
American government does or says about the dissemination
of erotic realism or obscenity or pornography.

A few years ago noted literary critic Malcolm Cowley
said that he was "not sorry to watch the continuing battle between artists and censors....   On the one hand, the artists
are defending originality, freedom, and their personal instinct about what is true and right.   They are, in a sense,
defending social change, or the possibility of change, since
we look to our artists for new values and perceptions.   On
the other hand, the censors are defending older values and
established institutions against what they regard as the threat
of moral chaos. "24   As a principled libertarian, Cowley
continues, 'Institutions have a right to defend themselves,
and older values may be the true ones. " He concludes, "all
we can hope is that the battle is conducted according to rules,
that the artists have a chance to be heard, and that their
personal visions ... will be exposed to logic and the light of
day. "

There will always be some kind of censorship, if only
in the minds of the artistic creators.   Indeed, it is likely
there will always be at least would-be censors.   But as long
as the "continuing battle" continues, somehow man will not
be denied his glimpse of Eden, his chance to be what there
is every indication he is: basically, a sexual animal.

There is every evidence that there is now going on
what has been variously called a "sexual renaissance, "25 a
"sex explosion, "26 and a sexual revolution, even a sexual

"wilderness. "27   These are much more than academic pronouncements; the mass media, as well as the professorial
journals, have featured almost ad nauseum what has been
characterized as "the acceptance of alternate means and to
some extent alternate goals that most sharply characterizes
the current sexual scene. "28

Granted a sharp break with such elements of our established social-religious tradition as premarital chastity,
monogamous marriage, evasion of genuine sex education, and
severely inhibited vocabulary--the whole idea that the pattern
of sexual behavior for all time was somehow set millenia
ago--the continuance of censorship of reading about sex is an
anachronism.   As British zoologist and sociologist Alex Comfort has put it, the barring or attempted barring of what he
calls "the natural history of sexual satisfaction and of human
sexual behavior" is due to its being "suppressed, destroyed,
or concealed by an active minority bent on seeing we did not
get it...."   He sees this as by no means reflecting the general taste or mores of our time. 29

The censor, Comfort says, extrapolates his own response to sexual representation, written or pictorial, on to
others, claiming that such writing or art is "...socially
dangerous and artistically unworthy, " because it produces
sexual excitement.   Comfort sees this, even if true, as only
part of the truth.   He says that "part of the popularity of
sexual literature today is due to a widespread conviction that
knowledge is being kept from us which would make for greater proficiency and enjoyment in our own experience: part is
the result of legitimate curiosity, the desire to compare our
habits with other people's and be liberated from the anxieties ... of our sexual pleasures. "30

His theory is that the wish to censor sexual art (in
the broadest sense) is really a sexual disability, comparable
to homosexuality or fetishism.   He grants that "sexually
squeamish people" are justified in requesting that what upsets
them regarding sex should not be forced on their attention.
But why does the censor fuss about written items dealing
with sex?   After all, as Comfort points out, "a book stays
closed until it is opened, and it can be voluntarily closed at
any moment. "31

The censor, then, is saying, among other things, that
the book about sex which talks about what bothers him must
necessarily bother all other possible readers the same way.

He is also saying that, although it is perfectly proper to
write and read about violence and killing and death, it is
definitely improper to write about anything that pertains to
the act which might lead to the creation of life.   He is for
Thanatos, rather than Eros.

     Comfort sees the basic causes of sexual censorship in
the fear of the word among primitives and "in the revival of
Oedipal anxieties in ill-adjusted numbers of the group. " Why
must those who are civilized enough to have outgrown the
fear of the word and who are normal (sexually speaking) conform to the censor's repressions and maladjustments?   Comfort says that it is simply wrong to permit a repressive,
limited sexual censorship to inhibit those (a vast majority)
who do not really want such a censorship. 32

     Dr. Helena Wright, viewing this whole issue, suggests
that it is behavior, rather than prohibition of behavior, that
is significant in a society as sexually charged as ours.   She
sees widespread availability and use of relatively effective
contraceptive measures as bringing about "the possibilities
for the kind of changes in society that could evolve when
sexual activity is freed from its conventional limitations. "33
First among these changes she sees the general acknowledge-
ment "that some degree of happy sexual experience is a universal need, except for certain rare individuals who have
successfully substituted some other creative form of activity. " Indeed she expresses the hope "that society will accept the findings of the psychiatrists and allow reasonable
sexual happiness to anyone who wants it. "34

     This offers an interesting set of alternatives, in
terms of the future of censorship: either it would no longer
be necessary to have any sex censorship, because there really would be nothing new or different for man (and woman) to
find out or have a "prurient" interest in, or else it would
not be necessary to have any censorship, because there
would be no censoriously-minded individuals or groups left.
It must be accepted as a reasonable probability that the censor and censorship would both vanish in a sexually-enlightened
society.

     The censor, the individual, or the group restraining
and inhibiting and limiting what other men may read are saying "no" to life.   The censor is offering negation and restriction as the right way to live; he is offering a distorted, mal-
formed picture as the complete mirror of what life is; he is,

in short, turning life into death.   Some facets of life may be
what some will call "evil"; but these facets exist, and hiding
them, masking them, pretending that all life is on the Elsie
Dinsmore level will, in the long run, cause more evil than
good.

     Given a choice between the free release of man's
creative and symbol-making abilities and the dead hand of
the censor, it is to be hoped that man will at least try to
see himself as he really is.   The social, historical, philosophical, psychological, ethnological, religious, legal, and
moralistic traditions of mankind surely indicate that the task
of the truth-facer is not an easy one.

     The fate of the censor and of censorship is not ca-
pable of precise prediction by any reasonable logic, whether
of reason or events.   Who, even as recently as two decades
ago, could have foreseen our present state of relative freedom?   More than technological improvement of contraceptive
methods was needed to bring about the U. S. Supreme Court's
almost invariable steady progression of majority anti-censorship decisions; or the indication by not one but several
major religious faiths, through their leadership, of a relaxation of strict sexual codes.   The general public, meanwhile,
by its expenditure of leisure-time funds and time (perhaps
the best criterion of taste in our capitalist society), has
continued to show its great and increasing interest in unin-
hibited fiction and non-fiction.   In a society that is changing
as rapidly in most respects as ours, it should not be a matter of surprise that a duly constituted Presidential Commission plumps for the abolition of all censorship of sexually-
oriented materials.   It just may be that the Obscenity and
Pornography Commission's majority report will be the first
major breakthrough towards eventually leaving all reading entirely up to individual choice.

14. THE CENSOR, THE INDIVIDUAL, AND MORALITY

"One year a State Senator introduced a bill into the Massachusetts legislature ... It began as follows:

'Any person acting as censor of either books, plays, pictures, music, or dancing, for the Commonwealth or any county, city or town thereof, shall first pass a civil-service examination including the standard Binet intelligence test for mentality of eighteen years, general information and language test similar to those required for employees of the Boston Public Library, and shall submit to the State Department of Public Health satisfactory evidence of normal sexual experience. '"

--Horace M. Kallen, Art and Freedom, 1942.

Chapter 14

THE CENSOR, THE INDIVIDUAL AND MORALITY

More and more, these days, morality is coming to be considered a matter for individual, rather than group or church or total societal concern. Such thinkers as Marc Oraison, Teilhard de Chardin, Martin Buber, Paul Tillich, and Jean-Paul Sartre, writing variously from French Catholic, Jewish, German Protestant, and French existentialist viewpoints, agree that one of the central problems of our time is the relationship of man and morality. Unless this is faced up to, the future of censorship, for example, can hardly be gauged in a modern context.

Oraison feels that between the ultra-rational, law-bound moralists and the ultra-clinical psychoanalytical psychologists somewhere lies the truth about morality, which is, for him, neither laid down in a hard and fast theological code nor in a semi-automatonized concept of the human psyche and unconscious. Oraison accepts this definition of morality: "Morality is the science of what man ought to be by reason of what he is. "[1] Despite any appearances to the contrary, this is a truly religious, God-centered definition.

Grant Oraison's premise--and that of Socrates!--that self-knowledge is really the most necessary of all knowledge, and it is easy to understand why he finds moral knowledge a necessity. He says that "for human beings ... it is imperative to learn, to grasp and to understand, and thus to engage ourselves.... " If morality is "the science of what man ought to be, " it, of course, can never be fully realized or achieved.

But we must, as humans, try. We are neither robots nor completely reasoning creatures; neither depth psychology nor theological rationalism has all the answers. British philosopher John Wilson has described man's "normal" or "natural" condition as one "which always needs improvement, "

"... of enlarging and thereby strengthening the consciousness, of recovering something of the strength and energy of our desires, of freeing them from guilt and fear which blended with them almost at their very inception. "[2]

This seems in perfect consonance with Oraison's illuminating insight that "the human person in the reality of his existence does not engage in relationships with principles or with a law. He rather binds himself to other persons. " This identification of morality as basically involving the individual's actions (in terms of his reactions to and from others) is a far cry from the Ten Commandments or the decrees of a Council of Trent.   Oraison quotes St. Paul on the "killing" power of the law (Romans 7). [3]

Oraison says that "the rise of moralism progressively obscured, penalized and falsified the Christian dynamics of behavior. " He questions whether so-called "Christian" morality is really Christian: he sees the values of Christian civilization as "vestiges of an ancient Stoicism ... "--an assumption which, in another connection, we have heard before. He mentions with scorn what "an eminent churchman" once said to him as "the last word in moral education (which, by the way, was reduced to sexual problems). " That statement was, "If you commit sin, you will go to hell. "[4]

The particular group which Oraison anathematizes are those he calls the "moralizing moralists, " people who "are fearful for themselves, without actually knowing it and without understanding what it is that they fear. " They are the ones who need a legalistic structure to underpin their own continued sense of insecurity. This "legalistic moralist" attitude, says Oraison, is really "a neurotic defense against life. ... "[5]

Another phase of what Oraison calls the "'fear of the other' which every human conscience must somehow overcome to live authentically" is that of complete rejection of any rules, any law whatsoever, people who are laws unto themselves.   This is just as improper, as unlikely to permit life to be what it should be, both humanly and spiritually. The "legalist" versus the "progressive" has produced a morality in our time which Oraison says "is no longer a morality to speak of.   There is only incoherent murmuring going on within a closed world. "[6]

If Oraison is correct, then we are really reaching an

impasse. He deplores the fact that Western civilization for
many centuries has based its morality on "a confused jumble
of valuable, rational truths and questionable (though unquestioned) traditions; of correct and fundamental intuitions, and
ignorances that loom large in the light of modern science;
of elaborated reasoning on good and evil and on a multiplicity
of taboos. " His call is for "a morality [which] is made for
man, not man for morality. " His redefinition of morality,
finally, is that "morality consists in studying the concrete
exigencies of charity ..., namely our relationships with our
neighbor and with God. "[7]

Using this as a working definition, modern man cannot possibly find censorship a moral act. The censor is
most concerned with society, least concerned with the individual. The individual who lives by Oraison's "modern" morality is really living by a standard which is both old and
new. It is pre-Paul and pre-Augustine, and also Freudian
and Fletcherian. The classic Greeks could live with this
morality, and do without the censor; modern America would
do well, in this regard at least, to learn by their example.

Martin Buber, a liberal Jewish theologian, has opened
many new roads in the trackless wastes of the study of morality. But his most central, most significant additions to
this century's re-ordering of priorities is his idea of the "I-
Thou" relationship. I and Thou[8] (originally published in
Germany in 1923, in English in 1937) has affected such important thinkers as Tillich and Barth, Reinhold Niebuhr and
Herbert Read. His "dialogical" philosophy has been important to philosophers and critics, theologians and educators
and psychoanalysts. But what is its import for the censor-
ship-freedom dispute?

It seems to me that Buber's 1957 postscript to his
original work is perhaps of most use here. Buber says
there that "every I-Thou relationship, within a relation which
specified as a purposive working of one part upon the other,
persists in virtue of a mutuality which is forbidden to be
full. "[9] Note that it is the mutuality which is "forbidden to
be full. " The relationship, however, must be mutual, must
really be one which is an "I-Thou" relationship. Buber is
concerned with the truest of freedoms, one which acknowl-
edges the reality--or the impossibility--of full mutuality of
understanding by anyone, but which still "persists. " It is
the attempt which is important.

Under censorship it would hardly be possible for true
mutuality even to be attempted, because without communication, how could it occur? Buber says, "Often enough we
think there is nothing to hear, but long before we have ourselves put wax in our ears. " When Ulysses resisted the
Sirens' songs by stopping up his crew's ears with wax, and
having himself bound to his own ship's mast, it did not save
him or his crew from all their subsequent vicissitudes. It
is only when he communicated with Nausicaa and the Phaea-
cians that he got the help he needed in order to head toward
home.

Buber is the great modern exponent of relationship,
of dualism, of "togetherness" (although he certainly does not
use that word himself). He says that "in the beginning is
relation. "[10] And how can censorship--the severing of com-
municative dialogue concerning man's most primary relationship, the sexual one--be possible along with an "I-Thou" relationship?

A much more pragmatic and less philosophical-mysti-
cal comment on the relationship of the individual to freedom
has been expressed by education professor Richard Ballou.
He feels that "from a psychological and educational point of
view, the maximum freedom must be found for individuals
to evolve and express their unique human purposes. " It is
the healthy society, he feels, which provides for "a continu-
ous creative process of revision and evolution ... between
... individual purpose and social welfare.... " So legalistic
laws are only good when they are positive and permissive,
rather than negative and forbidding. His developed definition
of a free society is interesting, in this context: "that society may be said to be most free which is able to permit the
maximum expression of purpose which is genuine to the individuals of the society. "[11]

As is readily apparent, Ballou is centering his interest on the individual, not the group. If the individual in a
society is limited in his efforts toward "the maximum expression of purpose"--whether that limitation inhibits his
reading, his writing, or his actions--and if that purpose is a
"genuine" one, not a societally-defeating one, that is, then
the society is not free. The role of the censor can never
be anything but a limiting, controlling one, in any society;
it would be difficult, if not impossible, to see any censor as
permitting "maximum human freedom. "

Ballou categorizes all human progress as of three types: "the urge to express an affinity with people" [which sounds a great deal like Buber's "I-Thou" principle], "the urge to express productive energies," and "the urge to express an awareness of meaning."[12] All of these are repelled and negated by censorship, in one way or another.

Certainly, censorship sets up barriers between people, even between sexes; the creative artist is unable to "express productive energies"; and surely, without the freedom to read, an individual or a society cannot find meaning in his or their fundamental drives. Ballou sees "the freedom of the individual to participate in a community of free men"[13] as the only hope for a future free world; can such individuals, can such a community exist in a censored society?

An outstanding theological philosopher of today, Paul Ramsey, has made a most interesting attempt to use Jean-Paul Sartre's existentialist philosophy as a basis for a truly modern religious approach to sex. In dealing with what he calls "the human significance of sexuality,"[14] Ramsey criticizes Christianity's traditional tendency to disparage sexual intercourse because it is not considered an act of the reason and will, but of the emotions--or of the Devil! Indeed, along with Sartre, Ramsey sees coitus as a transcendent act, one which serves "the unitive ends of marriage (as distinct from the ends of procreation)...." He disagrees with the traditional Roman Catholic view, for example, as held by St. Thomas Aquinas, that "sexuality cannot go to the heart of human existence."

For Ramsey, sexuality is so essential and centrally important to unifying human personality that he claims that "upon the reformation of the Church's sexual teaching depends not only the saving of Christianity from very much of its past, but perhaps also the prevention of the disappearance of passion from the life of modern man...."[15] To him sexuality is "God's great and good gift." To deny God's largesse, it would seem, is not only impious, it is also self-destructive. Certainly the kind of censorship which presumes that sex, per se, is bad is hardly compatible with the Ramsey-Sartre viewpoint.

The two leading exponents in this century of sexual freedom, Havelock Ellis and René Guyon, are much concerned with the problem of censorship. Guyon has set up

what he calls "indisputable laws" concerning sex; his point
is that he is looking at sexual acts as a physiological, rather
than psychological or theological or even moral matter.   His
"laws" (which some may consider shocking) are as follows:
"the exercise of the sexual organs for the avowed purpose
of procuring sexual pleasure, and ultimately also for the
purpose of reproduction, is natural, normal, proper, legitimate, and indeed necessitated by the demands of our constitution; ... failure to exercise these organs, as a consequence either of voluntary abstention or of external circum-
stance (chastity, legal prohibitions, etc.) is, on the contrary,
an artificial, abnormal, unhealthy, and unpleasant state";
and "... sexual pleasure, the immediate aim of sexual activity, is obtained through an appropriate mechanism.   This
mechanism presents certain variations; but, so far as the
general principle is concerned, and except for possible differences in the degree of pleasure obtained, it is independent
of the quality (and, above all, of the moral value) of the
methods or the partners employed for setting it in action; it
can function just as well without a partner (as in onanism),
or with any kind of partner (as in homosexuality or in-
cest). "[16]

Guyon feels that these "indisputable laws, " if followed, would let the individual realize, completely and satis-
factorily, what would, biologically speaking, be accepted as
sexuality's normal objectives.   He refers to any other rules
or laws regulating human sexual activity as founded on intellect or aesthetics or, most commonly, simply what convention calls for.   So the individual who follows these "laws"
and is not restrained by social conventions is, in Guyon's
view, much more normal than those who follow the "artificial
conventions (only too often accepted quite uncritically), "
whose worth Guyon strongly disputes.

He criticizes repression and censorship as resulting
in "an artificially-molded being, guided in all the more deliberate aspects of its behavior by taboo-like and illogical
conventions, conventions the toxic influence of which has
sapped its vitality and spirit, even though it still continues
to defend them. "[17]   Guyon points out how "more healthy, "
in the sexual sense, are most of the non-white, non-Western
civilizations, the non-believers in the Judeo-Christian ethic.
He claims that "from the ethical and social points of view,
we may say that, generally speaking, there has been more
happiness, less neurosis, and less tormenting conflict among
the Asiatic, African, and Polynesian races. "   He attributes

this in large part to their much lower incidence of sexual neuroses, which, he claims, is the direct outcome of the Judeo-Christian belief in sin. [18]

Once Guyon's major premises--that sexuality is divided into a sexual sense and a reproductive function, and that pleasure is an essential element of the sexual sense, but not of the reproductive one, are granted, many of his conclusions seem less revolutionary. Guyon prefers to describe the "sixth sense" as neural, rather than sexual, pleasure, which he describes in physiological terms as one where there is "a specific nervous mechanism of an absolutely autonomous kind, the full development of which constitutes sexual pleasure.... "[19]

For Guyon, "the moral elements in sex are all creations of the human mind which have been superimposed upon the original physiological facts. They have no basis in the facts themselves. "[20] Logically, one might expect Guyon to offer a sort of "new" morality which would have a basis in the "facts" of life as he sees it. He does, but not in so many words.

His is a morality of tolerance, of freedom. He is even willing that anyone who wants to should be against sex. As he says, "anyone has a right to adopt the anti-sexual taboo, with all its concomitant restrictions, if he so desires; but only on condition that he does not erect it into a doctrine with which to bully and to pester others. " And this is not a tenable condition. His conclusion is that the sexual morality of today is directly responsible for a whole string of evils, including "dangerous neuroses, shameful hypocrisies, and grave social injustice.... "[21]

The Guyon philosophy, while certainly not even today (nearly four decades after its first promulgation) very much known about or followed, has had some effects, although often their origins go unacknowledged. It is interesting to note that the eleven-page, double-column section of the otherwise quite modern Encyclopedia of Sexual Behavior dealing with "Sexual Freedom" refers to René Guyon neither in its text nor lengthy bibliography (although Guyon is cited in the book's index in reference to sex reform, art and sex, and prostitution). This may be because the author of this section differs with Guyon by stating flatly that there is no such thing as a human sexual instinct. Sociologist and anthropologist Robert M. Frumkin claims that "since man's sexual behavior

is symbolic, since it is social, learned, it is always shaped
in a particular cultural milieu and oriented by the values of
the society maintaining that milieu. "22

His evidence for this interesting-if-true statement is,
in large part, based on the studies of Leuba, and of Ford
and Beach, zoologists and biologists. Certainly, if one completely forgets or ignores the equally important research of
Freud, Jung, Adler and other important psychologists of our
time, it would be possible to grant that sexual behavior is
completely variable and cultural.

Frumkin defines sexual freedom as "the social-psy-
chologically based choice a person has among several alternatives of culturally defined action. "23 If one were to accept this definition, it would be fair to criticize censorship
as really not permitting any choice; obviously, if reading
about sex is limited or denied altogether, the individual's
choice of what to do, sexually speaking, is limited, too.

Between the Scylla and Charybdis of what Frumkin
calls "prosexual" societies (those "which have permissive attitudes toward sex and allow numerous alternatives in regard
to sexual behavior"), with modern Scandinavia as perhaps the
best current example, and "anti-sexual" societies (those
"which have extremely repressive and restrictive attitudes
toward sex"), exemplified today by "some segments of the
modern American population, " there can be seen a middle
ground, what Frumkin describes as "a strong, persistent
democratic trend toward more rational sexual behavior both
in the free world and certain areas behind the iron cur-
tain. "24 The accuracy of this view, expressed in 1967, is
evident in the current worldwide Women's Liberation movement, as well as in the worldwide anti-censorship wave.
What is being read and seen in the Western world (with, of
course, some exceptions) is circumscribed only very little.
And Guyon and Havelock Ellis were as much, perhaps more,
responsible for this as anyone.

The best-known modern philosopher of sex, Havelock
Ellis, has stated that there are really two functions involved
in the sexual relationship--the primary one, of course, being
reproduction, and the secondary, and not to be forgotten,
one, being what he describes as the "spiritual function of
furthering the higher mental and emotional processes. " This
one Ellis calls "the play-function" of sex. The important
part of this function, for anyone concerned about censorship,

is its relationship to "play as artistic creation. "25

Ellis decries the fact that to the average man in our society (he wrote this particular section of his book in 1921) "the notion of play in the sphere of sex ... is for him something quite low down, something to be ashamed of.... " He criticizes the "taboos and terrors, most tinged with artificial stains of impurity and degradation deprived from alien and antiquated traditions, " which adversely affect what he calls "the native impulses, ... the natural tendencies, " where activity is inhibited by such "taboos and terrors. "26

In discussing censorship directly, Ellis says that "it is law alone which makes pornography both attractive and profitable. " He believes that even the young would not suffer from abolition of all laws against obscenity and pornography: "Pornography has no meaning and no attraction for the healthy child who casually comes in contact with it; the reaction is one of indifference, if not of disgust. " He suggests that "parents and teachers must be trusted to aid the child in guiding himself safely through these risks, without injury to the freedom of adults. "27

To fortify this argument, consider the findings of an important recent study of family life in France through the sixteenth and seventeenth centuries. One chapter is unique in its revelations on this topic--revelations which have somehow been almost ignored by most other historians or social scientists. The French demographic historian, Philippe Aries, in a chapter entitled "From Immodesty to Innocence, " gives ample evidence to prove that at that time it was not thought that "references to sexual matters, even when virtually devoid of dubious meanings, could soil childish innocence, either in fact or in the opinion people had of it.... " Indeed, says Aries, "nobody thought that this innocence really existed. " In those days "broad talk was so natural that ... the strictest reformers would introduce into their sermons to children and students comparisons which would seem shocking today. "28

It was only towards the end of the seventeenth century that the idea of furnishing expurgated editions of the classics, specifically edited for the benefit of children, began. This was one of the many results of what Aries calls "an essential concept ... the innocence of childhood. " Another was this kind of injunction, found in a book on children's manners published in 1713: "Teach them to read books in

which purity of language and wholesome subject matter are
combined. "29 Novel-reading and singing of songs which expressed "dissolute passions" and were "full of indecent expressions" were banned, also.

The revelatory insight here is that a great many of
what somehow today are considered more or less "eternal
verities"--such as the possibility of corrupting children unless censorship is used--are really quite recent. As Aries
says, "the attitude to sex, and doubtless sex itself, varies
according to environment, and consequently according to
period and mentality." If we change again now, in the last
part of the twentieth century, it will not be the first time;
nor, likely enough, will it be the last. Let Aries have the
last word on this: "Our world is obsessed by the physical,
moral and sexual problems of childhood. "30 And both adults
and children are strongly affected by the results of this obsession, certainly as far as the freedom to read is concerned.

To return to Ellis, his case for non-censorship is
based on his massive and pioneering Studies in the Psychology of Sex, whose insights paved the way for the Kinseys,
the Dr. Albert Ellises, and the Masters and Johnsons of today. His judgment is certainly to be weighed and considered, especially when he states unequivocally, "the truth is--
one cannot too often repeat--that literature and art that are
'obscene' in any genuinely objectionable sense, will be unlikely to appeal to normally healthy minds when not surrounded by secrecy and prohibition. The market in pornography is artifically created [Ellis' italics]. That is the central fact of the situation. " And he claims that sexual censorship "has maimed the freedom of art, and hampered the
finest social and individual activities, alike in deed or
speech. "31

So far, this chapter's discussion has concentrated on
the last two parts of its heading: the individual and morality. How about the censor? It is not too common for a
censor to offer his own apologia pro vita sua. It might be
unkind, even if true, to say that censors are not always
literate, let alone capable of communicating their ideas on
their own profession.

One censor who did attempt to explain his own and
similar activities was William Joynson Hicks, Viscount Brentford, who, as Home Secretary in England during the Twenties,

had the responsibility for being more or less Great Britain's
literary censor. In a little 24-page pamphlet[32] Brentford
frankly stated his concept of his own job, and, more than
that, his feelings and reasonings on the whole theory of censorship.

          To begin with, Brentford is forthright in admitting
that "indecency in itself is, of course, not a crime"; what
is criminal, he says, is "indecency committed in public...."
He puts this legalistically by saying that the whole foundation
of his authority is based upon the right of the people not to
have "the amenities of their lives" affected by permitting
"certain acts" to be committed publicly. [33]

          Now this is quite a novel concept. Censorship is usu-
ally associated with keeping individuals from performing that
most private of actions, reading. Brentford attempts to explain his right to censor further by stating that "it is according to common law, that is, law without any statute, ...
that it is a misdemeanour to publish any indecent matter
tending to the destruction of the morals of society and to deprave and corrupt those whose minds are open to immoral
influence. " He claims that those who are responsible for
publishing obscene books "are as equally criminal as those
who commit obscene acts in public ... " but gives no reason
at all to support this claim. [34] Yet he was the censor in
England for a number of years, and was able to operate under this theory with no hindrance.

          He also declares his complete disagreement with a
rather interesting resolution approved by the World League
for Sexual Reform, which in 1929 held that "obscenity and
impropriety are matters too subjective and indefinite to serve
as a basis for laws. Human beings should be so educated as
to be able to meet all kinds of knowledge and decide for
themselves what they personally avoid or reject as obscene. "
Their reasoning was that "in literature and art judgment differs widely, and any form of censorship or subsequent persecution leads to the condemnation of works of artistic or
scientific importance. " They concluded by saying that "on
this ground we declare ourselves against all kinds of censorship on sex subjects in literature, scientific publications,
pictures, and other representations. "[35]

          The censor's rejoinder to this is most revelatory.
First, he says that he does not agree "to any criminal or
body of criminals deciding whether their own acts are, or

are not, criminal. " Next, after huffing and puffing that
"there are other matters in life of greater importance than
the free development of a particular form of art, " he waxes
quite indignant about the argument that a book that is a work
of art deserves different treatment from one that is not. His
conclusion on this point is that "a book which is well written,
even restrained in tone and delicate in treatment, may yet
be as corrupting in its influence, especially upon the young,
as the most miserable and disgusting literary production. "36
So the censor's thinking is clear; and it hardly seems necessary to report that during his stay as British Home Secretary, such great novelists as Aldous Huxley and D. H. Lawrence suffered from his reprobation.

Brentford gives his justification for censorship as his
"duty" to follow the law, which, he says, "is founded upon
public morality.... " Just what happens when that vague body
of thought, "public morality, " changes, he does not say.
For Brentford, it seems to be an everlasting, unchanging
standard, to which the censor may repair for backing at any
time.

The end of Brentford's slim but illuminating booklet--
one of the very few documents in existence wherein a modern censor attempts to justify his own existence--is rather
a surprising one.   After all his animadversions on "filth"
and "pernicious literature, " he offers a forecast, or perhaps
a plea, for the day to come when no censorship in any form
will be necessary.   That happy time will eventuate, he says,
when "by the spread of education and the extension of religion in the hearts of the people they will themselves learn to
reject all forms of unpleasant conduct, literature, art--and,
beyond all, of personal thought. "   When this Utopian time
comes, says Brentford, the people will learn "not merely to
disregard, but to detest all ... forms of indecency in thought,
word and deed.... "37

And, since the Viscount obviously equates unpleasant-
ness with evil and crime, the ideal world for Brentford will
be composed of eunuchs, all perfect gentlemen (if the last
part of the word is still applicable), and women who are
ladies first, and hardly, if ever, flesh-and-blood women.
As he says, "the people themselves will have attained, by
religion, by education and by personal thought, that cleanness
of heart which alone can ensure a cleanness of thought and
of action. "38

How was it Matthew Arnold described Shelley--"a beautiful and ineffectual angel beating in the void his luminous wings in vain"?   And isn't there at least a slight similarity to the World League for Sexual Reform's resolution in Brentford's almost identical plea for education of the populace as a preventative of censorship?

Sociologist Lewis A. Coser offers a rather different theory of the origin and spread of censorship, particularly in modern times.   He agrees with the Max Weber-R. H. Tawney idea that the necessarily "methodical and disciplined work habits" which an industrial society required just had to come from worker acceptance of the Puritan ethic, with its "morality of postponed gratification. "   Since unrepressed sexual appetite might have a deleterious effect on the "required discipline of the work force, " anything which might sharpen or encourage that appetite, such as so-called "obscene" literature, was bad.   (Coser points out the interesting coincidence that the New York Society for the Suppression of Vice became active about seventy years after its British countergroup, and that the American industrial society began its "takeoff" just about seventy years after the beginning of the British industrial revolution.)39

Coser says that censorship, in modern Anglo-American society, "was essentially an effort to maintain traditional sexual morality in the face of a rising new industrial social structure. "40   But with changing times, the manners, and the laws--and judicial opinion--also changed.   Coser feels that in today's sexual climate, "the battle of the censors to prevent the spread of ideas about sex was bound to fail. When there are so few 'pure' minds to protect, the very enterprise of protection is bound to appear ridiculous and quixotic. "

He sees a duty, even a responsibility, for censorship "during the period in which it was in tune with the dominant morality and the public opinion of the dominant strata in society. "   It certainly helped the ruling classes to hold down the proletariat as long as that was possible.   But the urbanization of our civilization has meant a decided change.   As Coser puts it, "the smalltown mind of the provincial backwoodsman, though still powerful in the backwaters, proved incapable of withstanding the mainstream of national ideas.... The morality of the industrial city had eroded the standards of repressive gentility. "41

The men who are groping their way toward the truth
about the relationship of morality and sex are part of a
tradition of one time's getting its inspiration from its pre-
decessors' ideas and codes.   The Judeo-Christian tradition
on morals, for example, was by no means a complete break
from the Hellenic and Roman traditions.   The teachings of
Jesus and Paul certainly showed the effects of the Judaism
in which both were born and trained, but also it was affected
by the Graeco-Roman culture which dominated their times.
As Crane Brinton puts it, "Nothing is easier than to draw
from the works of Graeco-Roman writers from Plato on expressions of ideas that seem clearly Christian. "[42]

What Christianity, at least in its beginnings, added is
discussed in chapter 5, and the subsequent Puritan influences
in chapter 6 of the present work, but there is one viewpoint,
soundly historically based, which deserves notice in this context.

British philosopher and moralist John Macmurray says
that "the Roman tradition, which is by far the strongest element in European civilization, is a Stoic tradition.   It lies
at the root of our moral conscience, particularly as regards
sex. "   This philosophy, as he expresses it succinctly, is
that sexual desire in itself is evil, and virtue "consists in
dominating and suppressing it on principle, by force of will,
in a lifelong struggle. "   So, Macmurray holds, "the orthodox
Christian tradition of sex-morality, what we refer to as
'Christian' morality, is essentially external and intellectual. "
He goes on to say that this is not really "Christian, " because "what Jesus did was to substitute an inner and emotional basis of behavior for an external and intellectual
one. "[43]   With love as a foundation, no morality can be bound
by rules and principles, and it is not likely that the censor
would have been quite as popular if Christ-related, rather
than Stoic-related, morality had prevailed in Christendom.

Macmurray asserts that "our civilization, for all its
scientific and administrative capacity, has remained emotionally vulgar and primitive, unchaste in the extreme. "   How
could it be otherwise, with "a morality based upon will and
reason, imposing itself upon the emotions and so destroying
their integrity? "   He is not promulgating licentiousness or
asking for the destruction of accepted Judeo-Christian sexual
standards.   Rather, he is pushing the cause of what he describes as "chastity, " by which he means "emotional sincer-
ity--sincerity in expression of what we feel. "[44]   For him, to

be unchaste is to be emotionally insincere, rather than sexually loose, in the accepted, common use of the word "unchaste. "

Macmurray is quite specific about the sexual relationship in this regard; he says, "It is neither something high
and holy, something to venerate and be proud of, nor is it
something low and contemptible, to be ashamed of. " Then
what is it? "It is a simple ordinary organic function to be
used like all the others, for the expression of personality in
the service of love. "

The philosopher is quite critical of what our civilization has done by singling out sex "as something very special
and wonderful and terrible.... " He says that this attitude
"has produced in us a chronic condition of quite unnatural
exasperation. " And, what is most pertinent in considering
the place of censorship in such a society, he states that "the
most powerful stimulant of sex is the effort to suppress it. "
Perhaps those last twelve words should be the permanent
slogan for any libertarian, anti-censorship individual or
group. Instead of suppression of sex, Macmurray recommends that we "take it up, simply, frankly, and naturally
into the circle of our activities.... "45

He admits there are some dangers to this position,
that there is no "security" in his way of dealing with the
sexual emotions. But he says the real danger is "spiritual
death; and it is possible to commit spiritual suicide from
fear of the terrors of spiritual reality. "46 That is quite a
choice, but it seems reasonable to be on the side of the ad-
venturous, chance-taking spirit, as against the security-lov-
ing, death-trending rule of pharisaical laws.

British moral philosopher John Wilson has said that
"no one is in a position to lay down a detailed code of sexual
morality with rational certainty. " Why? The key word in
the Wilson statement is "rational. " Wilson feels that it is
simply impossible to be "rational, " in the usual sense, about
any moral question, and, particularly, about the morality of
sexual behavior. If we are really looking for the truth about
sex, if we really want, as nearly as is humanly possible, to
find "rational certainty, " then, says Wilson, we must look at
sexual morality, of all things, logically. 47

Let us follow Wilson's argument. He asks first to
judge the "experts" in sex. Unlike experts in other fields,

our society will not accept the ones with the most actual experience in the subject as experts; they, of course, would
either be Casanovas or prostitutes. But, as Wilson says,
"experts in sex have to be socially respectable. " And their
social respectability, alas, may weigh more heavily in their
favor as acceptable sex experts than their actual expertise.

   The theologians, the anthropologists, the psychologists
--all of these are, or have been accepted as being, "experts, " in various ways, on sex. But the theologian, of
course, is dealing with beliefs, with faith, not facts and reason. The anthropologist collects facts about cultural diversity and similarity, but can not really prove their relevance
to a particular individual's sex morality. The psychologists,
alas, Wilson says, differ so widely in their opinions about
the human mind and its relationship to the body's intransi-
gence that, just like other, less-educated people, they "assert [their] own values and [their] own morality in a perennial
attempt to reassure ... [themselves] and to convince other
people. "48

   Of these types of experts, Wilson leans toward the
latter two, and particularly toward the psychologist. He
says that "in order to decide how we should think, feel, and
behave, it is obvious that we need to find out how and why
we actually do, think, feel, and behave, and with what results. " That is to say, "we need a science of human nature,
a science based, like every other science, on observation,
hypothesis, and prediction. "49 Certainly, the social sciences today are very far, as yet, from being such established
sciences.

   Granting Wilson's argument so far, where are we?
We are left, it would seem, as Wilson says, with a feeling
that no "authorities" can be more than "useful guides, " and
that "it is only we ourselves who can decide what is right
and wrong.... " The choices we make, he says, "relate to
our own desires, or to those of others as they relate to the
satisfaction of our desires. " An important point that Wilson
makes here is that "anyone who accepts life as a human being at all thereby accepts the whole apparatus of desire and
satisfaction.... " Indeed, Wilson stresses, "it is only in
terms of this apparatus that we can talk of justification for
morality at all. "50

   This begins to sound like religious morality upside
down, for how can we consider ourselves truly normal if we

are (a) selfish, or at least self-centered, and (b) hedonistic.
The very idea of equating morals with satisfaction rather
than denial somehow seems like an absolute inversion of
what most of us have hitherto considered the goals and
means of morality.   Probably this is why censorship really
offends so comparatively few; censorship, after all, is a
denial, it is the taking away of pleasure, and it applies to
society--what other moral models does it need?

Wilson exemplifies and reasons his way in some detail (not possible to repeat here) to the conclusion that "becoming more aware of our desires and how best to satisfy
them ... is making progress in morality. " In fact, he says,
"it would not be too misleading to say that what is 'really
right and wrong' (mature or immature, normal or abnormal,
healthy or unhealthy) is what the rational person, i.e., the
person who makes full use of these methods, comes to think
is right or wrong. "51

Another important consideration in all this is to be
aware that recognizing, being aware of one's own desires,
is not enough; morality, ordinarily (except in the case of
hermits or lone desert-island occupants, for example), must,
Wilson reminds us, be regarded as "essentially interpersonal. " To have a truly interpersonal morality, human beings must, basically, have two abilities and the chance to
use them.   These abilities are, Wilson says, "the ability to
love and to communicate. " What an interesting coincidence
that the censor, by his activities, can frustrate both at once!
Just possibly this proves the censor to be immoral--or, at
least, not concerned with what has been referred to before
as a most desirable human goal: that is, to make progress
in morality.   Wilson says that "moral progress ... essentially depends on the increased satisfaction of desire and on
good communications within the self. "52

Wilson follows this rather basic discussion of the logic
and reason behind morality with an interesting and not-too-
often-brought-up discussion of what he calls "the fallacy of
discrimination. " This, briefly stated, is the following series
of "logical" statements and conclusions: (1) X is an important, significant human activity, (2) therefore when X is
done, people ought to "use discrimination, " and (3) therefore
people should be taught to do X "only ... in forms restricted
by rules, precepts, principles, or ideals, because otherwise
X will become devalued, meaningless, irresponsible, or positively wicked. "53 In other words, reject some forms of sex,
because some are valuable and some are not.

As Wilson says, there are many who will view sexual activity as a necessary field for religious morality, or, if more "liberal," as "a matter of taking 'adult' attitudes, or ... of mutual perceptivity and awareness." But there are not many who will say that most of sexual activity is perfectly legitimate and proper, "including just good fun." Wilson sees the fallacy of discrimination as having such influence "that anyone who claims that sex should be, for the most part, just a matter of physical enjoyment would immediately be accused of insensitivity, immorality, incapacity for deep relationship, and practically every other crime."

But the fallacy is still a fallacy, regardless of how widespread its adherents. First, there is really no logical progression from number (2) above to number (3). Who knows what it is that we are discriminating about? Why is homosexuality, for instance, to be forbidden, and serial marriage (marriage, divorce, marriage, divorce, and so on) to be permitted? Why should a book that uses a four-letter word to help teach all the Judeo-Christian virtues (The Catcher in the Rye) to be considered "immoral," as against a book that uses "good" language to teach manifest immorality (and the examples, such as books about the Green Berets, have been legion)? As Wilson puts it, "any a priori sexual morality is a clear case of a pretence to knowledge where there is only ignorance."54

Also, Wilson points out, there is a definite ambiguity in the very concept of discrimination. To discriminate is not to reject. Just think of literary discrimination (sometimes referred to as literary criticism). To read Mann and Kafka and T. S. Eliot does not mean that one cannot acknowledge the relative values of Harold Robbins and Irving Wallace or even Jacqueline Susann! As Wilson reminds us, "one can look at people and things in more than one way ... no one way ... excludes the others."55

One argument that censors use is that it is "human nature" to feel guilty about sex and also that it is "human nature" to, as Wilson says, "coerce ourselves within some established framework of convention and morality...."56 Wilson says that there is little, if anything, that we cannot do to change ourselves. And any change should be of the liberating, freedom-making type. If changes are forced upon us, it is very unlikely that they will be for the real good of either the individual or society.

To achieve the real good, Wilson says, we must improve in two ways, "communication and experimentation. "
In other words, we must not be frozen into a particular set
of attitudes; there must be a means of trying out new ways
of living, as well as of telling each other about the proposed
innovations. Putting it very simply, we have to know what
it is we are doing, and whatever affects our lives at least
must not prevent us from such self-knowledge--or, in Wilson's phrase, from needed "liberating change. "[57]

If we accept the idea of "liberating change" as an individual and societal necessity, then certainly we cannot accept the idea of censorship. Censorship is bred in an atmosphere of confining sameness, of the status quo as an unalterable ideal. If censorship has a father, it is the Establishment; its maternal parent must, with equal logic, then, be
the fear of change. If either element is changed, censorship has little chance of even coming into being, let alone
being enforced.

I am indebted to Dr. Vernard Eller, professor of religion at La Verne College, and author of The Mad Morality,
or The Ten Commandments Revisited,[58] for the idea of commitments as opposed to, or replacing commandments for
modern man. His suggestion is that to have true freedom,
there must be some limits; in regard to moral freedom, in
particular, he says that what he calls "commitment-fences"
should be "accepted voluntarily. " The best way to do this,
he feels, is for the individual himself to build his own
fences and have them "installed in his own heart, mind, and
will. "[59]

This, of course, is the antithesis of the censor-prin-
ciple. Turning over the moral freedom of society, at least
in part, to the censor, will, among other things, vitiate the
instinct for freedom that all normal people have. Let someone else decide what you can or cannot read, and your "com-
mitment-fence" really is a boundary without an area to en-
close. Those who welcome the censor to think for them find
too often that they have lost the right to free action, along
with the power to have free thought.

No reasonable man says that censorship, historically
speaking, has not sometimes had its positive values. But
the question is whether censorship of writing about sex in
today's world serves anything but outmoded purposes and discarded values. Based on misconceptions about the statements

of top religious leaders, and quasi- or pseudo-scientific
"facts, " on a myriad of reasons that are mostly simply rationalizations or assumptions, censorship is one of many human aberrations which will some day be regarded as historically interesting but practically valueless.

Bedazzled by a phantasmagoria of inescapable and
hard-to-believe sights and sounds, bedeviled by the echoes
of ancient nationalist and theological quarrels, troubled by
the psychic after-shocks of personal anxieties of childhood,
traumatized by the successive hammer-blows of war after
war after war, apprehensive of a world-ending nuclear holo-
caust--surely even this partial list is enough and too much
for the men and women of today to have to endure. At
least they deserve to be able to face all these woes and
problems without the added headache of censorship. The
enemies one knows of and can identify are hard enough to
defeat; the blinders imposed by censorship make the truth
an enemy, and this is hardly reconciliable with our American heritage of freedom.

There is little in censorship, particularly censorship
of reading about sex, which can be defended on anything but
an emotional basis. No truly scientific or historical evidence exists to substantiate the hysterical, fanatical talk
(and that is all it is) of a direct, causal relationship between
reading about sex and sexual crimes. Indeed, there is some
scientific and historical evidence--strongly debated, it is
true, but still existent--that reading about sex is likely to
result in less sexual crime than what occurs under the rule
of censorship.

There is nothing inevitable or sacrosanct or sacred
or holy about censorship. There are societies which have
existed for a long time with it; there are equally viable and
active societies which have gone through their whole existence
without it; there are societies which have had periods in their
history of both strong censorship and, if there can be such
a term, strong anti- or non-censorship. No reasonable conclusions can be drawn from these facts, except that censorship is neither an essential nor a non-essential of people living together in a society, a culture. There is pretty good
evidence that strong, well-enforced, governmental censorship
is antithetical to true democracy.

15. THE SUPREME COURT, CENSORSHIP, AND EROS

"Of the forms of public education to which Americans recently have been exposed, none have been more expressive than the opinions of the Supreme Court, and especially in cases involving the interpretation of the First Amendment. The Supreme Court does not, normally, introduce into its reading of the Constitution explicitly 'moral' criteria. But according to the new conservatives it should do so."

--Donald Meiklejohn, Freedom and the Public: Public and Private Morality in America, 1965.

"However unhealthy we may think pornography to be, I do not believe the function of the law is to prohibit as such, nor to set itself up as the arbiter of what I may read or reject. The function of the law in the last ditch (and it is the last ditch) is to protect freedom."

--John A. T. Robinson, Christian Freedom in a Permissive Society, 1970.

Chapter 15

THE SUPREME COURT, CENSORSHIP, AND EROS

Here is an hypothesis and some tests of that hypothesis, and then an effort to see how well it can be supported as a theory. The hypothesis is this: the amount of censorship--legal and extra-legal--of writings on sexual matters in the United States increases in direct proportion to the level of authority which advocated censorship. In other words, when the president of the United States, the Senate and the House of Representatives, and, most of all, when the Supreme Court, countenance, indeed encourage, semi-vigilante censorship, something is going to happen.

The forces of censorship are always there, waiting for the forces of freedom to relax their vigilance, to give up, or to water down their efforts and concede victory. Indeed, the continuing struggle to weight one or the other sides of the ratio described in the above hypothesis is, to some extent, nearly the story, in its entirety, of the fight for the word in these United States.

One test of an hypothesis is to try it in reverse. Is it demonstrably true that as the level of authority that advocates censorship has gotten lower, the amount of U.S. censorship has decreased? There are two periods in American life when, practically speaking, there was little or no agitation or strong effort to censor most sex-related publications by any portion of the Federal government: nearly all of the first century of our history (1783-1873), and from 1957 to 1973.

During the first period, nearly a century before the so-called Comstock Law was passed, there were no Supreme Court decisions centering on sex-related literature; in fact, very little was recorded that would really be called serious censorship efforts by the courts of our nation. There is no record of any presidential comment concerning censorship,

211

nor, indeed, very much comment at all on the subject.   But, with the coming of Anthony Comstock there was quite a change in what the common citizen could read in relation to sex.   During the period between 1870 and 1957, actually, the fact that there was a Comstock Law on the Federal books seemed to be directly related to the fact that practically every state had its anti-obscenity law, and that it was usually left up to local and state courts to make decisions relative to obscenity.   There were some rather futile efforts by the Supreme Court to deal with this confused situation, but none worth any particular notice until 1957.

The problem of how to deal politically and practically with the moral issues supposedly involved in the publication and dissemination of supposedly obscene or/pornographic material is, of course, a most difficult one.   The solutions offered on the highest level of American jurisprudence, the Supreme Court, are interesting to the casual observer, but to the First Amendment devotee it is what the French call bouleversments (somehow a stronger term than flip-flops, the American equivalent) which are important.   It is really difficult to demonstrate any logical progression or reasonable succession in the various Supreme Court decisions in this country alone, on this complicated matter.

Or, is it really that difficult?   Is the dictum of "Mr. Dooley" that "Th' Supreme Court follows th' iliction returns, " as enunciated at the beginning of this century, the key to understanding Supreme Court activity, after all?   There are political scientists who feel strongly, as, for example, University of Minnesota professor Samuel Krislov has stated, that "the Court has indeed shown itself to be aware of the needs of group interaction and has consciously involved organized interests, at least in some small measure, in the deliberative processes of litigation.   It has explicitly adjusted remedies ... to practical exigencies and potential reaction of the populace. "[1]

These "explicitly adjusted remedies" have been confusing indeed.   Within the barely more than a decade spanning the landmark Roth decision and the Ginzburg case of 1968, there were less than fifty-five separate (and differing, to some extent) decisions in thirteen major cases involving obscenity and pornography. [2]

The dissenting opinion of Mr. Justice Harlan in Roth v. United States (1957) is illustrative of the state of almost

utter confusion resulting from the long string of conflicting
judicial opinions on obscenity and pornography by our top
Court's members.   Justice Harlan, in most legalistic language, made it clear that his solution to the dilemma of
whether the Supreme Court is or is not the "High Board of
Censors, " as one justice termed it, is a rather simple one:
he wanted the states to decide.

He shows his complete lack of knowledge of or willingness to accept the concept of freedom of reading as sub-
sumed in the First Amendment, with this truly remarkable
remark: "it seems to me that no overwhelming danger to
our freedom to experiment and to gratify our tastes in literature is likely to result from the suppression of a borderline
book in one of the States, so long as other states are free
to experiment with the same or bolder books. "3   And there
are fifty-four other equally individualistic opinions, which
certainly serve to give little, if any, followable guidance to
lower courts or, more importantly, to readers, writers, and
distributors of possibly "obscene" writings.

But let us get to the most recent Supreme Court in-
volvement with these matters.   One of these days your local
public, academic or school library--and, perhaps already,
your local bookstore or supermarket--are going to be invaded by men with stars on their chests who will remove
from the library or bookstore or newsstand such books as
Portnoy's Complaint, or Catcher in the Rye, or Brave New
World, or other contemporary classics, on the basis of the
precedent-making majority decisions of the U.S. Supreme
Court, as announced on June 21, 1973, in the cases of Miller v. California, Paris Adult Theater I v. Slaton, Kaplan v.
California, U.S. v. Orito, and U.S. v. 2200-Ft. Reels Film.
Slaton and Miller, in particular, will certainly effect the
reading, publishing, and distribution of sex-related materials
for Americans for years to come.

However, if precedent is any guide, they will not necessarily be operative for too many years.   There is no
guarantee that any decision by the Supreme Court will last
any particular length of time.   As of June 20, 1973, operat-
ing under a sixteen-year accumulation of relevant cases,
from Roth (1957) to Memoirs (1966), no library, no bookstore, no newsstand in the United States should have had any
qualms whatsoever about distributing or selling a wide variety of printed items which dealt quite explicitly, in language
and content, with sexual behavior.   After June 20, 1973,
even Playboy was under fire.

What had happened?   Putting it most directly, Richard
Nixon had happened.   During his first four years in office,
death and other circumstances gave him the opportunity to
fill no less than four Supreme Court seats.   A statistical
study has shown that since Congress stabilized the size of
the Court to nine justices in 1869, on the average a vacancy
in the Supreme Court has come up about every seventeen
months.   So the U.S. president serving two terms (ninety-
six months) could reasonably expect to appoint from four to
five members to the Supreme Court--but Nixon was fortunate
enough to be able to appoint four in less than forty-eight
months.   Statistically, he may be able to appoint four more
before his term ends on Inaguration Day, 1977.

His four appointees--Chief Justice Burger and Justices Blackmun, Rehnquist, and Powell, along with Kennedy-
appointed White--have combined to virtually reverse the comparatively libertarian trend of previous courts since 1957.
They chorused the Nixon feelings about the effects and significance of obscenity and pornography, as stated in his public comments on the report of the Commission on Obscenity
and Pornography.   When this commission issued its report
(which, by a majority vote, recommended repeal of all
"Federal, state, and local legislation prohibiting the sale,
exhibition, or distribution of sexual material to consenting
adults," President Nixon responded vigorously with his own
(undocumented) dictum that "pornography can corrupt society
and civilization.   The people's elected representatives have
the right and obligation to prevent that corruption."   He
didn't say anything about the Supreme Court at that point,
but it seems much more than a coincidence that his activities in recommending changes in the U.S. criminal code
(in relation to obscenity) as of March, 1973 almost exactly
pre-figured the statements by Chief Justice Burger in the
relevant decisions rendered only three months later.

But just what was the content and meaning of the
Burger decision in Slaton?   And how does it encourage the
censor?   In this decision, remarkable in many respects,
may be found a number of fascinating obiter dicta, each of
which merits individual attention:

1.   "The sum of experience, including that of the
past two decades, affords an ample basis for legislatures to
conclude a sensitive, key relationship of human existence,
central to family life, community welfare, and the development of human personality, can be debased and distorted by

crass commercial exploitation of sex.   Nothing in the Constitution prohibits a State from reaching such a conclusion
and acting on it legislatively simply because there is no conclusive evidence or empirical data. "

        Note particularly the second sentence.   Here, in a
few words, the prevailing rules of evidence of Anglo-American jurisprudence and the values, if any, of modern social
science methodology are disposed of.   The Supreme Court of
the United States, in a 1973 majority decision which becomes
the prevailing law of the land, has told us that state legis-
latures--in other matters, as well as in dealing with obscenity and pornography--need not act from now on upon
"conclusive evidence or empirical data. " The only logical
corollary must be that the state legislatures, with the approval and even urging of our highest Court, may act on in-
conclusive evidence and non-empirical data!

        Yet, in the first of this astonishing pair of non-
sequitur statements, we have been told that "the sum of experience" is to be the "ample basis" for anti-obscenity legislation from now on.   And "empirical, " any standard dictionary will tell you, means "probable or verifiable by experience
or experiment. " So, sentence one says to the legislators:
"Do it: experience backs you in your actions, " and sentence
two says: "Do it: don't wait for 'empirical' (experiential)
data. "

        Now there's an obiter dictum for you, fairly strad-
dling both sides of a problem and accepting absolutely opposed arguments to prove a point.

        2.   "Such laws [laws concerning obscenity] are to
protect the weak, the uninformed, the unsuspecting, and the
gullible from the exercise of their own volition. " Here is
a clear echo in this June 21 Supreme Court decision of the
Nixon statement (delivered in a pre-1972-election interview)
to the effect that Americans as a whole are to be treated as
children: certainly "the weak, the uninformed, the unsuspecting, and the gullible" need protection from those who
would and could exploit them.   But wouldn't it be a far greater protection to use the efforts of government to make the
weak strong, the uninformed informed, to warn the unsuspecting, and to see what can be done to make the gullible
less gullible?   We still permit cigarettes to be sold legally
and widely--but we do put a warning sign about health-im-
pairment danger on the advertisements for cigarettes, as
well as on their packages.

The question is, does the normal adult American
really need to be shielded from the so-called "facts of life?"
In their joint dissent in Paris v. Slaton, Justices Brennan,
Stewart, and Marshall reached quite different conclusions.
They based their dictum on the almost self-evident fact that
there is absolutely no way to define obscenity or even to
define the terms which seek to define the first term.   Referring to such "indefinite concepts as 'prurient intent,'
'patent offensiveness,' 'serious literary value,' and the
like ...," Justice Brennan's dissent (for the three justices)
says, "The meaning of these concepts necessarily varies
with the experience, outlook, and even idiosyncrasies of the
person defining them."   And, if the censoriously-minded
have so wide a choice as the five June 21, 1973 Supreme
Court majority decisions now permit, then we must really
begin to worry about the power of the censor over American
reading and writing and publishing.   As Justice Brennan
opined, "Although we have assumed that obscenity does exist
and that we know it when [we] see it, ... we are manifestly
unable to describe it in advance except by reference to concepts so elusive that they fail to distinguish clearly between
protected and corrupted speech."

There is an even more fundamental principle than
what Brennan calls the "void-for-vagueness doctrine" which
should be considered (although the majority opinion did not
consider it).   Brennan's dissent stresses Chief Justice Warren's important point in United States v. Harris (1954),
which was that "the Constitutional requirement of definiteness
is violated by a criminal statute that fails to give a person
of ordinary intelligence fair notice that his contemplated conduct is forbidden by the statute.   The underlying principle
is that no man shall be held criminally responsible for conduct which he could not reasonably understand to be proscribed."   Where does that leave the poor librarian, who,
presumably, under the five-case 1973 obscenity decisions
has really no way of knowing how "arbitrary and erratic enforcement of the law," which Brennan says is invited by
vague laws, will affect him.   Brennan calls "the resulting
level of uncertainty ... utterly intolerable."   And, one may
venture to guess, it may well, on this basis if no other,
eventually be reversed by a future, less moralistic, more
equity-seeking majority of the Supreme Court.

There is a post-Supreme Court-decision development
which should cast some light to clear away the murk of re-
vived Puritanism.   In August, 1973, the National Advisory

Commission on Criminal Justice Standards and Goals (a
"blue ribbon" group appointed by Nixon-appointed Jerris
Leonard, Administrator of the Law Enforcement Assistance
Administration of the U. S. Department of Justice) recommended that all "States review criminal statutes dealing with
gambling, marijuana use and possession for use, pornography, prostitution, and sexual acts between consenting adults
in private, to determine if current laws best serve the purposes of the State and the needs of the people; and, as a
minimum, States remove incarceration as a penalty for these
offences, except when these offences involve a willful attempt to affect others in these areas, such as pandering,
public lewdness, and sale or possession for sale of marijuana. "4

This Commission seems to be following on the pre-
viously-cited 1970 recommendation of the Commission on
Obscenity and Pornography, particularly in its suggestion,
in regard to pornography, that "some States may decide,
upon reevaluation of existing laws, to retain the laws or to
modify or repeal them altogether. " It does say that "there
may be some need to control pornography where children
could be exposed to explicit sexual material. " It describes
its list of victimless crimes as follows (and certainly por-
nography-distribution meets their definition): "these acts
usually consist of behavior that does not pose a direct threat
to others, but that often generates strong social disapproval. "5

The Commission, by the way, was a quite represen-
tative one, including the Governor of Delaware (Chairman),
the Sheriff of Los Angeles County, the Chief of Police of
Omaha, Nebraska, the 1968-72 Governor of Montana, a
woman D. C. Superior Court judge, a Professor of Criminal
Justice at the University of Illinois, the Chief of Police of
Dallas, Texas, a woman member of the National Advisory
Council on Vocational Education, the Chairman of the New
York State Narcotic Addiction Control Commission, a prominent Omaha lawyer, the mayor of Indianapolis, Indiana, the
Director of the Georgia State Board of Corrections, an Idaho
Supreme Court Justice, the Attorney General of Arizona, the
Director of the Kentucky Crime Commission, the Commis-
sioner of the Georgia Department of Public Safety, a Lutheran
minister, the President of the National Council on Crime
and Delinquency, the District Attorney of Philadelphia, the
president of a large manufacturing corporation, a Baptist
minister, and (ex officio) the Assistant Administrator of the

LEEA. But what influence, if any, these Commission recommendations will have remains to be seen.

Thus we end as we began, contemplating one of the
aspects of man that seems to be unlikely to be altered in
our time--but there is always hope. There need not be
such a demeaning of the human spirit, of the basic human
character, as to concede the ineluctable necessity for censorship; after all, murder and war and other human individual and social failings have continued throughout human history, but the vast majority of humans and the moral and
social and religious codes of most of mankind have inveighed
against these imperfections.

Early in this volume the insights of that great Egypt-
ologist and philosopher, James Henry Breasted, were adduced, relative to one of the earliest known inscribed statements on the importance of the Word. As Breasted reports,
in an Egyptian papyrus dating back to nearly 2,000 B. C. the
statement is made that "all things came into being through
that which the heart (mind) thought and the tongue (speech)
commanded. " Breasted translates this to signify that "the
agency by which mind became creative force was the spoken
word which enunciated the idea and gave it reality. The
idea thus took on being in the world of objective existence.
The god himself is identified with the heart which thinks,
and the tongue which speaks. "6

So that Word which was in the beginning, that Word
identified with deity by Egyptians four thousand years ago
and by Christians two millenia ago becomes a fearful and
sacred object--so much so that only certain privileged ones
can read some words and not be driven to immoral, unso-
cial, or even criminal action. The Censor fears the Word.
Must everyone do so in perpetuity?

In this year of 1973, when these final words of this
book were being written, a year when for the first time in
its history America was riven by a horrendous political
scandal involving, it seemed, almost every type of conceivable crime (except obscenity and pornography!), bringing low
some of the highest officials in the land, it appears to be
more than a coincidence that the same Americans who were
denied knowledge of some of the basic facts in the Watergate
scandal, by presidential fiat on the basis of "national security, " were also denied the right to read what they, as

consenting adults, wished to read, on the basis of <u>moral</u>
"security. "

The President of the United States, in a public newspaper interview just before the 1972 election, stated that he
regarded the average American as "just like a child in the
family, " to be treated as such by his government.   In
March, 1973 he recommended to Congress alterations in the
U. S. Criminal Code to convert this point of view into Federal law, as it related to the defining of the content and
punishing of writings deemed obscene and/or pornographic.

The Supreme Court of the United States, in a series
of 5-4 decisions in June, 1973, indicated they felt just about
the same way.   Local governmental authorities--censors--
moved swiftly to take advantage of these decisions to bar a
great deal of material which they had not dared to touch
within the sixteen years since <u>U. S. v. Roth.</u>

"In the Beginning was the Word, " and those who reverence several particular words--Truth and Freedom among
them--cannot let raw undiscerning Fear become <u>the</u> Word
which rules their lives and their nation.   The Censor thrives
on Fear--Fear of the Truth, Fear of freedom, Fear of human emotions, Fear, in particular, of the human body as a
sexual entity.   There is no use wishing that censors and
censorship will somehow vanish; it will take knowledge and
reason a long time, in this as in other human emotion-
rousing situations, to triumph.

But no one who believes in intellectual freedom can
with impunity overlook or denigrate the sheer power of the
censorial impulse and effort which has continued through recorded time.   It will take constant, undisturbing effort by
all who really desire to live with truth and freedom to fight
the Censor.   But such an unending enterprise is well worth
the effort required.   Without it, we may all well lose much
more than merely the right to read about sexually-involved
doings.   Political censorship is, and has been, all too often
in human history, the result or concomitant of sexual censorship.

But that is another story.   In a world composed of
men <u>and</u> women, mostly living in organized communities and
nations, the worship of Demos and of Eros are inextricably
and permanently intertwined.   And the Censor, really worshipping and reverencing only Mrs. Grundy, will, to a

greater or lesser extent, strive to place <u>his</u> god above all
others.

Just so long as we fear the Word, we may expect to
have to knuckle under to the Censor, and mankind, in the
ages-long quest for Truth, will continue to face almost in-
superable obstacles.

The Censor Fears the Word.   The Censor Fears the
Truth.   But the Truth is mighty, and shall prevail.

EPILOG: PORTRAIT OF THE CENSOR

"... at the bottom of it [Comstockery] ... there lies
that insistent presentation of the idea of sin, that enchant-
ment by concepts of carnality, which has enjoyed a certain
type of man, to the exclusion of all other notions, since the
dawn of history. "

--H. L. Mencken, A Book of Prefaces, 1917.

EPILOG

PORTRAIT OF THE CENSOR

There he stands--the Eternal Censor, the true believer in the Everlasting Nay. He is proud of his calling,
and willing, fanatically, to give up a great deal (sometimes
even his life) to keep the Bad from affecting the Good. He
knows intuitively what is evil, and he needs no legalistic
definitions to clarify his thinking. Only he, the Censor,
among all men, unerringly can tell the obscene and the pornographic and the scatological and the blasphemous and the
subversive from what is good, without more than a moment's
consideration. His mind has a built-in dowsing rod for all
the words of sin, and his divination of where the dirtiest of
dirt can be found is never less than accurate.

Through his eyes the world comes in just two shapes
--the lingam and the yoni--and the artistic creators always
seem to manage to mold whatever they are creating into
these two forms. There is no use trying to fool the Censor;
he can always tell what those rascally creatures, the imaginative artists, are really doing. What others might accept as
reality, he recognizes as exaggeration. What most might
consider artistic exaggeration, he can readily identify as obscene and pornographic. Whatever is obscene and pornographic by his standards must at least be expurgated, better
barred, at best obliterated for all time.

The Censor is not to be gulled by the literary fustian
which the critics and authors have draped around their presumably "artistic" goals. The Censor knows that there is
almost a direct correlation between practically anything
called "literature" and just plain filth--particularly today.
Nowadays, says the Censor (and he was saying this long before Kinsey or even Freud), only a very few authors are
writing about anything that doesn't come down, if properly
understood, to just raw sex. And the idea of sex promulgated
by these authors has nothing to do with the right way to think

222

and write about it; they dare to write about sex as if it were
--can you believe it?--pleasurable and joyous, fun and
games.

One cardinal tenet of the Censor is that, of all bad
things, sex is the worst. And the Censor is on intimate
terms with the truth about sex--the ultimate truth that is too
truthful for the mass of men.

The Censor never had to take lessons on that part of
Alice's Looking-Glass curriculum which included "Derision"
and "Uglification." As a literary critic, the Censor is always destructive; even if the destruction only succeeds in
eliminating a paragraph, a word, or a letter, it is eminently
worth doing. After all, the letter or word or paragraph removed from public view might be the very one which, if
read, would turn a moral, innocuous individual into an evil,
ravening sex-fiend.

The Censor alone is entitled to lower himself into
that cloacal abyss which is writing about sex; somehow the
filth which would enmire and besmirch the average man never affects him. He is thrice armed by his preordained and
appropriate roles of combined judge, jury, and appeals agency, a position which places him far above the average run
of impressionable men. It is from that lofty pinnacle that
he asserts his own purity and the innate impropriety of all
other men. His strength is both a result and a cause of the
weakness and impressionability of others.

The sock of comedy and the buskin of tragedy, to the
Censor, are both equally guilty accomplices in helping make
appealing and palatable to the masses the iniquitous, the
perverse, the base. Indeed, it is not really the morally unfit book or magazine or play which appalls the Censor, so
much as the very idea that sex exists. He dreads that
three-letter-word more than all the more explicit four-letter-
words put together.

Who is The Censor?

He is Cato, and St. Paul, and St. Augustine, and
Pope Paul IV, and Martin Luther. He is Savonarola, and
Torquemada, and Calvin, and Cromwell. He is Cotton
Mather, Thomas Bowdler, Lord Campbell, Chief Justice
Cockburn, Anthony Comstock, John S. Sumner, Senator Reed
Smoot, Joseph Stalin, Charles de Gaulle, Postmaster General
Arthur Summerfield, Congressman E. C. Gathings, Senator

Everett Dirksen, Senator McClellan, and President Richard Nixon. He is, indeed, not always "he." The Censor is Queen Victoria, Carry Nation, Congresswoman Kathryn Granahan. He is Catholic, Jewish, Protestant. He is Mormon, Christian Scientist, Seventh Day Adventist, Dowieite, Owenite. He is deistic and atheistic and agnostic. He is English and Irish and French and Scottish and Italian and German and Russian and Chinese and American. At various times he has worn skins, and armor, and monk's robes, and a tuxedo, and a suit "right off the rack."

He is Everyman, sometime, everywhere--and, to some extent always, he is the man or woman in <u>your</u> mirror!

APPENDIX A

AN ANTI-CENSORSHIP CHRESTOMATHY

"... any one brought up among Puritans knew that sex was sin. In any previous age, sex was strength. "
--Henry Adams, The Education of Henry Adams, 1918.

"... a strict censorship breeds scepticism and disrespect for state and society ... in a world which is being steadily integrated by the means of social communication many forms of censorship are simply ineffective.... "
--Michael Adams, Censorship: the Irish Experience, 1968.

"Man defends himself as much as he can against truth. "
--Henri Frederic Amiel, Private Journal, 1885.

"... all censorship is likely to be unenlightened, for ignorance and stupidity are usually implicit in the consent of persons to act as censors. "
--Harry Elmer Barnes, An Intellectual and Cultural History of the Western World, 1937.

"... absolute freedom does not exist. We are free in so far as the limitations of our culture do not oppress us; we are unfree when we become conscious of these limitations and are no longer willing to submit to them. "
--Franz Boas, "Liberty Among Primitive People, " 1940.

"If any word or expression is of such a nature that the first impression it excites is an impression of obscenity, that word ought not to be spoken nor written or printed; and, if printed, it ought to be erased. "
--Thomas Bowdler, 1818.

225

"... human sexual activities would seem to be an especially clear and often extreme example of the fact that the
word and the deed are not necessarily very closely united in
human life.   It may even be true that Homo sapiens spends
more time and energy fantasying, thinking, talking, and writing about sex then in doing anything about it. "
            --Crane Brinton, A History of Western Morals, 1959.

"... it is not unfair to say that most Christian thought
distrusts the whole natural man--his appetites for food,
drink, gaming, fighting, and vainglory, as well as for sexual indulgence.   Catholic Christianity has always provided a
place for the rare individual who wished to subdue the flesh.
Protestant Christianity has been less successful with such
people, who under Protestantism have generally had to turn
their ascetic drive toward reforming the conduct of others
on earth. "
            --Crane Brinton, John B. Christopher, and Robert
            Lee Wolff, A History of Civilization, 1955.

"... it does begin to appear that the case for legislation against obscenity rests, ultimately and solely, not upon
any hard factoral analysis of anti-social consequences but on
a vague generalised residual apprehension that sexual desire
is a form of depravity and should be depressed by law. "
            --British Arts Council Working Party Report on Ob-
            scenity, 1969.

'I should like very much to be able to live again and
to arrange for my own bringing up.   Under such circumstances I should provide that some parent, guardian, or
teacher should give me a dirty book as required reading.
This ought to happen at about the age of eight or nine, for
at the end the little scholar could hardly fail to say, 'And
is this all there is to it?'   Thereafter he might mature to
useful life, untroubled by vague speculations concerning the
exciting horrors of the unknown. "
            --Heywood Broun, Anthony Comstock, 1927.

"But now I'm going to be immoral; now
I mean to show things really as they are,
Not as they ought to be. "
            --Byron, Don Juan, 1824.

"... the habit of censorship is persistent and dangerous because it is so difficult to get agreement upon what
shall be censored. "
            --Henry Seidel Canby, American Memoir, 1947.

"I would confine myself to prohibiting public nuisances by law and hope that other institutions could raise the level of literary taste. Surely a liberal society is capable of distinguishing between art and trash.... The circulation of pornography, even of hard-core pornography, does not undermine this distinction or anything else that is fundamental to our social arrangements...."
> --Marshall Cohen, "On Pornography: Dissenting and Consenting Opinions," in: The Public Interest (Winter, 1971).

"Man is the only animal who arrives at sexual maturity before he achieves social maturity, so that every society develops codes which are designed to prevent a man's becoming a grandfather before he can vote."
> --William Graham Cole, Sex in Christianity and Psychoanalysis, 1955.

"Painting and literature which celebrate physical sexuality ... are not absent from our experience because artists had no inclination to produce them, or because there was no demand for them, but because they have been concealed, prohibited and destroyed by an active minority determined to see we did not get them. A whole segment of art, literature, and even everyday speech has been deleted, against the will and the real mores of our culture."
> --Alex Comfort, Darwin and the Naked Lady, 1961.

"If a culture encourages a form of sex expression--be it homosexuality or excessive prudery--all those will show it who can; in a culture which discourages it, only those will show it who must."
> --Alex Comfort, Sex in Society, 1966.

"I do not believe that Christians should advocate pre-censorship or the prohibition of any work of art, short story, picture or novel however questionable it may seem to us. We have erred too frequently in the past to allow ourselves to be the judges of another man's conscience."
> --Harvey G. Cox, Jr., "Sexuality and Responsibility: a New Phase," in: John Charles Wynn, ed., Sexual Ethics and Christian Responsibility, 1970.

"I believe that Christians should be just as vigorous in criticizing the deplorable taste, bad writing, and dehumanizing effects of much of the contemporary flood of pornographic literature as anyone else. We do this however by

pointing out its weaknesses and by encouraging the production
of better and more adequate depictions of human life, not by
preventing its publication. Also we object to it not because
of some shrinking violet attitudes about what should or should
not be published but because we have an unswerving commitment to the protection of intimacy and privacy in human
life. "
> --Harvey G. Cox, "Sexuality and Responsibility, "
> 1970.

"Biologically eroticism is a temporary phenomenon:
what lures us at night repels us at morning. Consequently
we are all tempted to be both readers of erotic books and
censors of sexual literature. Moral integrity and clear
thinking should enable modern communities to resolve the
tensions created by these opposing attitudes without hurt to
the spread of truth, the increase of beauty, and the furtherance of the good life. "
> --Alec Craig, Suppressed Books, 1963.

"I do know ... what censorship accomplishes, creating an unreal and hypocritical mythology, fomenting an attraction for forbidden fruit, inhibiting the creative minds
among us and fostering an illicit trade. Above all, it cur-
tails the right of the individual ... to satisfy his intellect
and his interest without harm. "
> --Judith Crist, in: Harold H. Hart, ed. Censorship:
> For & Against, 1971.

"Everybody has to choose, and no one will honor a
man who abstains from a vice of which he has no knowledge,
nor a teacher who feigns that pleasure does not exist. "
> --Edward Dahlberg, "On Passions and Asceticisms, "
> 1965.

"Censorship is not peculiarly Victorian; indeed, there
has probably not been a year since man became a social animal that it has not played an active role in government.... "
> --Clarence R. Decker, The Victorian Conscience,
> 1952.

"Censorship--that is, criticism enforced by political
action--is an index of official taste throughout the ages.... "
> --Clarence R. Decker, The Victorian Conscience,
> 1952.

"In the end, men do what they can do. They refrain

from doing what they cannot do. They do what their own
specific powers in conjunction with the limitations and resources of the environment permit. The effective control of
their power is not through precepts, but through the regulation of their conditions. "
    --John Dewey, "Intelligence and Morals, " 1910.

"... literature should not be suppressed merely because it offends the moral code of the censor. "
    --Justice William O. Douglas (Dissent, Roth v. U.S.,
    1957).

"It is fear--in reality a kind of fear-complex--which
dominates the people who practise secrecy and enforce repression in a matter where secrecy and repression are obviously against Nature and therefore certain to produce results which are worse than futile. "
    --Havelock Ellis, On Life and Sex, 1957.

"The code of decency of an age springs directly from
the people of that age; it represents a consensus; it cannot
be dictated by saints or sinners. If the majority of people
at any time and place want something which is objectionable
to those in power, they will get it no matter how rigorous
the interdict. "
    --Morris L. Ernst and Alexander Lindey, The Censor
    Marches On, 1940.

"While a minor's pornography law would satisfy many
of those who are still exercised over the effects of obscenity
on adolescence, we have faith that education, through school
and home, will prove the enduring solution. To be sure,
the method is slow, but its benefits are lasting. It is easier
to form the plastic child mind in the habits of decency than
to rely upon censorship legislation. "
    --Morris L. Ernst and William Seagle, To the
    Pure..., 1929.

"What artists we should be ... if from the outset
some guardian angel of the purity of our pens had kept us
from all contamination.... "
    --Gustave Flaubert, Letter to Louise Colet, 1846.

"... when a person calls a word obscene, indecent, or
dirty, this is an indication of his state of mind; neither the
words themselves nor the things they stand for can properly
be described as obscene, indecent, or dirty. "
    --Peter Fryer, Mrs. Grundy, 1964.

"The most injurious books are those that attempt to negate the strength of sex passion, to minimize the importance of the erotic element in life, and to impose impossible repression of thought. "
--Walter M. Gallichan, The Poison of Prudery, 1929.

". . . the only means of suppressing speech which some persons would describe as indecent would be the entire suppression of literature. "
--Walter M. Gallichan, The Poison of Prudery, 1929.

"It would be a bad state of affairs if reading had a more immoral effect than life itself, which daily develops scandalous scenes in abundance, if not before our eyes then before our ears. Even with children we need not by any means be too anxious about the effects of a book or a play. As I have said, daily life is more effective than the most effective book. "
--Goethe, Dialogues with Eckermann, 1832.

"Prohibiting is prohibited. Liberty begins with prohibition: feed not on the liberty of others. "
--Graffiti written on the walls of a Paris university building during the French student rioting, 1968.

"The constant state of prohibition, of denunciation, of interference with private life, of strife, of public inquiry, which is characteristic of the American conception of sex, constitutes in itself a neurosis of a very specific kind; a neurosis in which the mind is continually obsessed by sexual thoughts, the omnipotence of which is testified by the frantic efforts that are made to overcome them.
--René Guyon, The Ethics of Sexual Acts, 1934.

"To put thought in leash to the average conscience of the time is perhaps tolerable, but to fetter it by the necessities of the lowest and least capable seems a fatal policy. "
--Judge Learned Hand, in: U. S. v. Kennerley, 1913.

"Government restraint of culture is being replaced by a smiling, very genteel dictatorship of private citizens who seek to do what the law cannot do. "
--Robert W. Haney, Comstockery in America, 1960.

"Are we to have a censor whose imprimatur shall say what books may be sold, and what we may buy? ... Whose foot is to be the measure to which ours are all to be cut or

stretched? ... For God's sake, let us freely hear both
sides, if we choose. "
      --Thomas Jefferson, A Letter to Dufief, 1814.

"Liberals must educate, or others will censor. "
      --Iredell Jenkins, "The Laissez-Faire Theory of
        Artistic Censorship, " 1944.

"Censorship of books ... is an advantageous katharsis
for the semi-literate. "
      --Gerald W. Johnson, "The Devil Is Dead and What a
        Loss, " 1947.

"Puritanism ... is a religion that prevents nobody
from sinning, but does prevent anybody from enjoying it. "
      --Gerald W. Johnson, "The Devil Is Dead and What
        a Loss, " 1947.

"The activity of censoring not only permits but mor-
alizes and glorifies ... preoccupation with sex. "
      --Horace M. Kallen, Indecency and the Seven Arts,
        1930.

"So long as culture and morality are seen as the
Sacred Superego, unassailable by doubt, we are imprisoned
in eternal childhood by the fathers of the past. "
      --Weston La Barre, The Human Animal, 1954.

"There are ... synthetic fathers in every age who
promise to purvey The Truth--in return for a docile child-
like faith, prayerful dependent obedience, and sometimes the
surrender of goods and the abnegation of sexuality. "
      --Weston La Barre, The Human Animal, 1954.

"...in an increasingly impersonal world, we should
be increasingly wary of handing over decisions to any form
of Authority--not least decisions about what we ourselves,
and our children, should be allowed to see, hear and read. "
      --J. W. Lambert, "The Folly of Censorship, "
        Encounter, July, 1967.

"Man is the animal which by nature is ashamed of
its sexual attributes, goes in fear of their consequences and
regards its female half as inferior, if not degenerate. Why
this is so is the problem of psychology.... "
      --John Langdon-Davies, Sex, Sin and Sanctity, 1954.

"One of the great differences between civilised and savage communities is that the latter obey the law and the priests, whereas we do not. We may disapprove of the savage's idea of what is proper with regard to sexual intercourse, but we must admit that he is good according to his light whereas we are not. We approve our code and have a tacit understanding with one another that it shall not be kept."

--John Langdon-Davies, Sex, Sin and Sanctity, 1954.

"The only way to stop the terrible mental itch about sex is to come out quite simply and naturally into the open with it."

--D. H. Lawrence, Pornography and Obscenity, 1930.

"The laws as to 'obscenity' and so forth are ... perfectly irrelevant, and completely unenforceable, though one cannot hope for their total disappearance without the disappearance also, or at least the desuetude, of anti-sexual Western religion."

--Gershon Legman, The Horn Book, 1964.

"The principal periods of erotic publishing have, historically, almost always preceded and followed revolutions, depressions, protracted wars, and similar upheavals."

--Gershon Legman, The Horn Book, 1964.

"... when writers are allowed to write anything they please and publishers to put it in circulation, then the great responsibility for discrimination rests with the reader."

--Harry Levin, Refractions, 1966.

"Barring the universal crimes against life and property, a society will bear down most heavily upon those actions toward which its members are most vividly drawn, but which some ghostly superstition causes them to fear."

--Ludwig Lewisohn, Expression in America, 1932.

"It is undeniable that numerous classes of readers still regard books as either a pastime or as an illustration of their antecedent certainties. For these classes it is not illogical to demand that a censorship suppress or an Index condemn books which, conflicting with their antecedent certainties, they must conceive of as false and therefore harmful."

--Ludwig Lewisohn, Expression in America, 1932.

"So far as morals go, the law is concerned with the minimum. It sets the standard below which civilization should not sink, but it cannot pretend to say how the best of men should live."
     --Walter Lippmann, "Law and Order," 1915.

"There is no itch in the religion of the spirit to make men good by bearing down on them with righteousness and making them conform to a pattern. Its social principle is live and let live ... Its principle is to civilize the passions, not by regulating them imperiously, but by transforming them with a mature understanding of their place in an adult environment."
     --Walter Lippmann, A Preface to Morals, 1929.

"Nothing is so galling to a people, not broken in from the birth, as a paternal or, in other words, a meddling government, a government which tells them what to read and say and eat and drink and wear."
     --Thomas Babington Macaulay, Southey's Colloquies, 1830.

"Sex is a great and wonderful power for evil and for good, and we must deal with it as we deal with other forces of nature: understand, respect and control it in the light of truth and not in the shadows of prejudice and preconception."
     --Bronislaw Malinowski, "Havelock Ellis," 1931.

"...who or what makes anybody anywhere at any time for any reason indignant is obscene."
     --Ludwig Marcuse, Obscene, 1965.

"To achieve a pseudo-homogeneity, modern man must outlaw and suppress, purge and interdict, those persons and ideas who challenge a falsely over-simplified scheme. At best he achieves only a precarious and synthetic homogeneity, built not upon the honesty of limited knowledge, but upon a dogmatic selection from a wide range of knowledge which will not fit upon his Procrustean bed. And at the same time, any attempt at a single standard sacrifices all the hard-won gains of heterogeneity--freedom of thought, with resulting freedom of inquiry into the natural world, respect for contrasting and complementary values, all the new values which are constantly born of intricacy and complexity--all would go."
     --Margaret Mead, From the South Seas, 1939.

"Pornography exists, not because unscrupulous fiends print and sell it, but because it is a part of our nature. There is, therefore, no question of whether we will have pornography. We will have it, as we have it now, and as we have always had it. The question is quite simply whether we can stand our own humanity."
>   --Peter Michelson, The Aesthetics of Pornography,
>   1971.

"The responsibility of society, if it accepts poetry as a mode of knowledge, is to remain open to what poets of all genres, including the pornographic, have to say. Otherwise all mirrors will soon reflect the same imbecilic smile."
>   --Peter Michelson, The Aesthetics of Pornography,
>   1971.

"The artist must conform to the current, and usually hypocritical, attitude of the majority. He must be original, courageous, inspiring, and all that--but never too disturbing. He must say Yes while saying No."
>   --Henry Miller, Remember to Remember, 1947.

"Puritans did not think that the state was merely an umpire.... The state to them was an active instrument of leadership, discipline, and, whenever necessary, of coercion; it legislated over any or all aspects of human behavior, it not merely regulated misconduct but undertook to inspire and direct all conduct."
>   --Perry Miller, Errand into the Wilderness, 1956.

"The morality of a given society is not the morality of the writer of genius: he would simply not be a writer of genius if it were."
>   --John Middleton Murry, Pencillings, 1923.

"The trouble is that we cannot talk on sexual matters without making the waters turbid. We must be able to think on this subject and speak of it in a way that is really natural ... This subject is the vital center of society. It is the soul of the fine arts."
>   --John Humphrey Noyes, quoted in: Gilbert Seldes,
>   The Stammering Century, 1928.

"... much of the rejection of pornography can be traced to the fact that this is a kind of information a great many individuals do not want to have about themselves."
>   --Morse Peckham, Art and Pornography, 1969.

"...whatever the government decides to do about pornography, we may be reasonably sure that at best it will
barely avoid making a bad mistake. "
    --Morse Peckham, Art and Pornography, 1969.

"Considering the instruments at its command, government will sometimes most effectively serve liberty by leaving the regulation of private interests to private institutions,
such as church, school, or charitable organization, or to the
unofficial power of the social conscience ... the mechanisms
of public enforcement are ill suited to distinguish between
art and pornography.... "
    --Ralph Barton Perry, "Liberty in a Democratic
      State, " 1940.

"...because the great sex-taboo, in place of liberating us from ... over-preoccupation with sex, increases and
intensifies it, it is to the advantage of simple human happiness that this taboo shall be criticized and analyzed if not
modified and relaxed. "
    --John Cooper Powys, Psychoanalysis and Morality,
      1923.

"The evil man meddles, interferes, and insists on
regulating a person's life. "
    --John Cooper Powys, In Defence of Sensuality, 1930.

"The Index (including under this term the whole system of censorship) came to constitute one of the more important of the influences which have worked through the centuries towards the narrowing of the Church Universal (the
magnificent ideal of the Middle Ages) into the organization
known in our twentieth century as the Church of Rome. "
    --George Haven Putnam, The Censorship of the
      Church of Rome, 1906.

"Censorships ... are never to be judged or their
effects measured by ... what they have excised from
material before them.   What evil they do is done partly
by distortion of what does come through, but principally by
the general influence that they exercise upon the future
course of production.   A policy line pursued by a censorship
may be only negative in the first place; but regularly per-
sisted in it becomes positively creative, since men will
shape their output to what is likely to be accepted. "
    --C. J. R. Radcliffe, Censors, 1961.

"Whatever one's attitude to sex is, it cannot be denied that a great part of its attraction arises from curiosity, from its being kept secret and forbidden."
--Otto Rank, Modern Education, 1932.

"Repression surrounds the desired objects with an allure they do not have otherwise, and attributes to them power and peril beyond reality."
--Theodor Reik, Myth and Guilt, 1957.

"The true censor has objectives beyond the masking of the erotic and the indecent. The end in view is an established principle of suppression, available anywhere in the world of the mind."
--Charles Rembar, The End of Obscenity, 1968.

"...the irrationality of regarding sex as something dirty is becoming inescapable."
--Theodor Roseburg, Life on Man, 1969.

"...the only obligation of the artist is between himself and his piece of paper. Morals, ethics, society, institutions of behavior--all these impinge upon his work but only by chance."
--Karl Shapiro, "A Malebolge of Fourteen Hundred Books," 1968.

"All censorships exist to prevent anyone from challenging current conceptions and existing institutions. All progress is initiated by challenging current conceptions, and executed by supplanting existing institutions. Consequently the first condition of progress is the removal of censorships. There is the whole case against censorships in a nutshell."
--George Bernard Shaw, Preface to Mrs. Warren's Profession, 1902.

"...all support of censorship should be considered as problems of abnormal psychology."
--Theodore Schroeder, A Challenge to the Sex Censors, 1938.

"In one word, it must always be foul to tell what is false; and it can never be safe to suppress what is true."
--Robert Louis Stevenson, "The Morality of the Profession of Journalism," 1898.

"To deceive the young and deprive them of their

inheritance for fear of corruption is risky indeed, far more
risky than to endow them with what is rightfully theirs, even
when this includes error and evil, for they are called to be
men. "
> --Irving and Cornelia Sussman, How To Read a Dirty
> Book, 1966.

"I would rather have all the risk which comes from
free discussion of sex than the great risk we run by a con-
spiracy of silence.... We want to liberate the sex impulse
from the impression that it is always to be surrounded by
negative warnings and restraints, and to place it in its
rightful place among the great creative and formative things. "
> --William Temple, Archbishop of Canterbury (quoted
> in: David Mace, The Christian Response to the
> Sexual Revolution, 1970), 1930.

"The relevant question at any stage of human history
is not 'Does censorship exist?' but rather, 'Under what sort
of censorship do we now live?'"
> --Donald Thomas, A Long Time Burning, 1969.

"History teaches us that the accursed of to-day may
be--perhaps is likely to be--the blessed of tomorrow; yet
we continue to curse and excommunicate and to fancy that
in so doing we are sending up grateful incense to the God of
peace and love. "
> --W. P. Trent, "Some Remarks on Modern Book-
> Burning, " 1905.

"...the man who cares only for the books that ex-
pound and defend the causes he espouses is really a foe,
and a very dangerous one, to literature. "
> --W. P. Trent, Greatness in Literature, 1905.

"The early documents of the Reformation contain bril-
liant declarations of the rights of conscience; it was, of
course, only by an appeal to those rights that the Reformers
could justify their own attitude toward Roman Catholicism.
But it is one thing to claim liberty for oneself, and another
to accord it to others. "
> --Edward Westermarck, Christianity and Morals,
> 1939.

"The highest regard for truth is not to profess it, but
to seek for it. In this respect the Christian Churches have
been most lamentably deficient. "
> --Edward Westermarck, Christianity and Morals, 1939.

"I am quite incapable of understanding how any work of art can be criticized from a moral standpoint. The sphere of art and the sphere of ethics are absolutely distinct and separate; and it is to the confusion between the two that we owe the appearance of Mrs. Grundy...."
        --Oscar Wilde, "Letter to the Editors," St. James Gazette, June 25, 1890.

"In the cases of violence and obscenity, it is unlikely that social science can either show harmful effects or prove that there are no harmful effects. It is unlikely, in short, that considerations of utility or disutility can be governing. These are moral issues and ultimately all judgments about the acceptability of restrictions on various media will have to rest on political and philosophical considerations."
        --James Q. Wilson, "Violence, Pornography, and Social Science," in: The Public Interest, Winter, 1971.

"The most tragic thing in life would be to lie in one's death bed thinking of all the things one had not done, the experiences one had not had, but would have liked to. So, if I had to push people at all, I should try to push them into fuller life, to persuade them to say 'Yes' to life and not to say 'No.' On this earth, at least, we only have one life: and we might as well make the most of it."
        --John Wilson, Logic and Sexual Morality, 1965.

"It is a feeble, blind, and tense culture that withdraws its vision, which is art, from anything. When that from which art is withdrawn is that which continues life, and therefore culture, the culture wills its own extinction."
        --Wayland Young, Eros Denied, 1964.

The following quotations are from the nine volumes of the Technical Report of the Commission on Obscenity and Pornography.

"... efforts to restrict or censor have the psychological effect of increasing the desirability of the material. Increasing the difficulty of obtaining erotic materials, harassing and punishing pornographers and purveyors of pornography, setting minimum age limits for the purchase of these

materials, and so on, may have the unwanted effect of increasing interest in the materials, rendering them more
desirable, and producing a greater impact on the recipients,
than if none of these measures were utilized. "
>   --Timothy C. Broch, "Erotic Materials, " in: __Tech-
>   nical Report of the Commission on Obscenity and__
>   __Pornography__, vol. I, __Preliminary Studies__, 1971.

"in the specific case of pornography ... the effect
will be determined by the reader in combination with the
material.   Some readers will become sexually aroused, but
any miniskirt might do the same thing.... There is ... no
way to isolate a pathology associated with a literary text
alone.   There is, therefore, no social or therapeutic basis
for interfering with the freedom to read, or, more exactly,
the freedom to do one's own defending against anxiety-
arousing fantasies. "
>   --Norman N. Holland, "Pornography of the Mechan-
>   isms of Defense, " in: __Technical Report of the__
>   __Commission on Obscenity and Pornography__, vol. I,
>   __Preliminary Studies.__

"Censors ... always work on the assumption that
they, presumably, are safely immune to the moral perils of
the materials they must examine in order to pronounce them
morally dangerous for someone else.   In self-defense, unless
they are megalomaniac, they must admit that there are at
least a few collaborators and assistants among their colleagues and friends who are as morally safe as they are.
The censors do not have any absolute criteria by which to
identify those who constitute this safe audience.   By the
same token, they lack absolute criteria as to who constitute
the unsafe audience.   Since, however, they must protect
someone from moral danger, they usually elect to protect
someone who has no power to answer back--someone who is
younger or politically impotent, for example--and who must
accept the status of being unable to make his own decision. "
>   --John Money, "The Positive and Constructive Ap-
>   proach to Pornography in General Sex Education,
>   in the Home, and in Sexological Counselling, " in:
>   __Technical Report of the Commission on Obscenity__
>   __and Pornography__, vol. V, __Societal Control Mechan-__
>   __isms__, 1971.

"... sex attitudes and practices are more likely to be
influenced by cultural and familial factors than by exposure
to pornography ... a reasonable exposure to erotica,

particularly during adolescence, reflects a high degree of
sexual interest and curiosity. Sexual curiosity is correlated
with an adult pattern of acceptable heterosexual practice.
Less than average adolescent exposure [to erotica] ... reflects either avoidance of heterosexual stimuli ... or childhood development in an extremely restrictive atmosphere in
which contact with such stimuli was prohibited and punished
... unresolved sexual conflicts in adolescence relate to adult
sexual patterns in which erotica is a necessary stimulant
(in the case of users [of illegal drugs], homosexuals, sex offenders, for example) to obtain gratification. In the normally developed male, the adolescent use of erotica as an adjunct to sexual actions declines, and the sexual partner becomes the primary source of arousal and gratification. "
> --Michael J. Goldstein, H. S. Kant, L. L. Judd,
> C. J. Rice, and R. Green, "Exposure to Pornog-
> raphy and Sexual Behavior in Deviant and Normal
> Groups, " in: Technical Report of the Commission
> on Obscenity and Pornography, vol. VII, Erotica
> and Antisocial Behavior, 1972.

"... sex offenders ... tend to have less experience
with pornography than other groups ... a small minority of
sex offenders report that pornography did figure in as part
of the motivation that led them to commit a sexual offense.
However, expert clinical judges did not note the fantasy productions of the sex offenders in response to projective stimuli as indicating significantly more pathological sexual thought,
sexual arousal, or aggressive sexual inclinations. "
> --C. Eugene Walker, "Erotic Stimuli and the Aggres-
> sive Sex Offender, " in: Technical Report of the
> Commission on Obscenity and Pornography, vol.
> VII, Erotica and Antisocial Behavior, 1972.

"... the contention that pre-adolescent and adolescent
exposure to pornography contributes to later commitment of
a sexual offense is simply not supported by this research.
On the contrary, if there is a relationship between early exposure to pornography and the tendency to commit a sex
crime, it would appear to be negative. "
> --Robert F. Cook and Robert H. Fosen, "Pornography
> and the Sex Offender: Patterns of Exposure and
> Immediate Arousal Effects of Pornographic Stimuli, "
> in: Technical Report of the Commission on Ob-
> scenity and Pornography, vol. VII, Erotica and An-
> tisocial Behavior, 1972.

"... the sex offenders examined did not differ substantially from nonoffender adult males of the same age group in the general population in regard to amount, frequency, or circumstances of experience with erotic materials. These data suggest that if sex offenders and nonoffenders differ in certain initial respects, ... their experience with erotic material is not one of the differentiating factors."

> --Weldom T. Johnson, Lenore R. Kupperstein, and Joseph J. Peters, "Sex Offenders' Experience with Erotica," in: Technical Report of the Commission on Obscenity and Pornography, vol. VII, Erotica and Antisocial Behavior, 1972.

"What seems indisputable, and what should be worthy of consideration, by State and Federal legislators here in the United States, is that pornography of the type disseminated in Denmark apparently has caused no increase in the rate of sex crimes. It follows that this type of pornography should not be considered a cause of sex crimes ... While there may be some valid reasons for the prohibition of Danish pornography in our society, fear that it will inspire potential sex offenders to act criminally should not be one of them."

> --Richard Ben-Veniste, "Pornography and Sex Crime: the Danish Experience," in: T. R. C. O. P., vol. VII, Erotica and Social Behavior, 1971.

THE RECOMMENDATIONS OF
THE COMMISSION ON OBSCENITY AND PORNOGRAPHY

On September 30, 1970 the Commission on Obscenity and Pornography, set up by President Lyndon B. Johnson in 1968 in response to a Congressional request (Public Law 90-100, October, 1967), issued a report which included a comprehensive set of recommendations (approved by a 12-6 majority of the Commission members) for actions on legislative, administrative, group and individual levels. Since these recommendations, despite their almost immediate rejection by the U. S. Senate (by a 60-5 vote) and President Nixon, seem likely to have a strong influence on the future of censorship in America, they are herewith included:*

I. Non-Legislative Recommendations

The Commission believes that much of the "problem" regarding materials which depict explicit sexual activity stems from the inability or reluctance of people in our society to be open and direct in dealing with sexual matters. This most often manifests itself in the inhibition of talking openly and directly about sex. Professionals use highly technical language when they discuss sex; others of us escape by using euphemisms--or by not talking about sex at all. Direct and open conversation about sex between parent and child is too rare in our society.

Failure to talk openly and directly about sex has

*The Report of the Commission on Obscenity and Pornography, (Washington, D. C.: Government Printing Office, 1970), pp. 47-69. All footnotes from the Report itself are listed at the end of these recommendations.

several consequences. It overemphasizes sex, gives it a magical, non-natural quality, making it more attractive and fascinating. It diverts the expression of sexual interest out of more legitimate channels, into less legitimate channels. Such failure makes teaching children and adolescents to become fully and adequately functioning sexual adults a more difficult task. And it clogs legitimate channels for transmitting sexual information and forces people to use clandestine and unreliable sources.

The Commission believes that interest in sex is normal, healthy, good. Interest in sex begins very early in life and continues throughout the life cycle although the strength of this interest varies from stage to stage. With the onset of puberty, physiological and hormonal changes occur which both quicken interest and make the individual more responsive to sexual interest. The individual needs information about sex in order to understand himself, place his new experiences in a proper context, and cope with his new feelings.

The basic institutions of marriage and the family are built in our society primarily on sexual attraction, love, and sexual expression. These institutions can function successfully only to the extent that they have a healthy base. Thus the very foundation of our society rests upon healthy sexual attitudes grounded in appropriate and accurate sexual information.

Sexual information is so important and so necessary that if people cannot obtain it openly and directly from legitimate sources and through accurate and legitimate channels, they will seek it through whatever channels and sources are available. Clandestine sources may not only be inaccurate but may also be distorted and provide a warped context.

The Commission believes that accurate, appropriate sex information provided openly and directly through legitimate channels and from reliable sources in healthy contexts can compete successfully with potentially distorted, warped, inaccurate, and unreliable information from clandestine, illegitimate sources; and it believes that the attitudes and orientations toward sex produced by the open communication of appropriate sex information from reliable sources through legitimate channels will be normal and healthy, providing a solid foundation for the basic institutions of our society.

The Commission, therefore, presents the following positive approaches to deal with the problem of obscenity and pornography.

1. The Commission recommends that a massive sex education effort be launched. This sex education effort should be characterized by the following:

a) its purpose should be to contribute to healthy attitudes and orientations to sexual relationships so as to provide a sound foundation for our society's basic institutions of marriage and family;

b) it should be aimed at achieving an acceptance of sex as a normal and natural part of life and of oneself as a sexual being;

c) it should not aim for orthodoxy; rather it should be designed to allow for a pluralism of values;

d) it should be based on facts and encompass not only biological and physiological information but also social, psychological, and religious information;

e) it should be differentiated so that content can be shaped appropriately for the individual's age, sex, and circumstances;

f) it should be aimed, as appropriate, to all segments of our society, adults as well as children and adolescents;

g) it should be a joint function of several institutions of our society: family, school, church, etc.;

h) special attention should be given to the training of those who will have central places in the legitimate communication channels--parents, teachers, physicians, clergy, social service workers, etc.;

i) it will require cooperation of private and public organizations at local, regional, and national levels with appropriate funding;

j) it will be aided by the imaginative utilization of new educational technologies; for example, educational television could be used to reach several members of a family in a family context.

The Commission feels that such a sex education program would provide a powerful positive approach to the
problems of obscenity and pornography. By providing accurate and reliable sex information through legitimate sources,
it would reduce interest in and dependence upon clandestine
and less legitimate sources. By providing healthy attitudes
and orientations toward sexual relationships, it would provide
better protection for the individual against distorted or
warped ideas he may encounter regarding sex. By providing
greater ease in talking about sexual matters in appropriate
contexts, the shock and offensiveness of encounters with sex
would be reduced.

   2. The Commission recommends continued open discussion, based on factual information, on the issues regarding obscenity and pornography.

   Discussion has in the past been carried on with few
facts available and the debate has necessarily reflected, to
a large extent, prejudices and fears. Congress asked the
Commission to secure more factual information before making recommendations. Some of the facts developed by the
Commission are contrary to widely held assumptions. These
findings provide new perspectives on the issues.

   The information developed by the Commission should
be given wide distribution, so that it may sharpen the issues
and focus the discussion.

   3. The Commission recommends that additional factual information be developed.

   The Commission's effort to develop information has
been limited by time, financial resources, and the paucity of
previously existing research. Many of its findings are tentative and many questions remain to be answered. We trust
that our modest pioneering work in empirical research into
several problem areas will help to open the way for more
extensive and long-term research based on more refined
methods directed to answering more refined questions. We
urge both private and public sources to provide the financial
resources necessary for the continued development of factual
information so that the continuing discussion may be further
enriched.

   The Federal Government has special responsibilities
for continuing research in these areas and has existing

structures which can facilitate further inquiry. Many of the
questions raised about obscenity and pornography have direct
relevance to already existing programs in the National Institute of Mental Health, the National Institute of Child Health
and Human Development, and the United States Office of Education. The Commission urges these agencies to broaden
their concerns to include a wider range of topics relating to
human sexuality, specifically including encounters with explicit sexual materials.

     4. The Commission recommends that citizens organ-
ize themselves at local, regional, and national levels to aid
in the implementation of the foregoing recommendations.

     The sex education effort recommended by the Com-
mission can be achieved only with broad and active citizen
participation. Widespread discussion of the issues regarding
the availability of explicit sexual materials implies broad
and active citizen participation. A continuing research program aimed at clarifying factual issues regarding the impact
of explicit sexual materials on those who encounter them
will occur only with the support and cooperation of citizens.

     Organized citizen groups can be more constructive
and effective if they truly represent a broad spectrum of the
public's thinking and feeling. People tend to assume, in the
absence of other information, that most peoples' opinions are
similar to their own. However, we know that opinions in
the sexual realm vary greatly--that there is no unanimity of
values in this area. Therefore, every group should attempt
to include as wide a variety of opinion as is possible.

     The aim of citizen groups should be to provide a
forum whereby all views may be presented for thoughtful
consideration. We live in a free, pluralistic society which
places its trust in the competition of ideas in a free market
place. Persuasion is a preferred technique. Coercion, repression and censorship in order to promote a given set of
views are not tolerable in our society.

II.   Legislative Recommendations

     On the basis of its findings, the Commission makes
the following legislative recommendations. The disagreements of particular Commissioners with aspects of the Commission's legislative recommendations are noted below,

where the recommendations are discussed in detail. Commissioners Link, Hill, and Keating have filed a joint dissenting statement. In addition, Commissioners Keating and Link have submitted separate remarks. Commissioners Larsen and Wolfgang have filed statements explaining their dissent from certain Commission recommendations. A number of other Commissioners have filed short separate statements. [1]

In general outline, the Commission recommends that federal, state, and local legislation should not seek to interfere with the right of adults who wish to do so to read, obtain, or view explicit sexual materials. [2] On the other hand, we recommend legislative regulations upon the sale of sexual materials to young persons who do not have the consent of their parents, and we also recommend legislation to protect persons from having sexual materials thrust upon them without their consent through the mails or through open public display.

The Commission's specific legislative recommendations and the reasons underlying these recommendations are as follows:

A. STATUTES RELATING TO ADULTS

The Commission recommends that federal, state, and local legislation prohibiting the sale, exhibition, or distribution of sexual materials to consenting adults should be repealed. Twelve of the 17 participating members[3] of the Commission join in this recommendation. [4] Two additional Commissioners[5] subscribe to the bulk of the Commission's Report, but do not believe that the evidence presented at this time is sufficient to warrant the repeal of all prohibitions upon what adults may obtain. Three Commissioners dissent from the recommendation to repeal adult legislation and would retain existing laws prohibiting the dissemination of obscene materials to adults. [6]

The Commission believes that there is no warrant for continued governmental interference with the full freedom of adults to read, obtain or view whatever such material they wish. Our conclusion is based upon the following considerations:

1. Extensive empirical investigation, both by the

Commission and by others, provides no evidence that exposure to or use of explicit sexual materials play a significant
role in the causation of social or individual harms such as
crime, delinquency, sexual or nonsexual deviancy or severe
emotional disturbances.[7] This research and its results are
described in detail in the Report of the Effects Panel of the
Commission and are summarized above in the Overview of
Commission findings. Empirical investigation thus sup-
ports the opinion of a substantial majority of persons pro-
fessionally engaged in the treatment of deviancy, delinquency
and antisocial behavior, that exposure to sexually explicit
materials has no harmful causal role in these areas.

Studies show that a number of factors, such as disor-
ganized family relationships and unfavorable peer influences,
are intimately related to harmful sexual behavior or adverse
character development. Exposure to sexually explicit materials, however, cannot be counted as among these determina-
tive factors. Despite the existence of widespread legal prohibitions upon the dissemination of such materials, exposure
to them appears to be a usual and harmless part of the process of growing up in our society and a frequent and non-
damaging occurrence among adults. Indeed, a few Commission studies indicate that a possible distinction between sexual offenders and other people, with regard to experience with
explicit sexual materials, is that sex offenders have seen
markedly less of such materials while maturing.

This is not to say that exposure to explicit sexual materials has no effect upon human behavior. A prominent effect of exposure to sexual materials is that persons tend to
talk more about sex as a result of seeing such materials.
In addition, many persons become temporarily sexually
aroused upon viewing explicit sexual materials and the frequency of their sexual activity may, in consequence, increase
for short periods. Such behavior, however, is the type of
sexual activity already established as usual activity for the
particular individual.

In sum, empirical research designed to clarify the
question has found no evidence to date that exposure to explicit sexual materials plays a significant role in the causation of delinquent or criminal behavior among youth or
adults. [8]

2. On the positive side, explicit sexual materials are
sought as a source of entertainment and information by

substantial numbers of American adults. At times, these
materials also appear to serve to increase and facilitate
constructive communication about sexual matters within marriage. The most frequent purchaser of explicit sexual materials is a college-educated, married male, in his thirties
or forties, who is of above average socio-economic status.
Even where materials are legally available to them, young
adults and older adolescents do not constitute an important
portion of the purchasers of such materials.

     3.   Society's attempts to legislate for adults in the
area of obscenity have not been successful. Present laws
prohibiting the consensual sale or distribution of explicit
sexual materials to adults are extremely unsatisfactory in
their practical application. The Constitution permits material to be deemed "obscene" for adults only if, as a whole,
it appeals to the "prurient" interest of the average person,
is "patently offensive" in light of "community standards,"
and lacks "redeeming social value." These vague and highly
subjective aesthetic psychological and moral tests do not provide meaningful guidance for law enforcement officials, juries
or courts. As a result, law is inconsistently and sometimes
erroneously applied and the distinctions made by courts between prohibited and permissible materials often appear in-
defensible. Errors in the application of the law and uncertainty about its scope also cause interference with the communication of constitutionally protected materials.

     4.   Public opinion in America does not support the
imposition of legal prohibitions upon the right of adults to
read or see explicit sexual materials. While a minority of
Americans favors such prohibitions, a majority of the American people presently are of the view that adults should be
legally able to read or see explicit sexual materials if they
wish to do so.

     5.   The lack of consensus among Americans concern-
ing whether explicit sexual materials should be available to
adults in our society, and the significant number of adults
who wish to have access to such materials, pose serious
problems regarding the enforcement of legal prohibitions upon
adults, even aside from the vagueness and subjectivity of
present law. Consistent enforcement of even the clearest
prohibitions upon consensual adult exposure to explicit sexual
materials would require the expenditure of considerable law
enforcement resources. In the absence of a persuasive
demonstration of damage flowing from consensual exposure to

such materials, there seems no justification for thus adding
to the overwhelming tasks already placed upon the law enforcement system.   Inconsistent enforcement of prohibitions,
on the other hand, invites discriminatory action based upon
considerations not directly relevant to the policy of the law.
The latter alternative also breeds public disrespect for the
legal process.

      6.   The foregoing considerations take on added signif-
icance because of the fact that adult obscenity laws deal in
the realm of speech and communication.   Americans deeply
value the right of each individual to determine for himself
what books he wishes to read and what pictures or films he
wishes to see.   Our traditions of free speech and press also
value and protect the right of writers, publishers, and booksellers to serve the diverse interests of the public.   The
spirit and letter of our Constitution tell us that government
should not seek to interfere with these rights unless a clear
threat of harm makes that course imperative.   Moreover,
the possibility of the misuse of general obscenity statutes
prohibiting distributions of books and films to adults constitutes a continuing threat to the free communication of ideas
among Americans--one of the most important foundations of
our liberties.

      7.   In reaching its recommendations that government
should not seek to prohibit consensual distributions of sexual
materials to adults, the Commission discussed several arguments which are often advanced in support of such legislation.   The Commission carefully considered the view that
adult legislation should be retained in order to aid in the
protection of young persons from exposure to explicit sexual
materials.   We do not believe that the objective of protecting youth may justifiably be achieved at the expense of denying adults materials of their choice.   It seems to us wholly
inappropriate to adjust the level of adult communication to
that considered suitable for children.   Indeed, the Supreme
Court has unanimously held that adult legislation premised
on this basis is a clearly unconstitutional interference with
liberty.

      8.   There is no reason to suppose that elimination of
governmental prohibitions upon the sexual materials which
may be made available to adults would adversely affect the
availability to the public of other books, magazines, and
films.   At the present time, a large range of very explicit
textual and pictorial materials are available to adults without

legal restrictions in many areas of the country. The size of
this industry is small when compared with the overall industry in books, magazines, and motion pictures, and the business in explicit sexual materials is insignificant in compari-
son with other national economic enterprises. Nor is the
business an especially profitable one; profit levels are, on
the average, either normal as compared with other busi-
nesses or distinctly below average. The typical business
entity is a relatively small entrepreneurial enterprise. The
long-term consumer interest in such materials has remained
relatively stable in the context of the economic growth of the
nation generally, and of the media industries in particular.

9. The Commission has also taken cognizance of the
concern of many people that the lawful distribution of explicit
sexual materials to adults may have a deleterious effect upon
the individual morality of American citizens and upon the
moral climate in America as a whole. This concern appears
to flow from a belief that exposure to explicit materials may
cause moral confusion which, in turn, may induce antisocial
or criminal behavior. As noted above, the Commission has
found no evidence to support such a contention. Nor is
there evidence that exposure to explicit sexual materials adversely affects character or moral attitudes regarding sex
and sexual conduct. 9

The concern about the effect of obscenity upon morality is also expressed as a concern about the impact of sexual
materials upon American values and standards. Such values
and standards are currently in a process of complex change,
in both sexual and nonsexual areas. The open availability of
increasingly explicit sexual materials is only one of these
changes. The current flux in sexual values is related to a
number of powerful influences, among which are the ready
availability of effective methods of contraception, changes of
the role of women in our society, and the increased education and mobility of our citizens. The availability of explicit
sexual materials is, the Commission believes, not one of the
important influences on sexual morality.

The Commission is of the view that it is exceedingly
unwise for government to attempt to legislate individual moral
values and standards independent of behavior, especially by
restrictions upon consensual communication. This is certainly true in the absence of a clear public mandate to do so,
and our studies have revealed no such mandate in the area
of obscenity.

The Commission recognizes and believes that the existence of sound moral standards is of vital importance to individuals and to society. To be effective and meaningful, however, these standards must be based upon deep personal commitment flowing from values instilled in the home, in educational and religious training, and through individual resolutions of personal confrontations with human experience. Governmental regulation of moral choice can deprive the individual of the responsibility for personal decision which is essential to the formation of genuine moral standards. Such regulation would also tend to establish an official moral orthodoxy, contrary to our most fundamental constitutional traditions. [10]

Therefore, the Commission recommends the repeal of existing federal legislation which prohibits or interferes with consensual distribution of "obscene" materials to adults. These statutes are: 18 U.S.C. Section 1461, 1462, 1464, and 1465; 19 U.S.C. Section 1305; and 39 U.S.C. Section 3006. [11] The Commission also recommends the repeal of existing state and local legislation which may similarly prohibit the consensual sale, exhibition, or the distribution of sexual materials to adults.

B. STATUTES RELATING TO YOUNG PERSONS

The Commission recommends the adoption by the States of legislation set forth in the Drafts of Proposed Statutes in Section III of this Part of the Commission's Report prohibiting the commercial distribution or display for sale of certain sexual materials to young persons. Similar legislation might also be adopted, where appropriate, by local governments and by the federal government for application in areas, such as the District of Columbia, where it has primary jurisdiction over distributional conduct.

The Commission's recommendation of juvenile legislation is joined in by 14 members of the Commission. Two of these[12] feel the legislation should be drawn so as to include appropriate descriptions identifying the material as being unlawful for sale to children. Three members disagree. [13] Other members of the Commission, who generally join in its recommendation for juvenile legislation, disagree with various detailed aspects of the Commission's legislative proposal. These disagreements are noted in the following discussion.

The Commission's recommendation of juvenile legislation flows from these findings and considerations:

A primary basis for the Commission's recommendation for repeal of adult legislation is the fact that extensive empirical investigations do not indicate any causal relationship between exposure to or use of explicit sexual materials and such social or individual harms such as crime, delinquency, sexual or nonsexual deviancy, or severe emotional disturbances. The absence of empirical evidence supporting such a causal relationship also applies to the exposure of children to erotic materials. However, insufficient research is presently available on the effect of the exposure of children to sexually explicit materials to enable us to reach conclusions with the same degree of confidence as for adult exposure. Strong ethical feelings against experimentally exposing children to sexually explicit materials considerably reduced the possibility of gathering the necessary data and information regarding young persons.

In view of the limited amount of information concerning the effects of sexually explicit materials on children, other considerations have assumed primary importance in the Commission's deliberations. The Commission has been influenced, to a considerable degree, by its finding that a large majority of Americans believe that children should not be exposed to certain sexual materials. In addition, the Commission takes the view that parents should be free to make their own conclusions regarding the suitability of explicit sexual materials for their children and that it is appropriate for legislation to aid parents in controlling the access of their children to such materials during their formative years. The Commission recognizes that legislation cannot possibly isolate children from such materials entirely; it also recognizes that exposure of children to sexual materials may not only do no harm but may, in certain instances, actually facilitate much needed communication between parent and child over sexual matters. The Commission is aware, as well, of the considerable danger of creating an unnatural attraction or an enhanced interest in certain materials by making them "forbidden fruit" for young persons. The Commission believes, however, that these considerations can and should be weighed by individual parents in determining their attitudes toward the exposure of their children to sexual materials, and that legislation should aid, rather than undermine, such parental choice.

Taking account of the above considerations, the model
juvenile legislation recommended by the Commission applies
only to distributions to children made without parental consent.   The recommended legislation applies only to commercial distributions and exhibitions; in the very few instances
where noncommercial conduct in this area creates a problem,
it can be dealt with under existing legal principles for the
protection of young persons, such as prohibitions upon contributing to the delinquency of minors.   The model legislation also prohibits displaying certain sexual materials for
sale in a manner which permits children to view materials
which cannot be sold to them.   Two members of the Commission, [14] who recommend legislation prohibiting sales to
juveniles, do not join in recommending this regulation upon
display; one member of the Commission[15] recommends only
this display provision, and does not recommend a special
statute prohibiting sales to young persons.

The Commission, pursuant to Congressional direction,
has given close attention to the definitions of prohibited material included in its recommended model legislation for
young persons.   A paramount consideration in the Commission's deliberations has been that definitions of prohibited
materials be as specific and explicit as possible.   Such
specificity aids law enforcement and facilitates and encourages voluntary adherence to law on the part of retail dealers
and exhibitors, while causing as little interference as possible with the proper distribution of materials to children and
adults.   The Commission's recommended legislation seeks to
eliminate subjective definitional criteria insofar as that is
possible and goes further in that regard than existing state
legislation.

The Commission believes that only pictorial material
should fall within prohibitions upon sale or commercial display to young persons.   An attempt to define prohibited
textual materials for young persons with the same degree of
specificity as pictorial materials would, the Commission believes, not be advisable.   Many worthwhile textual works,
containing considerable value for young persons, treat sex
in an explicit manner and are presently available to young
persons.   There appears to be no satisfactory way to distinguish, through a workable legal definition, between these
works and those which may be deemed inappropriate by some
persons for commercial distribution to young persons.   As a
result, the inclusion of textual material within juvenile legislative prohibitions would pose considerable risks for dealers

and distributors in determining what books might legally be
sold or displayed to young persons and would thus inhibit
the entire distribution of verbal materials by those dealers
who do not wish to expose themselves to such risks.   The
speculative risk of harm to juveniles from some textual material does not justify these dangers.   The Commission believes, in addition, that parental concern over the material
commercially available to children most often applies to pictorial matter.

       The definition recommended by the Commission for
inclusion in juvenile legislation covers a range of explicit
pictorial and three-dimensional depictions of sexual activity.
It does not, however, apply to depictions of nudity alone,
unless genital areas are exposed and emphasized.   The
definition is applicable only if the explicit pictorial material
constitutes a dominant part of a work.   An exception is provided for works of artistic or anthropological significance.

       Seven Commissioners would include verbal materials
within the definition of materials prohibited for sale to
young persons. 16   They would, however, also include a broad
exception for such textual materials when they bear literary,
historical, scientific, educational, or other similar social
value for young persons.

       Because of changing standards as to what material,
if any, is inappropriate for sale or display to children, the
Commission's model statute contains a provision requiring
legislative reconsideration of the need for, and scope of,
such legislation at six-year intervals.

       The model statute also exempts broadcast or telecast
activity from its scope.   Industry self-regulation in the past
has resulted in little need for governmental intervention.   If
a need for governmental regulation should arise, the Commission believes that such regulations would be most appropriately prepared in this specialized area through the
regulating power of the Federal Communications Commission,
rather than through diverse state laws.

       The Commission has not fixed upon a precise age lim-
it for inclusion in its recommended juvenile legislation, believing that such a determination is most appropriately made
by the States and localities which enact such provisions in
light of local standards.   All States now fix the age in juvenile obscenity statutes at under 17 or under 18 years.   The

recommended model statute also excludes married persons,
whatever their age, from the category of juveniles protected
by the legislation.

The Commission considered the possibility of recommending the enactment of uniform federal legislation requiring a notice or label to be affixed to materials by their publishers, importers or manufacturers, when such materials
fall within a definitional provision identical to that included
within the recommended state or local model juvenile statute.
Under such legislation, the required notice might be used by
retail dealers and exhibitors, in jurisdictions which adopt
the recommended juvenile legislation, as a guide to what
material could not be sold or displayed to young persons.
The Commission concluded, however, that such a federal
notice or labelling provision would be unwise. [17] So long as
definitional provisions are drafted to be as specific as possible, and especially if they include only pictorial material,
the Commission believes that the establishment of a federal
regulatory notice system is probably unnecessary; specific
definitions of pictorial material, such as the Commission
recommends, should themselves enable retail dealers and
exhibitors to make accurate judgments regarding the status
of particular magazines and films. The Commission is also
extremely reluctant to recommend imposing any federal system for labelling reading or viewing matter on the basis of
its quality or content. The precedent of such required
labelling would pose a serious potential threat to First
Amendment liberties in other areas of communication. La-
bels indicating sexual content might also be used artificially
to enhance the appeal of certain materials. Two Commissioners[18] favor federally imposed labelling in order to advise
dealers as clearly and accurately as possible about what material is forbidden for sale to young persons, placing the
responsibility for judging whether material falls within the
statute on the publisher or producer who is completely
aware of its contents and who is in a position to examine
each item individually.

Finally, the Commission considered, but does not af-
firmatively recommend, the enactment by the federal government of juvenile legislation which would prohibit the sale of
certain explicit materials to juveniles through the mails.
Such federal legislation would, the Commission believes, be
virtually unenforceable since the constitutional requirement
of proving the defendant's guilty knowledge means that a
prosecution could be successful only if proof were available

that the vendor knew that the purchaser was a minor. Except in circumstances which have not been found to be prevalent, as where a sale might be solicited through a mailing list composed of young persons, mail order purchases are made without any knowledge by the vendor of the purchaser's age. Certificates of age by the purchaser would be futile as an enforcement device and to require notarized affidavits to make a purchase through the mails would unduly interfere with purchase by adults. The Commission has found, moreover, that at present juveniles rarely purchase sexually explicit materials through the mail, making federal legislative machinery in this area apparently unnecessary.

C. PUBLIC DISPLAY AND UNSOLICITED MAILING

The Commission recommends enactment of state and local legislation prohibiting public displays of sexually explicit pictorial materials, and approves in principle of the federal legislation, enacted as part of the 1970 Postal Reorganization Act, regarding the mailing of unsolicited advertisements of a sexually explicit nature. The Commission's recommendations in this area are based upon its finding, through its research, that certain explicit sexual materials are capable of causing considerable offense to numerous Americans when thrust upon them without their consent. The Commission believes that these unwanted intrusions upon individual sensibilities warrant legislative regulation and it further believes that such intrusions can be regulated effectively without any significant interference with consensual communication of sexual material among adults.

PUBLIC DISPLAY

The Commission's recommendations in the public display area have been formulated into a model state public display statute which is reproduced in the Drafts of Proposed Statutes in Section III of this Part of the Commission Report. Three Commissioners dissent from this recommendation. [19]

The model state statute recommended by the Commission (which would also be suitable for enactment in appropriate instances by local government units and by the federal government for areas where it has general legislative jurisdiction) prohibits the display of certain potentially offensive, sexually explicit, pictorial materials in places easily visible from public thoroughfares or the property of others. [20]

Verbal materials are not included within the recommended prohibition. There appears to be no satisfactory way to define "offensive" words in legislation in order to make the parameters of prohibition upon their display both clear and sufficiently limited so as not to endanger the communication of messages of serious social concern. In addition, the fact that there are few, if any, "dirty" words which do not already appear fairly often in conversation among many Americans and in some very widely distributed books and films indicates that such words are no longer capable of causing the very high degree of offense to a large number of persons which would justify legislative interference. Five Commissioners disagree[21] and would include verbal materials in the display prohibition because they believe certain words cause sufficient offense to warrant their inclusion in display prohibitions.

Telecasts are exempted from the coverage of the statute for the same reasons set forth above in connection with discussion of the Commission's recommendation of juvenile legislation.

The recommended model legislation defines in specific terms the explicit sexual pictorial materials which the Commission believes are capable of causing offense to a substantial number of persons. The definition covers a range of explicit pictorial and three-dimensional depictions of sexual activity. It does not apply to depictions of nudity alone, unless genital areas are exposed and emphasized. An exception is provided for works of artistic or anthropological significance. The Commission emphasizes that this legislation does not prohibit the sale or advertisement of any materials, but does prohibit the public display of potentially offensive pictorial matter. While such displays have not been found by the Commission to be a serious problem at the present time, increasing commercial distribution of explicit materials to adults may cause considerable offense to others in the future unless specific regulations governing public displays are adopted.

UNSOLICITED MAILING

The Commission, with three dissents,[22] also approves of federal legislation to prevent unsolicited advertisements containing potentially offensive sexual material from being communicated through the mails to persons who do not wish to receive such advertisements. The Federal

Anti-Pandering Act, which went into effect in 1968, imposes
some regulation in this area, but it permits a mail recipient to protect himself against such mail only after he has
received at least one such advertisement and it protects him
only against mail emanating from that particular source.
The Commission believes it more appropriate to permit mail
recipients to protect themselves against all such unwanted
mail advertisements from any source.   Federal legislation
in this area was enacted just prior to the date of this report
as part of the 1970 Postal Reorganization Act.   Public Law
91-375, 91st Cong. , 2nd Sess. , 39 U. S. C. Sections 3010-
3011; 18 U. S. C. Sections 1735-1737.

        The Commission considered two possible methods by
which persons might be broadly insulated from unsolicited
sexual advertisements which they do not wish to receive.
One approach, contained in the 1970 Postal Reorganization
Act, authorizes the Post Office to compile and maintain current lists of persons who have stated that they do not wish
to receive certain defined materials, makes these lists available at cost to mailers of unsolicited advertisements, and
prohibits sending the defined material to persons whose
names appear on the Post Office lists.   A second approach,
described in detail in the Commission's Progress Report of
July, 1969, would require all mailers of unsolicited advertisements falling within the statutory definition to place a
label or code on the envelope.   Mail patrons would then be
authorized to direct local postal authorities not to deliver
coded mail to their homes or offices.

        In principle, the Commission favors the first of these
approaches employed by Congress in the 1970 Postal Reorganization Act.   The Commission takes this view because it
believes that the primary burden of regulating the flow of
potentially offensive unsolicited mail should appropriately fall
upon the mailers of such materials and because of its reluctance to initiate required federal labelling of reading or
viewing matter because of its sexual content.   The Commission believes, however, that under current mail-order practices it may prove financially unfeasible for many smaller
mailers to conform their mailing lists to those compiled by
the Post Office.   Use of computers to organize and search
mailing lists will apparently be required by the new law;
few, if any, small mailers utilize computers in this way
today.   If the current lists maintained by the Post Office
came to contain a very large number of names--perhaps one
million or more--even a computer search of these names,

to discover any that were also present on a mailing list
sought to be used by a mailer, might be prohibitively ex-
pensive.   If such were the case, the Commission would believe the second possible approach to regulation to be more
consistent with constitutional rights.   This approach, however, might place serious burdens upon Post Office person-
nel.   The Commission was not able to evaluate the practical
significance of these burdens.

In considering the definition appropriate to legislation
regulating unsolicited sexual advertisements, the Commission
examined a large range of unsolicited material which has
given rise to complaints to the Post Office Department in
recent years.   A definition was then formulated which quite
specifically describes material which has been deemed offensive by substantial numbers of postal patrons.   This definition is set forth in the footnote. [23]   The Commission prefers
this definitional provision to the less precise definitional
provision in the 1970 Postal Reorganization Act.

D.   DECLARATORY JUDGMENT LEGISLATION

The Commission recommends the enactment, in all
jurisdictions which enact or retain provisions prohibiting the
dissemination of sexual materials to adults or young persons,
of legislation authorizing prosecutors to obtain declaratory
judgments as to whether particular materials fall within
existing legal prohibitions and appropriate injunctive relief.
A model statute embodying this recommendation is presented
in the Drafts of Proposed Statutes in Section III of this Part
of the Commission Report.   All but two[24] of the Commissioners concur in the substance of this recommendation.
The Commission recognizes that the particular details governing the institution and appeal of declaratory judgment actions will necessarily vary from State to State depending
upon local jurisdictional and procedural provisions.   The
Commission is about evenly divided with regard to whether
local prosecutors should have authority to institute such actions directly, or whether the approval of an official with
state-wide jurisdiction, such as the State Attorney General,
should be required before an action for declaratory judgment
is instituted.

A declaratory judgment procedure such as the Commission recommends would permit prosecutors to proceed
civilly, rather than through the criminal process, against

suspected violations of obscenity prohibition. If such civil procedures are utilized, penalties would be imposed for violation of the law only with respect to conduct occurring after a civil declaration is obtained. The Commission believes this course of action to be appropriate whenever there is any existing doubt regarding the legal status of materials; where other alternatives are available, the criminal process should not ordinarily be invoked against persons who might have reasonably believed, in good faith, that the books or films they distributed were entitled to constitutional protection, for the threat of criminal sanctions might otherwise deter the free distribution of constitutionally protected material. The Commission's recommended legislation would not only make a declaratory judgment procedure available, but would require prosecutors to utilize this process instead of immediate criminal prosecution in all cases except those where the materials in issue are unquestionably within the applicable statutory definitional provisions.

WITHDRAWAL OF APPELLATE JURISDICTION

The Commission recommends against the adoption of any legislation which would limit or abolish the jurisdiction of the Supreme Court of the United States or of other federal judges and courts in obscenity cases. Two Commissioners[25] favor such legislation; one[26] deems it inappropriate for the Commission to take a position on this issue.

Proposals to limit federal judicial jurisdiction over obscenity cases arise from disagreement over resolution by federal judges of the question of obscenity in litigation. The Commission believes that these disagreements flow in largest measure from the vague and subjective character of the legal tests for obscenity utilized in the past; under existing legal definitions, courts are required to engage in subjective decision making and their results may well be contrary to the subjective analyses of many citizens. Adoption of specific and explicit definitional provisions in prohibitory and regulatory legislation, as the Commission recommends, should eliminate most or all serious disagreements over the application of these definitions and thus eliminate the major source of concern which has motivated proposals to limit federal judicial jurisdiction.

More fundamentally, the Commission believes that it would be exceedingly unwise to adopt the suggested proposal from the point of view of protection of constitutional rights.

The Commission believes that disagreements with court results in particular obscenity cases, even if these disagreements are soundly based in some instances, are not sufficiently important to justify tampering with existing judicial institutions which are often required to protect constitutional rights. Experience shows that while courts may sometimes reverse convictions on a questionable basis, juries and lower courts also on occasion find guilt in cases involving books and films which are entitled to constitutional protection, and state appeals courts often uphold such findings. These violations of First Amendment rights would go uncorrected if such decisions could not be reversed at a higher court level.

The Commission also recommends against the creation of a precedent in the obscenity area for the elimination by Congress of federal judicial jurisdiction in other areas whenever a vocal majority or minority of citizens disagrees strongly with the results of the exercise of that jurisdiction. Freedom in many vital areas frequently depends upon the ability of the judiciary to follow the Constitution rather than strong popular sentiment. The problem of obscenity, in the absence of any indication that sexual materials cause societal harm, is not an appropriate social phenomenon upon which to base a precedent for removing federal judicial jurisdiction to protect fundamental rights guaranteed by the Bill of Rights.

III.   Drafts of Proposed Legislation

A.   RECOMMENDED FEDERAL LEGISLATION

REPEAL OF EXISTING LAWS

The following federal statutes prohibiting the consensual distribution of "obscene" material to adults are hereby repealed: 18 United States Code, Sections 1461, 1462, 1464, 1465; 19 United States Code, Section 1305; 39 United States Code, Section 3006.

B.   RECOMMENDED STATE LEGISLATION

SECTION 1.   REPEAL OF EXISTING LAWS

The following statutes prohibiting the distribution of obscene material to adults are hereby repealed:

[cite appropriate state statutes].27

SECTION 2. SALE AND DISPLAY OF EXPLICIT SEXUAL
MATERIALS TO YOUNG PERSONS

(a) Purpose. -- It is the purpose of this section to
regulate the direct commercial distribution of certain explicit
sexual materials to young persons in order to aid parents
in supervising and controlling the access of children to such
material. The legislature finds that whatever social value
such material may have for young persons can adequately be
served by its availability to young persons through their
parents.

(b) Offenses Defined. -- A person is guilty of a misdemeanor if he

(i) knowingly disseminates explicit sexual material, as hereinafter defined, to young persons or
(ii) if he knowingly displays explicit sexual material for sale in an area to which young persons have access,
unless such material has artistic, literary, historical, scientific, medical, educational or other similar social value
for adults.

(c) Penalty. -- Whoever violates the provisions of
this section shall be liable to [left to state option].

(d) Definitions. -- For the purposes of this section:

(i) "Young person" means any person less than___
years of age;
(ii) "Explicit sexual material" means any pictorial
or three dimensional material including, but not limited to,
books, magazines, films, photographs and statuary, which
is made up in whole or in dominant part of depictions of human sexual intercourse, masturbation, sodomy (i. e. , bestiality or oral or anal intercourse), direct physical stimulation
of unclothed genitals, or flagellation or torture in the context of a sexual relationship, or which emphasizes the depiction of uncovered adult human genitals; provided however,
that works of art or of anthropological significance shall not
be deemed to be within the foregoing definition.
(iii) "Disseminate" means to sell, lease or exhibit
commercially and, in the case of an exhibition, to sell an
admission ticket or pass, or to admit persons who have
bought such a ticket or pass to the premises whereon an

exhibition is presented.

(iv) "Display for sale" in an area to which young persons have access means display of material for sale so that young persons may see portions of the material constituting explicit sexual pictorial material.

(v) An offense is committed "knowingly" only if (A) the defendant knew that the recipient of material was a young person, as herein defined, or had grounds to believe it probable that the recipient was a young person as herein defined and failed to make reasonable inquiries to determine the age of the recipient; and if (B) (1) the defendant was aware of contents of the material clearly within the definition of explicit sexual material contained in part (ii) of this subsection, or (2) had reason to know that the contents of the material were likely to fall within the definition of explicit sexual material and failed to examine the material to ascertain its contents.

(e)   Defenses. -- It shall be an affirmative defense to a prosecution under this section for the defendant to show:

(i) That the dissemination was made with the consent of a parent or guardian of the recipient, that the defendant was misled as to the existence of parental consent by a misrepresentation of parental status, or that the dissemination was made to the recipient by his teacher or clergyman in the discharge of official responsibilities;

(ii) That the recipient was married, or that the defendant was misled in this regard by a misrepresentation of marital status.

(f)   Exemption for Broadcasts. -- The prohibition of this section shall not apply to broadcasts or telecasts through facilities licensed under the Federal Communications Act, 47 U.S.C. Section 301 et seq.

(g)   Limitation Upon Effective Period of Legislation. -- This Act shall be effective for six years from the date of enactment and shall become null and void thereafter unless reenacted.

SECTION 3.   PUBLIC DISPLAYS OF EXPLICIT SEXUAL
             MATERIALS

(a)   Purpose. -- It is the purpose of this section to prohibit the open public display of certain explicit sexual

materials, in order to protect persons from potential offense
through involuntary exposure to such materials.

(b) Offense Defined. -- A person is guilty of a misdemeanor if he knowingly places explicit sexual material
upon public display, or if he knowingly fails to take prompt
action to remove such a display from property in his possession after learning of its existence.

(c) Penalty. -- Whoever violates the provisions of
this section shall be liable to [left to state option].

(d) Definitions. -- For the purposes of this section:

(i) "Explicit sexual material" means any pictorial
or three-dimensional material depicting human sexual intercourse, masturbation, sodomy (i. e., bestiality or oral or
anal intercourse), direct physical stimulation of unclothed
genitals, flagellation or torture in the context of a sexual
relationship, or emphasizing the depiction of adult human
genitals; provided, however, that works of art or of anthropological significance shall not be deemed to be within the
foregoing definition. In determining whether material is
prohibited for public display by this section such material
shall be judged without regard to any covering which may be
affixed or printed over the material in order to obscure
genital areas in a depiction otherwise falling within the definition of this subsection.

(ii) Material is placed upon "public display" if it
is placed by the defendant on or in a billboard, viewing
screen, theater marquee, newsstand, display rack, window,
showcase, display case or similar place so that matter
bringing it within the definition of subparagraph (i) of this
subsection is easily visible from a public thoroughfare or
from the property of others.

(e) Exception for Broadcasts. -- The prohibition of
this section shall not apply to broadcasts or telecasts through
facilities licensed under the Federal Communications Act, 47
U. S. C. Section 301 et seq.

(f) Limitation Upon Effective Period of Legislation.
-- This Act shall be effective for six years from its date of
enactment and shall become null and void thereafter unless
reenacted.

C.   MODEL DECLARATORY JUDGMENT AND
INJUNCTION STATUTE[28]

(a) Creation of Remedy. -- Whenever material is
being or is about to be disseminated in violation of [insert
citation to applicable legal prohibition or prohibitions], a
civil action may be instituted by the State against any disseminator or disseminators of the material in order to obtain a declaration that the dissemination of such material is
prohibited. Such an action may also seek an injunction appropriately restraining dissemination. Such action may be
initiated by any county prosecutor [or other prosecuting official authorized to represent the State in criminal proceed-
ings]. [29]

(b) Venue. -- Such an action may be brought only in
the _____ Court of the county in which any disseminator resides,
or where the dissemination is taking place or is about to
take place.

(c) Parties. -- Any disseminator of or person who
is about to be a disseminator of the material involved may
intervene as of right as a party defendant in the proceedings.
In addition to the named defendant, the Attorney General
shall undertake to give notice to the producer, manufacturer
or importer of the material, and the wholesale distributor
(if any), that they may exercise this right.

(d) Procedure. -- [The court of initial jurisdiction]
shall give expedited consideration to actions brought pursuant
to this section. A hearing shall be held within____days of
the filing of the complaints and final judgment rendered
within____days of the termination of the hearing. Appeal
from the decision of the [court of initial jurisdiction] lies
only to the [highest court of the jurisdiction]. [30] A notice
of appeal shall be filed within____ days of the final judgment
of the [court of initial jurisdiction] and the [highest court]
shall hear and consider the appeal within____days of the filing of a notice of appeal and shall render final decision
within____days after hearing the appeal. A declaration in an
action brought pursuant to this section shall not be deemed
final for any purpose until the final decision of the [highest
court] is rendered or until the time to file a notice of appeal
from the decision of the [court of initial jurisdiction] has
expired. No restraining order or injunction of any kind
shall be issued restraining the dessimination of any work on
the ground of its obscenity prior to the completion of the
adversary hearing required by this subsection.

Any defendant may assert a right to the trial of the issue of obscenity by jury in actions brought pursuant to this section.

(e) Use of Declaration. -- A final declaration obtained pursuant to this section may be used to establish scienter or to form the basis for an injunction and for no other purposes. The Attorney General may undertake to notify any person of final judgment pursuant to this section as a means of affording such person actual notice of that judgment, but such notice shall not have effect in establishing scienter if the person to whom it is communicated was known to the Attorney General as a producer, manufacturer, importer or wholesale distributor of the material involved and was not given notice of his right to intervene pursuant to subsection (c) of this section.

(f) Definitions. -- For purposes of this section:

(i) "Disseminate" means to sell, lease, or exhibit commercially

(ii) "Disseminator" means any person who imports, produces, manufactures or engages in wholesale distribution of any material intended to be disseminated, or any person who disseminates any material.

(g) Inconsistent Laws Superseded. -- All laws regulating the procedure for obtaining declaratory judgments or injunctions which are inconsistent with the provisions of this section shall be inapplicable to proceedings brought pursuant to this section.

(h) Prosecution Policy. -- From and after the enactment of this Act criminal prosecutions shall be brought prior to the obtaining of a declaration under this Act only in cases of material which is unquestionably within the applicable definitional provision. In all other cases, the provisions of this Act shall be used prior to prosecution, which shall not be based upon conduct engaged in before notice of a declaration obtained pursuant to this Act. Prosecutions brought contrary to this subsection shall be dismissed by the trial court; the trial court's decision in this regard shall not be reviewable in appeal.

Notes

1.   Commissioners Joseph T. Klapper, Morris A. Lipton,
      G. William Jones, Edward D. Greenwood and Irving
      Lehrman.

2.   The term explicit sexual materials is used here and
      elsewhere in these recommendations to refer to the
      entire range of explicit sexual depictions or descrip-
      tions in books, magazines, photographs, films,
      statuary, and other media.   It includes the most ex-
      plicit depictions, or what is often referred to as
      "hard-core pornography."   The term, however, re-
      fers only to sexual materials, and not to "live" sex
      shows, such as strip tease or on-stage sexual activ-
      ity or simulated sexual activity.   The Commission
      did not study this phenomenon in detail and makes
      no recommendations in this area.   See Preface to
      this Report.

3.   Commissioner Charles H. Keating, Jr., chose not to
      participate in the deliberation and formulation of any
      of the Commission's recommendations.

4.   Commissioner Edward E. Elson joins in this recom-
      mendation only on the understanding that there will
      be prior enactment of legislation prohibiting the pub-
      lic display of offensive sexual materials both pic-
      torial and verbal, that there will be prior enactment
      of legislation restricting the sales of explicit sexual
      materials to juveniles, and that there be prior pub-
      lic and governmental support for the Commission's
      nonlegislative recommendations before such repeal
      is enacted.

5.   Commissioners Irving Lehrman and Cathryn A. Spelts.

6.   Commissioners Morton A. Hill, S. J., Winfrey C.
      Link, and Thomas C. Lynch.

7.   See footnote 4 in the Overview of Effects.

8.   See footnote 4 in the Overview of Effects.

9.   See footnote 4 in the Overview of Effects.

10.   Commissioner Thomas D. Gill has amplified his position

with reference to this finding as follows: Legislation primarily motivated by an intent to establish or defend standards of public morality has not always been, as the Report of the Commission would have it, inappropriate, unsound, and contrary to "our most unsound, and contrary to "our most fundamental constitutional traditions."

In fact for at least 140 years after its adoption, the Constitution never appears to have been considered a barrier to the perpetuation of the belief held in the 13 original colonies that there was not only a right but a duty to codify in law the community's moral and social convictions. Granted homogeneous communities and granted the ensuing moral and social cohesiveness implied in such uniformity of interest the right of these solid and massive majorities to protect their own values by legislation they deemed appropriate went unchallenged so long as it did not impinge upon the individual's right to worship and speak as he pleased.

Only in the 20th century has an increasingly pluralistic society begun to question both the wisdom and the validity of encasing its moral and social convictions in legal armour, and properly so, for if all laws to be effective must carry into their implementation the approval of a majority, this is peculiarly and all importantly the case with laws addressed to standards of morality, which speedily become exercises in community hypocrisy if they do not embody the wishes and convictions of a truly dominant majority of the people.

The Commission's studies have established that on a national level no more than 35% of our people favor adult controls in the field of obscenity in the absence of some demonstrable social evil related to its presence and use.

The extensive survey of the prosecutorial offices of this country gives added affirmation of the principle that acceptable enforcement of obscenity legislation depends upon a solid undergirding of community support such as may be and is found in the smaller, more homogeneous communities, but is increasingly difficult to command in the largest urban areas where the divisiveness of life leads to splintered moral and social concepts. In effect this report tells us that where you have substantial community concern you don't require the law, but lacking

such concern, the law is a substitute of uncertain
effectiveness.

If, then, legal rules controlling human conduct
are designed to emphasize and reinforce society's
moral convictions only in those areas where the
pressures for transgression are the greatest and
the resulting social consequences the most serious,
there is a notable lack of justification for such intervention in the Commission's findings as to the
magnitude of the public's concern and the efficacy
of the enforcement of current obscenity laws. As
has so often occurred, an approach which was both
defendable and workable in one era has become vul-
nerable and suspect in another.

Fairness, however, requires that despite these
formidable considerations something more be said
and therein is to be found the primary reason for
this individual statement. It is by no means certain that the Commission's national study, accurate
as it has every reason to be in presenting a national
consensus, has an equal validity in depicting the
group thinking of a given geographical area, state,
or community. It is believable, therefore, that
notwithstanding the findings in the national reports,
and quite consistent with them, there well may be
found geographical pockets of homogeneous conviction, various regional, state, and local units where
the requisite massive majority support essential for
the legal codification of community standards does
exist. My concurrence in the recommendation for
the abolition of obscenity controls for consenting
adults is not intended to express my disapproval of
the right of any such group, so constituted, to challenge and attempt to override the substantial findings
of law and fact which the Commission has determined to be persuasive in order to sustain their
own deeply and widely held beliefs: a very considerable body of legislation in this country rests on just
such a base of moral and social traditions.

It is a base, however, which is being undercut
and eroded by the currents of the time and because
this is so it may not now upon fair and objective
examination be found to be of sufficient dimensions
to sustain its burden.

11. The broadcasting or telecasting of explicit sexual material has not constituted a serious problem in the

past. There is, however, a potential in this area
for thrusting sexually explicit materials upon un-
willing persons. Existing federal statutes imposing
criminal and civil penalties upon any broadcast of
"obscene" material do not adequately address this
problem because they do not describe with sufficient
specificity what material would be prohibited, or
under what conditions. Hence, the repeal of these
statutes is recommended, upon the understanding
that the Federal Communications Commission either
already has, or can acquire through legislation,
adequate power to promulgate and enforce specific
rules in this area should the need arise.

12. Commissioners Edward E. Elson and Winfrey C. Link.

13. Commissioners Otto N. Larsen and Marvin E. Wolfgang disagree for reasons stated in their separate
statement. Commissioner Morton A. Hill, S. J.
disagrees for reasons stated in his separate statement.

14. Commissioners Edward E. Elson and Freeman Lewis
believe that segregating that material prohibited for
sale to juveniles from that which is available to all
would only enhance its appeal. Further, Commissioner Elson believes that juveniles would be protected from viewing sexually explicit materials if
the Model Public Display Statute were extended to
apply to those places technically private but public
in the sense that they offer free and open access
to all. Moreover, such an extension would significantly insulate the general public from such materials being thrust upon them without their consent.

15. Commissioner Morton A. Hill, S. J. See his separate
statement for his reasons.

16. Commissioners Edward E. Elson, Thomas D. Gill,
Joseph T. Klapper, Irving Lehrman, Winfrey C.
Link, Thomas C. Lynch, and Cathryn A. Spelts.

17. Commissioners Thomas D. Gill finds this conclusion
acceptable at the present time, but if experience
demonstrates that the effective enforcement of juvenile statutes which proscribe written as well as pictorial material is hampered by the problem of

scienter he believes the labelling statute promises
to be an appropriate method of correction and should
be tried.   Commissioners Irving Lehrman and
Cathryn A. Spelts join in this footnote.

18.   Commissioners Edward E. Elson and Winfrey C. Link.

19.   Commissioners Otto N. Larsen, Freeman Lewis, and
        Marvin E. Wolfgang believe that a public display
        statute specifically aimed at erotic material is un-
        necessary.   Very few jurisdictions have such a
        statute now.   The execution of existing statutes and
        ordinances concerned with the projection of generally
        offensive objects, erotic or not, before the public
        provides all the spatial boundaries on public display
        of offensive erotica that is needed.   Moreover,
        these three Commissioners believe that the offen-
        siveness which may be caused by undesired exposure
        to sexual depictions is not so serious in scope or
        degree to warrant legislative response.

20.   Commissioners Edward E. Elson and Winfrey C. Link
        believe that the model display statute should be so
        extended as to apply to those places technically pri-
        vate but public in the sense that they offer free and
        open access to all.   The statute would then cover,
        for example, retail stores, transportation terminals,
        and building lobbies.   It would then prevent poten-
        tially offensive sexually explicit materials from be-
        ing thrust upon the public unexpectedly at any time.

21.   Commissioners Edward E. Elson, Morton A. Hill,
        S. J. , Winfrey C. Link, Thomas C. Lynch, and
        Cathryn A. Spelts.

22.   Commissioners Otto N. Larsen and Marvin E. Wolf-
        gang.   See their separate statement.   Commissioner
        Freeman Lewis dissents for two reasons: (1) that
        legislation restricting only the mailing of sexually
        oriented materials when so many other kinds of un-
        solicited mail also produce offense is bad public
        policy because it is too particular and too arbitrary;
        and (2) that the frequency of offense caused by un-
        solicited sexually oriented mail is demonstrably so
        minute that it does not warrant either the costs of
        the requisite machinery for operation and enforce-
        ment or the exorbitant expenses which would be

forced upon this particular small category of mailers in order to comply. In his opinion, the most effective resolution of this problem is to employ the same technique commonly used for any other kinds of unwanted, unsolicited mail: throw it in the garbage pail.

23. Potentially offensive sexual advertisement means:
"(A) Any advertisement containing a pictorial representation or a detailed verbal description of uncovered human genitals or pubic areas, human sexual intercourse, masturbation, sodomy (i. e., bestiality or oral or anal intercourse), direct physical stimulation of unclothed genitals or flagellation or torture in the context of a sexual relationship; or
"(B) Any advertisement containing a pictorial representation or detailed verbal description of an artificial human penis or vagina or device primarily designed physically to stimulate genitals;
"Provided that, material otherwise within the definition of this subsection shall not be deemed to be a potentially offensive sexual advertisement if it constitutes only a small and insignificant part of the whole of a single catalogue, book, or other work, the remainder of which does not primarily treat sexual matters and, provided further, that the Postmaster General shall, from time to time, issue regulations of general applicability exempting certain types of material, or material addressed to certain categories of addressees, such as advertisements for works of fine art or solicitations of a medical, scientific, or other similar nature addressed to a specialized audience, from the definition of potentially offensive sexual advertisement contained in this subsection, where the purpose of this section does not call for application of the requirements of this section. "

24. Commissioners Morton A. Hill, S. J. and Winfrey C. Link.

25. Commissioners Morton A. Hill, S. J. and Winfrey C. Link.

26. Commissioner Cathryn A. Spelts.

27. The state statutes which appear to the Commission

presently to impose prohibitions upon the consensual
distribution of sexual material to adults are the fol-
lowing: Ala. Code tit. 14, Section 374(4) (1958);
Alaska Stat. Section 11.40.160 (1962); Ariz. Reg.
Stat. Ann. Section 13-532 (1956); Ark. Stat. Ann.
Section 41-2701, 2703, (1947); Cal. Penal Code
Section 311.2 (West 1969); Colo. Rev. Stat. Ann.
Section 40-9-16 (1963); Conn. Gen. Stat. Ann. Section 53-244 (1958); Del. Code Ann. tit. 11, Section
711 (1953); Fla. Stat. Ann. Section 847.011 (1965);
Ga. Code Ann. Section 26-2101 (1969); Hawaii Rev.
Stat. Section 727-8 (1968); Idaho Code Ann. Section
18-4101 (3, 4, 5), 4102 (1947); Ill. Ann. Stat. Ch.
38, Section 11-20 (Smith-Hurd 1954); Ind. Ann.
Stat. Section 9-601 (Fifth); Section 9-604(b); Section
10-2803 (1956); Iowa Code Ann. Section 725.3-6
(1950); Kan. Stat. Ann. Sections 21-1102, 1115,
1118 (1964); Ky. Rev. Stat. Section 436.101 (1962);
La. Rev. Stat. Section 14.106 (1950); Me. Rev.
Stat. Ann. tit. 17, Sections 2901, 2904, 2905 (1964);
Md. Ann. Code Art. 27, Section 418 (1957); Mass.
Ann. Laws Ch. 272, Section 28A, B, Section 31,
32 (1932); Mich. Comt. Laws Section 750.343a-b
(1968); Minn. Stat. Ann. Section 617.241; Section
617.26 (1964); Miss. Code. Ann. Sections 2280,
2286, 2288, 2674.03 (1942); Mo. Ann. Stat. Sections
563.270, .280, .290 (1953); Mont. Rev. Codes Ann.
Sections 94.3601, .3602 (1969); Neb. Rev. Stat.
Sections 28.921, .922 (1964); Nev. Rev. Stat. Section 201.250 (1969); N.H. Rev. Stat. Ann. Section
571A (1955); N.J. Rev. Stat. Section 2A: 115-2
(1951); N.Y. Penal Law Sections 235.00, .05, .10,
.15 (McKinney's 1967); N.C. Gen. Stat. Sections
14-189, 189.1, .2, 14-190 (1969). N.D. Cent. Code
Section 12-21-09 (1960); Ohio Rev. Code Ann. Sections 2905.34, .342(A), .36, .40, .41 (Page 1953);
Okla. Stat. Ann. tit. 21, Sections 1021(3)(4), 1040.8,
.13 (1958); Ore. Rev. Stat. Section 167.151 (1969);
Pa. Stat. Ann. tit. 18 Sections 4524, 4528 (1963);
R.I. Gen. Laws Ann. Sections 11-31-1, 3, 4 (1956);
S.C. Code Ann. Section 16-414.1 (1962); S.D. Compiled Laws Ann. Sections 22-24-11, 12 (1967);
Tenn. Code Ann. Section 39-3003 (1955); Tex.
Penal Code Art. 527(1) (1948); Utah Code Ann. Section 76-39-5(1-5) (1953); Va. Code Ann. Sections
18.1-228, 229, 230 (1950); Wash. Rev. Code Sec-
tions 9.68.010, .020 (1961); W. Va. Code Ann.

Sec. 61-8-11 (1966); Wis. Stat. Sections 944.21,
.22, .23 (1958); Wyo. Stat. Ann. Sections 6-103,
104 (1957); D. C. Code Ann. Section 22-2001 (Supp.
III, 1970).

28. This statute could also be adapted to use in connection
with federal legislation.

29. About half the members of the Commission favor requiring local prosecutors to obtain the approval of a
law enforcement official with state-wide jurisdiction,
such as the Attorney General, before instituting an
action.

30. A different appeal route or procedure may be deemed
appropriate in States with three levels of courts.

APPENDIX C

STATEMENTS FOR AND ON THE COMMISSION
ON OBSCENITY AND PORNOGRAPHY

1. Statement of the American Library Association,
    Prepared for the Commission ..., May 4, 1970*

Background

      Founded in 1876, the American Library Association
is the oldest and largest library association in the world.
A non-profit, educational organization, it represents more
than 39,000 librarians, trustees, institutions, and friends of
libraries from the United States, Canada, and over eighty
other countries. It is, furthermore, the chief spokesman
for the modern library movement in North America and, to
a considerable extent, throughout the world.

      The Association was created for the purpose of pro-
moting library service and librarianship. In support of this
purpose, the Association seeks to make ideas, particularly
through printed matter, vital forces in American life and to
make libraries, the storehouses of ideas and knowledge,
easily accessible to all people. The Association also seeks
to improve professional standards of librarianship and to
create and publish professional literature.

"Library Bill of Rights" and "Freedom to Read Statement"

      Library service in the United States is built on the
concept of intellectual freedom. The term is defined in the
Library Bill of Rights, the Association's basic policy statement concerning the concept. This document states that it

*As prepared and offered by Mrs. Judith F. Krug, Director,
Office of Intellectual Freedom, American Library Association.

is the responsibility of library service to provide books and
other materials representing all points of view concerning
the problems and issues of our times. It further states
that no library materials should be proscribed or removed
from libraries because of partisan or doctrinal disapproval.
In pursuance of the fulfillment of this philosophy, the document contends that the rights of an individual to the use of
a library should not be denied or abridged because of his
age, race, religion, national origins or social or political
views.

Originally adopted in 1939, the Library Bill of Rights
was extensively revised in 1948.   Further revisions were
approved by the Council, the governing body of the Association, in 1961 and 1967.   Each revision, while broadening the
Association's interpretation of intellectual freedom, also reflected changes that had occurred in regard to the concept
of the library.   This institution is no longer the stronghold
of the printed word, but now accommodates all materials
that can help provide information and enlightenment.   This
means that not only books, magazines, and newspapers, but
also tapes, pictures, films, recordings--indeed, all expressions regardless of form--have a valid, if not required,
place in a library.

The same concern that led the Association to adopt
the Library Bill of Rights led it, in 1940, to establish the
Intellectual Freedom Committee.   The Committee was
charged with the responsibility "to recommend such steps
as may be necessary to safeguard the rights of library users
in accordance with the Bill of Rights of the United States
and the Library Bill of Rights as adopted by the ALA Council. " Among its many activities, the Intellectual Freedom
Committee has developed supportive and interpretive documents relating to the Association's position on intellectual
freedom.   Prime among these is the Freedom to Read Statement, formulated in conjunction with the American Book Publishers Council.   The Statement stresses the necessity for
free access to all information and ideas, regardless of the
form the expression takes.

Association Position Regarding Obscenity and Pornography

With particular reference to obscenity, the Freedom
to Read Statement asserts the Association's belief that Americans can be trusted to recognize and reject obscenity.   It

further states that individuals in a free society do not need
the help of organized censors to assist them in this task.
One reason for this belief is that the Association cannot determine the individual or group in whom this power over all
other individuals and groups can be vested.

As public servants, librarians are required to act in
accordance with existing laws relating to obscenity. Such
legislation, however, is directly in conflict with the goal of
librarians to make available the widest diversity of views
and expressions, including those which are unorthodox or
unpopular with the majority. In this context, the Freedom
to Read Statement implies that such legislation--insofar as
it coerces the tastes of others, confines adults to materials
deemed suitable for adolescents, or inhibits the efforts of
creative people to achieve artistic expression--must be challenged by librarians through every legal means available.

In addition, it seems to the Association that laws
dealing with so-called obscenity are contrary to the main-
tenance of a free society and, therefore, are contrary to
the public interest. The Bill of Rights, particularly the
First Amendment, has given to each citizen the right to
think what he pleases on any subject and to express his
point of view in whatever manner he deems appropriate, be
it orally or graphically, publicly or privately. To utilize
this "right" effectively, a man must have something to think
about, something on which to base his own opinions and decisions. Generally, this is in terms of other men's thinking. Access to the ideas of other men, therefore, is a
necessity.

This, then, is the philosophy guiding librarians in ac-
quiring and making available information representing all
points of view on all questions and issues. Freedom keeps
open the path of novel and creative solutions and enables
change to come by choice.

Alleged Gravity of "Situation" Constitutes Specious Argument

At the present time, the American Library Association does not view the alleged situation regarding obscenity
and pornography as a grave one. It views it, rather, as
one that is impossible to assess in objective terms. This
view is predicated on three significant aspects of the situation.

First, to state that the situation is grave is to imply that an acceptable definition of obscenity and pornography is available.   As the Commission, itself, stated in its Progress Report of July, 1969, there is no generally accepted definition of either "obscenity" or "pornography. " The Association believes, furthermore, that it is a practical impossibility to define these words.   Each human being is an individual with his own wants, needs, and desires.   These, in turn, have been determined by the various environments in which the individual has lived; by the values, principles, and goals instilled in him by his parents and others who were or are in positions to influence him; and finally, by the experiences that one has throughout his life.

To allow for human diversity, the Association, in the Freedom to Read Statement, assigned the responsibility of defining "obscene and pornographic materials" to the individual citizen, in accordance with his own judgment and tastes.

The Association reaffirms its belief in this Statement and suggests that if individuals can ever be considered identical to one another, perhaps it will be possible to determine a definition of "obscenity and pornography. " Of course, if such a definition were to be imposed, that day when all individuals were alike would be much closer.

Secondly, to state that the situation is grave is to imply that there is a demonstrable relationship between allegedly obscene and pornographic materials and overt, antisocial acts.   The Commission, however, has recognized in its Progress Report (July, 1969) that there is little, if any, reliable, empirical evidence to substantiate a belief in such a causal relationship.   The Association contends that what an individual hears, sees, or reads serves to reinforce previously learned behavior.   Seeing and hearing, and particularly reading, are acts of the mind.   It does not follow that thought processes are invariably translated into overt action.

Furthermore, the Association adheres to the belief that it is the right and the responsibility of parents--not public officials--to guide their children, and only their children, to informational sources for any subject in which the children express a need or an interest.   In line with this belief, the Library Bill of Rights specifically states that an individual shall not be restricted in his use of the library, whether materials or services, because of his age.

Thirdly, to state that the situation is grave is to imply that it somehow requires enforced legislative control. It implies further that there is a necessity for such suppression and that this necessity outweighs the benefit of continuing our national tradition of freedom of speech and freedom of the press. Implicit, furthermore, in this advocation of legal suppression is the belief that restrictions upon publication and dissemination of one kind of materials will not adversely affect the publication and dissemination of other kinds of materials. This, however, does not seem to be the case.

Censorship Attempts

A review of the history of censorship attempts and a survey of contemporary conditions indicates that suppression of one kind of materials does lead to the extension of the license to other kinds of materials. In effect, the acceptance of one kind of suppression fosters a climate for the acceptance and perpetuation of suppression in other areas.

To illustrate, the Association believes that our culture would have suffered if would-be censors in the past had succeeded in their attempts to eradicate or bowdlerize certain creative works which were repugnant to various segments of the society. Among these works are the comedies of Aristophanes, the plays of Shakespeare, the "Song of Songs" from the Bible, Chaucer's Canterbury Tales, Walt Whitman's Leaves of Grass, James Joyce's Ulysses, D. H. Lawrence's Lady Chatterley's Lover, J. D. Salinger's Catcher in the Rye, and more recently, Claude Brown's Manchild in the Promised Land. The writers of these works each expressed, with superlative skill, some aspect of our common humanity. Still, each of these works has been banned or mutilated at one time or another. Who is to say what pieces of outrageous literature will someday gain respectability and acceptance?

That suppression of allegedly obscene materials leads easily to suppression of other kinds of ideas is illustrated by the popular view and treatment of the underground, "dissident," or "alternative" press. Many historians and educators have pointed out the social and historical value of the underground press as a recorder of a movement which escapes objective coverage in the conventional news media. It is estimated that, in an average underground newspaper, 30% may be morally objectionable to some. The remaining 70%

deals with social and political issues.   Yet, courts have
found particular issues of the underground newspapers to be
obscene.   This leads the Association to believe that some
individuals are utilizing the moral question which--granted--
is able to arouse great emotions, as a screen from behind
which social and political ideas, somewhat contrary to those
currently in vogue, can be attacked.

Self-Censorship

        As a result of their controversial nature, underground
newspapers have been banned from the library collections of
some institutions.   Printers, on occasion, have refused to
handle the papers.   Certain principals and college adminis-
trators have attempted to suppress the production of "underground" publications at their institutions.   Police have ar-
rested street vendors, sometimes confiscating their publications through extra-legal methods.   College editors have re-
signed to protest administrational censorship.   Well-known
underground publications have ceased activity completely because of an inability to withstand legal and extra-legal in-
timidation and censorship.   The long-range result may be
the eventual curtailment or extinction of a valuable historical
record and a truly "alternative" voice.

        What effect has "creeping censorship" had on the li-
brary?   During the summer of 1969, the mayor of Memphis,
Tennessee received national news coverage when he pro-
claimed Portnoy's Complaint to be a "dirty book. "   He did
not believe that it should be in the library, and certainly
was against using taxpayers' money for "this kind" of material.   It did not matter that the book was #1 on the Best-
seller List, nor did it matter that the Memphis Public Library had almost 100 requests for the book.

        Just three months ago, the mayor of Madison, Wis-
consin, launched a crusade against the public library to remove all allegedly obscene materials.

        A librarian in a Chicago Public High School placed
Claude Brown's Manchild in the Promised Land in her office
and required any student wishing to read it to bring a note
from his teacher.   She believed the book to be detrimental
to any individual in the school who would read it, since it
clearly reflected the individual's current situation.

A librarian from a small Chicago suburb refused to have "Portnoy's Complaint or any books like that" in her collection. Books "like that" included medical texts and particularly, art books.

A librarian in the Missouri State Library was fired for writing a letter to the local newspaper protesting the suppression of an underground newspaper published and distributed by University of Missouri students.

In St. Louis County (Missouri), some book dealers and librarians are finding it politically expedient to remove "controversial books from their shelves at the suggestion of police."

In New Orleans, a new ordinance, which combines the provisions of Ginzberg v. New York, the "variable obscenity law," with certain provisions of the 1968 Postal Law, allows any individual to walk into a book store or a public library and demand that any piece of material be removed from the shelf. We understand that if the bookstore owner or the librarian should not carry out this directive, he is liable to criminal prosecution.

In the Los Angeles Public Library, the professional staff asked the city attorney for an opinion in regard to California's "variable obscenity law," which went into effect November 10, 1969. The Assistant City Attorney, in response, stated that if a librarian is in doubt, he must--for his own good--censor the materials.

Closing

All of these examples, occurring in rapid succession, leads the Association to believe that we are functioning in a "repressive" climate and that any further controls may prove completely stifling. Of particular concern to the Association is that individual or group of individuals who would be chosen to determine what the general public is permitted to read, see, and hear. Some of the finest minds in our society have wrestled with the problem of exactly what is to be deemed "obscene and pornographic." We are no closer to a generally acceptable definition today than we were when the Bill of Rights was adopted. Of course, this is undoubtedly one of the reasons for the First Amendment to the United States Constitution.

Since a definition of the term or terms seems impossible and since, as noted previously, there is little, if any, reliable empirical evidence to substantiate the belief of a causal relationship between certain materials and behavior, it would seem to the Association that any further concrete action must be based on a strictly personal point of view. We strongly advocate personal points of view--and, in fact, the entire profession is geared to helping people arrive at personal points of view. But we do not believe that we have yet reached the juncture where citizens in this country must be dictated to by individuals and/or groups of individuals in accordance with the beliefs that these persons hold.

The Association recognizes that many people find much of what is uttered or printed in the various communications media to be offensive or objectionable. That there is fear and concern is easily documented by reference to reactions in the press and other media. The success of nationally organized community efforts to rally large numbers of supporters of "decent literature" to their cause is further evidence of the widespread concern. The Commission, itself, is a visible manifestation of the fact that the tastes of many people have been offended. The fear is obvious. The justification for this fear is not obvious.

The American Library Association contends that the dangers of legislative control of any materials are far easier to prove and much more significant in their implications. We maintain that it is the responsibility of those who believe in repression to show, beyond a reasonable doubt, that their way is superior to free choice.

In accordance with these beliefs and its basic philosophy regarding intellectual freedom, the American Library Association urges the Commission on Obscenity and Pornography not to recommend any further controls on the population's access to materials of any kind.

2.   Resolution on the Report of the Commission on Obscenity and Pornography (Adopted January 20, 1971, by the ALA Council)

WHEREAS, The Commission on Obscenity and Pornography performed a difficult and historically significant service for the nation by initiating the first, broad scientific inquiry into the nature of obscene and pornographic materials and their effect upon users, and

WHEREAS, The Commission's efforts resulted in an important body of empirical data which should serve as the basis for sound and continuing evaluation and study of an area of social and legislative concern too long ignored, and

WHEREAS, The U. S. Senate rejected the REPORT OF THE COMMISSION ON OBSCENITY AND PORNOGRAPHY by a 60-5 vote, and the President of the United States, said, "I have evaluated that report and categorically reject its morally bankrupt conclusions and major recommendations, " be it therefore

RESOLVED, That the American Library Association commends the success of the Commission on Obscenity and Pornography for amassing a significant body of empirical evidence in an area of great social concern heretofore excluded as a subject for serious scientific investigation, and be it

FURTHER RESOLVED, That the American Library Association urges the Senate and the President of the United States to reconsider their categorical rejection of this significant data and to encourage the dissemination and evaluation of these materials by the citizenry of the United States, and be it

FURTHER RESOLVED, That the American Library Association urges all libraries to provide their users with complete access to the REPORT OF THE COMMISSION ON OBSCENITY AND PORNOGRAPHY and to the important supportive volumes and critical evaluations of the REPORT and its research in consonance with the library's role in the dissemination of information vital to the communities they serve.

3. Coalition Statement on the Report of the Federal
    Commission on Obscenity and Pornography
    (Released January, 1971)

The recently-issued Report of the Federal Commission on Obscenity and Pornography, created by the Congress
three years ago, was greeted with criticism based mainly on
pre-conceived premises and personal attacks on Commission
members.

The organizations which sign this statement deplore
this reaction, which contravenes the process of rational discussion through which decisions on public issues should be
made in a democracy. We agree with the wise words of
Thomas Jefferson: "If the book be false in its facts, disprove them; if false in its reasoning, refute it. But for
God's sake, let us hear freely from both sides. "

The Commission's Report represents two years of in-
tensive efforts by dedicated men and women, working under
a Congressional mandate which instructed them to explore
facets of a social issue which disturbs various segments of
the national community. They have produced a 646-page
Report and ten volumes of supporting factual evidence which
are an exhaustive treatment of the subject. That in itself
is a praise-worthy contribution to public understanding.

But the Commission's Report is not entitled to auto-
matic acceptance simply because of its thorough study. Some
of the undersigned organizations hold different views from
the Commission, and may ultimately reject certain of its
recommendations. But, despite our varying views on the
question of obscenity, we all agree that the Report must receive a full, fair hearing; that its findings and recommendations should be tested in even-tempered dialogue; and that
those who debate the Report should read it--and deal with
its specific findings and recommendations.

The Report did not--as critics have erroneously
charged--recommend abolition of all laws regulating obscenity. On the contrary, the Commission recommended laws to
prohibit the distribution of sexually explicit pictorial material
to minors, the public display of sexually explicit material,
and the mailing of unsolicited advertising for such material.
The Commission emphasized that adults who do not wish to
receive obscene material should be protected from having it
thrust upon them against their wishes. In short, the

Commission did not, as some opponents suggested, recommend opening the floodgates for a wave of obscenity to engulf the public.

What the Report did recommend was the abolition of those obscenity laws which prohibit the distribution of materials to adults who choose to receive them.   This is not a radical innovation.   The Supreme Court has ruled that the First Amendment protects an adult's right to read and see whatever he chooses, and we believe the same constitutional principles necessarily protect the publisher or bookseller who sells these materials to consenting adults.

While others disagree with this conclusion, these differences are legitimate subjects of debate.   And there should be debate also on the Commission's conclusions that obscenity statutes, because of their vagueness, suppress non-obscene works, and that scientific studies provide no evidence that obscene books or motion pictures incite adults to criminal conduct, sexual deviancy, or emotional disturbances.   There should also be discussion of the Commission's proposals for a broad-scale program of sex education and for further scientific investigation.

The undersigned do not necessarily agree with each other about the issue of obscenity and its significance in American life.   But we are united in our concern about censorship, and the need for freedom of thought and freedom of expression--freedom of choice--in all areas of human existence.   This is why, without endorsing or opposing the Commission's Report, we commend it for serious study and debate by legislators, courts, community leaders and the general public.   We urge that proponents and opponents of the Report participate fully and rationally in this process, a venture which can enlarge intelligent understanding of a social question that requires wise decision-making.

American Civil Liberties Union
American Federation of Teachers
American Jewish Committee
American Library Association
American Orthopsychiatric Association
American Public Health Association
Association of American University Presses, Inc.
Association of American Publishers, Inc.
Authors League of America, Inc.
Bureau of Independent Publishers and Distributors

*John Donovan, Executive Director, The Children's Book
    Council, Inc.
*Charlton Heston, President, Screen Actors Guild
 International Reading Association
 Jewish War Veterans of the USA
 National Association of Theatre Owners, Inc.
 The National Book Committee, Inc.
 National Council for Social Studies
 National Council of Churches of Christ in the USA
 National Council of Jewish Women
 National Council of Teachers of English
 National Education Association
 National Library Week Program
 National Board, YWCA
*Lewis I. Maddocks, Executive Director, Council for
    Christian Action of United Church of Christ
*The Rev. Everett Parker, Director, Office of Communi-
    cation, The United Church of Christ
 Periodicals and Book Association of America, Inc.
 P.E.N. American Center
 Sex Information and Education Council of the United
    States, Inc.
 Union of American Hebrew Congregations
 Women's National Book Association
 Speech Communication Association

---

*Organization's name for identification only

APPENDIX D

BRITISH ARTS COUNCIL
"WORKING PARTY" RECOMMENDATIONS

The following statements are the main recommendations of the "Working Party" of the Arts Council of Great
Britain, as submitted to the Home Secretary and Parliament
in 1969.

(1) It is not for the state to prohibit private citizens from
     choosing what they may or may not enjoy in literature
     or art unless there were incontrovertible evidence that
     the result would be injurious to society.   There is no
     such evidence.

(2) No crystal ball can lay down dogmatically whether more
     or less pornography would result from Repeal but in any
     case there is complete absence of evidence to suggest
     that sex in the arts, even when aphrodisiac in intention,
     has criminal or anti-social repercussions.

(3) Though it is sometimes conjectured with no indisputable
     evidence that heavy and prolonged exposure to the por-
     trayal of violence may not only reflect but also influence
     the standards of society, violence has been ubiquitous in
     the art, literature and press of the civilised world for
     so long that censorship must by now be recognised as a
     totally inadequate weapon to combat it.   Indeed laws
     available for the purpose including the Obscenity Acts
     are virtually never even invoked against it. *

*The only case concerning violence under the 1959 and 1964
Obscenity Acts was "D. P. P. v. A. & B. C. Chewing Gum
Ltd. , with this firm being convicted for issuing, inside
packets of bubble-gum, cards picturing atomic atrocities
considered likely to deprave their juvenile customers. "

288

(4) Since judges have to work in what is in effect a legal vacuum, the prosecution of an occasional book--usually the wrong one--often succeeds only in bringing the law into disrepute, without effectively preventing the distribution even of that book.

(5) The very objective of the law is not even established, let alone identified in concrete meaningful terms that could command acceptance. Although judges emphasise that an article cannot be condemned because it shocks or disgusts, in practice that is precisely what happens, since juries have no other criteria to guide them.

(6) It is impossible to devise a definition of obscenity that does not beg the question or a rational procedure for weighting depravity and corruption against artistic merit and the "public good."

(7) When juries and defendants are without a comprehensible definition of the crime alleged, the defendant is left at the mercy of a personal opinion; which is a system of censorship rather than a system of law.

(8) It is intolerable that a man should be criminally punished for an action that he has no means of ascertaining in advance is criminal.

(9) Incitement to criminal behavior is sufficiently covered by the ordinary law of incitement. To that extent the Obscenity Acts are redundant. In so far as they add to the concept of an unintentional tendency toward crime as a punishable offence they are to be deplored.

(10) It is an affront both to legal and common sense that incitement to a non-crime should be punishable as a crime; and worse when this doctrine is extended to a mere tendency.

(11) No encouragement should be given to the concept of the State as a custos morum [guardian of morals] with its corollary that merely to shock is a criminal offence.

(12) The proper sanction for breaches of taste or non-conformity with current mores should be social reprobation and not penal legislation.

APPENDIX E

CHAPTER NOTES

Chapter 1

1. Joseph Wood Krutch, "Introduction," in: Eliseo Vivas, The Moral Life and the Ethical Life (Chicago: Henry Regnery, 1963), p. 9.
2. James Harvey Robinson, The Mind in the Making (N. Y.: Harper, 1921), p. 205.

Chapter 2

1. V. Gordon Childe, Man Makes Himself (N. Y.: New American Library, 1951), p. 94.
2. Ibid., p. 55.
3. Ibid.
4. Sigmund Freud, Totem and Taboo (N. Y.: Vintage Books, 1946), p. 44.
5. Fritz Steiner, Taboo (Baltimore, Md.: Penguin Books, 1967), p. 20.
6. Edward Westermarck, Ethical Relativity (Patterson, N. J.: Littlefield, Adams, 1960), p. 166.
7. Georges Bataille, Death and Sensuality (N. Y.: Ballantine Books, 1969), p. 1.
8. Freud, op. cit., p. 44.
9. Bataille, op. cit., p. 44.
10. Ibid., pp. 44-45.
11. Sir James E. Frazer, Taboo (N. Y.: Macmillan, 1935), p. 11.
12. Ibid., p. 142, 156, 166-167, 188, 196, 200.
13. Freud, op. cit., p. 128.
14. Kaj Birket-Smith, The Paths of Culture (Madison, Wisc.: University of Wisconsin Press, 1965), p. 232.
15. Ibid., p. 100.
16. Ibid., p. 181.

17. Robert H. Lowie, Primitive Society (N.Y.: Horace
     Liveright, 1920), p. 414.
18. Bronislaw Malinowski, Sex and Repression in Savage
     Society (Cleveland, Ohio: World Publishing Com-
     pany, 1968), p. 73, 74-75.
19. Emile Durkheim, The Elementary Forms of the Reli-
     gious Life (Glencoe, Ill.: Free Press, 1947), p.
     300.
20. Ibid., p. 301.
21. Ibid., p. 311.
22. Malinowski, op. cit., p. 173, 174-175.
23. Ibid., pp. 175-176.
24. Ibid., p. 177.
25. Bataille, op. cit., p. 5.
26. Ibid., p. 25.
27. Ibid., p. 44.
28. Ibid., p. 35.
29. Ibid., p. 57.
30. V. F. Calverton and S. D. Schmalhausen, eds., Sex
     in Civilization (Garden City, N.Y.: Garden City
     Publishing Company, 1929), p. 9.
31. Lucien Lévy-Bruhl, Primitive Mentality (N.Y.: Mac-
     millan, 1923), p. 266.
32. Ibid., p. 268.
33. J. C. Flugel, Man, Morals and Society (N.Y.: Viking
     Press, 1961), pp. 123-143.
34. Leslie A. White, The Science of Culture (N.Y.: Grove
     Press, 1949), p. 356.
35. Frazer, op. cit., p. 218.

Chapter 3

1. Walter J. Ong, The Presence of the Word (N.Y.:
    Simon and Schuster, 1970), p. 22.
2. Ibid., p. 23.
3. The New English Bible (N.Y.: Oxford University Press,
    1961), p. 15.
4. Ong, op. cit., pp. 182-188.
5. Ibid., p. 190.
6. S. J. Tambih, "The Magic Power of Words," Man,
    N.S., vol. 3, no. 2 (June 2, 1968), p. 184.
7. Sir James Frazer, op. cit., p. 318.
8. Margo Astrov, The Winged Serpent (N.Y.: John Day,
    1946), pp. 19-52, passim.
9. John C. Condon, Semantics and Communication (N.Y.:
    Macmillan, 1966), p. 97.

10. Otto Jespersen, Language: Its Nature, Development, and Origin (N. Y.: Norton, 1964), (first published 1921), p. 239.
11. Paul Radin, Primitive Man as a Philosopher (N. Y.: Appleton, 1920), p. 59.
12. J. C. Flugel, op. cit., p. 140, 142.
13. Quoted in: Flugel, op. cit., p. 142.
14. Flugel, op. cit., p. 143.
15. Edward Sagarin, The Anatomy of Dirty Words (N. Y.: Paperback Library, 1969), p. 103.
16. Edward Sagarin, "An Essay on Obscenity and Pornography," Humanist (July-August, 1967), p. 10.
17. Ibid., p. 11.
18. James Henry Breasted, The Dawn of Conscience (N. Y.: Scribner's, 1933), p. 37.
19. Ibid.
20. V. Gordon Childe, op. cit., p. 148, 150.
21. Joshua Trachtenberg, Jewish Magic and Superstition (Philadelphia: Meridian Books and Jewish Publication Society, 1961), p. 104 et seq.
22. Julius Guttmann, Philosophies of Judaism (Garden City, N. Y.: Anchor Books, Doubleday, 1966), pp. 28-32.
23. Ibid., p. 28.
24. A Handbook of Christian Theology (Cleveland: World Publishing Co., 1958), p. 214.
25. Samuel Sandmel, A Jewish Understanding of the New Testament (Cincinnati: Hebrew Union College Press, 1957), p. 51.
26. Rudolf Bultmann, Jesus and the Word (N. Y.: Scribner's, 1934), p. 217, 218.
27. Ibid., p. 12, 13.
28. Eberhard and Phyllis Kronhausen, Pornography and the Law (N. Y.: Ballantine Books, 1959), p. 26.
29. Ibid., p. 143.
30. Ibid., p. 55.
31. C. K. Ogden and I. A. Richards, The Meaning of Meaning (N. Y.: Harcourt, Brace, 1956), 8th Edition, pp. 24-47, 29.
32. Bronislaw Malinowski, "Supplement I: the Problem of Meaning in Primitive Languages," in: Ogden and Richards, op. cit. p. 322.

Chapter 4

1. Gilbert Murray, Greek Studies (London: Oxford University Press, 1946), p. 3.

2. Ibid., pp. 4-5.
3. It is true that one of Plato's last dialogues, the Laws, put literature (indeed, all the arts) under censorship, forbidding any ideas to be expressed which the rules of the state deemed dangerous to public morals and faith. But Will Durant, in his Life of Greece (N.Y.: Simon and Schuster, 1939), says (p. 523): "A long life is not always a blessing; it would have been better for Plato to have died before writing ... these prolegomena to all future Inquisitions."
4. Murray, op. cit., p. 15.
5. Ibid., p. 75.
6. G. Lowes Dickinson, The Greek View of Life (Garden City, N.Y.: Doubleday, Doran, 1931), pp. 24, 27, 28.
7. Dickinson, op. cit., p. 148.
8. Ibid., p. 158.
9. Crane Brinton, A History of Western Morals (N.Y.: Harcourt Brace, 1959), pp. 105-106.
10. Will Durant, Caesar and Christ (N.Y.: Simon and Schuster, 1944), p. 29.
11. Livy, History, quoted in: William Stearns Davis, Readings in Ancient History, vol. II, (Boston: Allyn and Bacon, 1913), pp. 99-100.
12. Davis, op. cit. (note 11), p. 97.
13. Durant, op. cit., p. 90.
14. Brinton, op. cit., p. 112.
15. Durant, Caesar and Christ (N.Y.: Simon and Schuster, 1944), p. 274.
16. Ibid., p. 97.
17. Bertrand Russell, A History of Western Philosophy (N.Y.: Simon and Schuster, 1945), p. 266.
18. Marcus Aurelius Antonius, The Meditations, in: Whitney J. Oates, ed., The Stoic and Epicurean Philosophers (N.Y.: Random House, 1940), pp. 510, 575, 577.
19. Epictetus, The Manual, in: Oates, op. cit., pp. 475, 478.

Chapter 5

1. F. R. Tennant, The Sources of the Doctrines of the Fall and Original Sin (N.Y.: Schocken Books, 1968). First published 1903.
2. Ibid., p. 10.
3. Ibid., p. 13.

4.   Theodor Reik, Myth and Guilt (N. Y.: Grosset and Dun-
        lap, 1970), p. 32.
5.   Tennant, op. cit., p. 249.
6.   Cf. Bultmann, op. cit., pp. 99-105, 197-200.
7.   Shailer Matthews, The Social Teachings of Jesus (N. Y.:
        Macmillan, 1905), pp. 81-82.
8.   Ernst Troeltsch, The Social Teaching of the Christian
        Church (N. Y.: Harper and Row, 1960), v. 1, p.
        61.
9.   W. D. Davies, Paul and Rabbinic Judaism (N. Y.:
        Harper and Row, 1968), p. 22.
10.   Tennant, op. cit., p. 272.
11.   Erich Fromm, Escape from Freedom (N. Y.: Avon
        Books, 1965 - first printed 1941), pp. 193-194.
12.   Edward Westermarck, Christianity and Morals (Free-
        port, N. Y.: Books for Libraries Press, 1969), p.
        106-7.
13.   Samuel Sandmel, The Genius of Paul (N. Y.: Schocken
        Book, 1970), p. 22.
14.   Westermarck, op. cit., p. 125.
15.   Ibid., pp. 125-128, passim.
16.   Ibid., pp. 128-129.
17.   Tertullian, De Patientu, 5, quoted in: Tennant, op.
        cit., p. 333, footnote 2.
18.   Robert M. Hawkins, The Recovery of the Historical
        Past (Nashville, Tenn.: Vanderbilt University
        Press, 1943), p. 176.
19.   Will Durant, The Age of Faith (N. Y.: Simon and
        Schuster, 1950), p. 976.
20.   Frank Thilly, History of Philosophy (N. Y.: Henry
        Holt, 1914), p. 153.
21.   Norman P. Williams, The Ideas of the Fall and of
        Original Sin (N. Y.: Longmans, Green, 1927), p.
        365.
22.   Ibid.
23.   Harry Elmer Barnes, An Intellectual and Cultural His-
        tory of the Western World (N. Y.: Random House,
        1937), pp. 303-304.
24.   Durant, op. cit., p. 76.
25.   Ibid., p. 77.
26.   Barnes, op. cit., p. 293.
27.   Alvin Boyd Kuhn, Shadow of the Third Century (Eliza-
        beth, N. J.: Academy Press, 1949), p. 453, 464.
28.   Westermarck, op. cit., p. 178.
29.   Quoted in: Morton M. Hunt, The Natural History
        of Love (N. Y.: Grove Press, 1959), pp. 108, 110.
30.   Ibid., p. 115.

31. Ibid., p. 109.
32. Paraphrased in: Ibid., p. 116.
33. Westermarck, op. cit., p. 179.
34. Ibid., p. 181.
35. Hunt, op. cit., p. 175.
36. Peter Brown, Augustine of Hippo (Berkeley, Calif.: University of California Press, 1967), p. 238-239.
37. G. C. Coulton, Five Centuries of Religion (Cambridge (Eng.): Cambridge University Press, 1923), v. 1, p. 17.
38. Durant, The Age of Faith, p. 112.
39. Coulton, op. cit., p. 209.
40. Durant, op. cit., p. 519.
41. Coulton, op. cit., p. 176.
42. Ibid., p. 179.
43. Durant, op. cit., p. 519.
44. Ibid., p. 523.
45. Quoted in: C. H. and Winifred Whitley, Sex and Morals (N. Y.: Basic Books, 1967), p. 42.
46. Ibid., p. 43.
47. Will Durant, The Reformation (N. Y.: Simon and Schuster, 1957), p. 929.
48. Reik, op. cit., p. 332.
49. Durant, op. cit., p. 932.
50. Crane Brinton et al., A History of Civilization (N. Y.: Prentice-Hall, 1955), vol. 1, p. 490.
51. Ralph Roeder, The Man of the Renaissance (N. Y.: Time, Inc., 1966), p. 68.
52. Ibid., p. 75.
53. Will Durant, The Renaissance (N. Y. Simon and Schuster, 1953), p. 156.
54. George Haven Putnam, The Censorship of the Church of Rome (N. Y.: Benjamin Blom, 1967), 2 vols.
55. Ibid., vol. 1, p. 182, 184.
56. Redmond Burke, What Is the Index? (Milwaukee, Wisc.: Bruce, 1952).
57. Putnam, op. cit., p. 169.
58. Ibid., vol. 2, pp. 310-311.
59. Ibid., vol. 1, p. 49.
60. Ibid., pp. 236-269, passim.
61. Westermarck, op. cit., p. 184.
62. Durant, The Reformation, p. 364.
63. Ibid., p. 374.
64. Ibid., p. 419.
65. Ibid., p. 419-420.
66. Ibid., p. 452.
67. Putnam, op. cit., vol. 1, p. 267.

Chapter 6

1. Will Durant, The Reformation, p. 474.
2. Ibid.
3. Francois Wendel, Calvin, (N.Y.: Harper, 1963), p. 84.
4. Durant, op. cit., p. 474.
5. Sydney Clark, All the Best in Switzerland (N.Y.: Dodd, Mead, 1954), p. 110.
6. Preserved Smith, The Age of the Reformation (N.Y.: Henry Holt, 1970), p. 133.
7. Ibid., p. 175.
8. Durant, op. cit., p. 459.
9. Smith, op. cit., pp. 161-162.
10. Durant, op. cit., p. 462.
11. John Calvin, Institutes of the Christian Religion, (Philadelphia: Presbyterian Board of Christian Education, 1928), vol. 2, chapter V, p. 19.
12. Williams, op. cit., p. 433.
13. Durant, op. cit., p. 474.
14. Ibid., pp. 476-477.
15. Ibid., p. 420.
16. Max Weber, The Protestant Ethic and the Spirit of Capitalism (N.Y.: Charles Scribner's Sons, 1958), p. 80.
17. H. H. Gerth and C. Wright Mills, eds., From Max Weber (New York: Oxford University Press, 1946), p. 349.
18. Brinton et al., op. cit., p. 515.
19. Ibid.
20. Ibid.
21. Morris L. Ernst and William Seagle, To the Pure: a Study of Obscenity and the Censor (N.Y.: Viking, 1928), pp. 14-15.
22. Durant, op. cit., pp. 475-476.
23. Ibid., pp. 479-484.
24. Smith, op. cit., p. 176.
25. Ibid., p. 174.
26. Ibid., p. 165.
27. Ibid., p. 345.
28. Winston S. Churchill, The New World (N.Y.: Dodd, Mead, 1962), vol. 2, The History of the English-Speaking Peoples, p. 312.
29. Churchill, op. cit., p. 248.
30. Percy H. Boynton, Literature and American Life (Boston: Ginn, 1936), p. 12, 22.
31. Ibid., p. 837.

32. Edmund S. Morgan, "The Puritans and Sex," in: Carl
    N. Degler, ed., Pivotal Interpretations of American
    History (N.Y.: Harper and Row, 1966), vol. 1, pp.
    1-16.
33. Ibid., p. 16.
34. Carl N. Degler, op. cit., p. 2.
35. The American Heritage Dictionary of the English Lan-
    guage (Boston: American Heritage Publishers and
    Houghton Mifflin, 1969), p. 1061.
36. The Random House Dictionary of the English Language
    (N.Y.: Random House, 1967), p. 1167.
37. Michael Adams, Censorship: the Irish Experience
    (University, Ala.: University of Alabama Press,
    1968), p. 106.
38. Ibid., p. 24, 26.
39. Ibid., pp. 29-37.
40. Ibid., p. 50, 60.
41. Ibid., p. 99, 101, 220 (footnote 53).
42. Ibid., p. 119, 132.
43. Ibid., p. 150.
44. Ibid., p. 154.
45. Norman St. John Stevas, Obscenity and the Law (Lon-
    don: Secker & Warburg, 1956), p. 188.
46. Adams, op. cit., p. 191, 194, 195.
47. Ibid., p. 199.
48. John Langdon-Davies, Sex, Sin and Sanctity (London:
    Victor Gollancz, 1954), pp. 69-70, 84.
49. Bergen Evans, ed., Dictionary of Quotations (N.Y.:
    Delacorte Press, 1968), p. 567.
50. Thomas Babington Macaulay, History of England (Lon-
    don, 1849), vol. I, p. ii (quoted in: Evans, op. cit.,
    p. 566).

Chapter 7

1. David R. Mace, The Christian Response to the Sexual
   Revolution (Nashville, Tenn.: Abingdon Press, 1970),
   pp. 112-113, 126.
2. Ibid., pp. 126-127.
3. Ibid., p. 90.
4. Derrick Sherwin Bailey, Sexual Relations in Christian
   Thought (N.Y.: Harper, 1959), p. 233.
5. Ibid., p. 252.
6. Ibid., p. 254.
7. Ibid., p. 255.
8. The Lambeth Conference 1958 (Greenwich, Conn.:

Seabury Press, 1958), pp. 2.144-2.145.

9.   Ibid., p. 2.160.
10. Sex and Morality: a Report to the British Council of
     Churches, October 1966 (Philadelphia: Fortress
     Press, 1966), p. 5.
11. Ibid., p. 77.
12. Alastair Horn, ed., Towards a Quaker View of Sex
     (London: Friends Home Service Committee, 1964),
     rev. ed.
13. Ibid., pp. 9, 12.
14. Ibid., pp. 44-45.
15. Ibid., p. 46.
16. Ibid., p. 56.
17. David H. X. Read, Christian Ethics (Philadelphia:
     Lippincott, 1969), p. 79.
18. Ibid., pp. 102, 106.
19. Ibid., p. 107.
20. E. Clinton Gardner, "Responsibility in Freedom," in:
     John C. Bennett, et al., Storm over Ethics (N.Y.:
     United Church Press, 1967.
21. Ibid., pp. 52-54.
22. Ibid., pp. 58-59, 66.
23. Robert W. Gleason, "Situational Morality," in: Ben-
     nett, et al., op. cit., pp. 115, 122-123, 129.
24. Gerald Kennedy, "The Nature of Heresy," in: Bennett,
     et al., op. cit., pp. 130, 144, 148.
25. Joseph Fletcher, "Situation Ethics under Fire," in:
     Bennett, et al., op. cit., pp. 149-173.
26. Ibid., pp. 169-170.
27. William Dunphy, ed., The New Morality (N.Y.: Herd-
     er and Herder, 1967), p. 9.
28. Michael Sheehan, "History: the Context of Morality,"
     in: Dunphy, ed., op. cit., pp. 9, 54.
29. Stanley Kutz, "The Demands of the Present: Education
     of the Emotions," in: Dunphy, ed., op. cit., p.
     151.
30. Ibid., p. 154.
31. Robert Grimm, Love and Sexuality (N.Y.: Association
     Press, 1964).
32. Ibid., p. 39.
33. Ibid., pp. 42-43.
34. Ibid., p. 44.
35. Ibid., p. 117.
36. Marc Oraison, et al., Sin (N.Y.: Macmillan, 1962),
     p. 27.
37. Ibid., p. 136.
38. Pierre Teilhard de Chardin, quoted in: Roger Garaudy

From Anathema to Dialogue (N. Y.: Herder and Herder, 1966), pp. 42-43.

39.   Paul Ricoeur, ed., "Sexuality Today," Cross Currents (Spring, 1964), entire issue.

40.   Paul Ricoeur, "Wonder, Eroticism, and Enigma," in: Ricoeur, ed., op. cit., pp. 134, 135, 138.

41.   Ibid., p. 140.

42.   Alphonse H. Clemens, "Catholicism and Sex," in: Albert Ellis and Albert Abarbanel, eds., The Encyclopedia of Sexual Behavior (N. Y.: Hawthorn Books, 1967), p. 229, 232, 234.

43.   Henry V. Sattler, Parents, Children and the Facts of Life (Garden City, N. Y.: Doubleday, 1956).

44.   Ibid., pp. 75, 77.

45.   Ibid., p. 187.

46.   Ibid., pp. 89, 96.

47.   John Courtney Murray, "Literature and Censorship," in: Robert B. Downs, ed., The First Freedom (Chicago: American Library Association, 1960), pp. 216, 219, and see pp. 219-220 of The First Freedom for Father Murray's suggested rules for censorship by minority groups (by which term he means all religious groups in America, incidentally).

48.   Robert Gordis, Sex and the Family in the Jewish Tradition (N. Y.: Burning Bush Press, 1967), p. 28.

49.   Ibid., pp. 28, 34.

50.   "Books, Prohibited," in: New Standard Jewish Encyclopedia (Garden City, N. Y.: Doubleday, 1970), p. 339.

51.   Richard L. Rubinstein, After Auschwitz; Radical Theology and Contemporary Judaism (Indianapolis, Ind.: Bobbs-Merrill, 1966), pp. 149, 282.

52.   Herman Wouk, This Is My God (N. Y.: Dell, 1964), p. 125.

53.   Cole, op. cit., p. 285.

54.   Ibid., p. 297.

55.   Ibid., p. 311.

56.   Nicolas Berdyaev, The Destiny of Man (N. Y.: Harper and Row, 1960), p. 68.

57.   Oscar E. Feucht, ed., Sex and the Church (St. Louis, Mo.: Concordia Publishing House, 1961), p. 235.

Chapter 8

1.   Rollo May, Man's Search for Himself (N. Y.: New

American Library, 1953), p. 13.
2.   Sigmund Freud, Totem and Taboo (N. Y. :   Vintage,
     1946, copyright 1918), p. 207.
3.   Sigmund Freud, "Libidinal Types, " Psychoanalytic
     Quarterly, vol. 1 (1936), pp. 3-6.
4.   Sigmund Freud, "Civilized, Sexual Morality and Modern
     Nervousness, " (1908), in his: Collected Papers
     (London: Hogarth Press, 1953), vol. II, pp. 81-2.
5.   Ibid., pp. 83-4.
6.   Ibid., p. 86-7.
7.   Ibid., p. 95.
8.   J. C. Flugel, Man, Morals, and Society: A Psycho-
     Analytical Study (N. Y. :   Viking Press, 1961), 2nd
     ed., p. 37.
9.   Ibid., pp. 245, 246, 248.
10. Ludwig Marcuse, Obscene (London: MacGibbon and
     Kee, 1964).
11. Ibid., pp. 20-21.
12. Peter Fryer, Private Case--Public Scandal (London:
     Secker and Warburg, 1966), pp. 11, 13 says that
     the British Museum Collection of "erotical and
     sexological works" numbers only about 5,000, but
     is "without a doubt the most comprehensive in the
     world. "
13. The Report of the Commission on Obscenity and Por-
     nography (N. Y. : Bantam Books, 1970), p. 85.
14. Quoted in: Ludwig Marcuse, op. cit., p. 32.
15. Ibid., p. 35.
16. Otto Rank, The Myth of the Birth of the Hero and Oth-
     er Writings (N. Y. : Vintage Books, 1959), p. 271.
17. Ibid., pp. 275, 282, 286.
18. Ibid., p. 259.
19. Herbert Marcuse, One-Dimensional Man (Boston:
     Beacon Press, 1964).
20. Herbert Marcuse, Eros and Civilization (N. Y. : Vin-
     tage Books, 1955), p. 180.
21. T. W. Adorno, Else Frankel-Brunswick, et al., The
     Authoritarian Personality (N. Y. : Harper and Row,
     1950), pp. 233, 241.
22. Ibid., p. 232.
23. Ibid., p. 480, 483.
24. Ibid., pp. 372, 373, 376.
25. Ian D. Suttie, The Origins of Love and Hate (London:
     Kegan, Paul, Trench, Traebner, 1935), p. 73.
26. Ibid., p. 126.
27. Ibid., p. 125.
28. Abram Kardiner, Sex and Morality (Indianapolis, Ind. :

Bobbs-Merrill, 1962).

29. Ibid., p. 87.
30. Ibid., pp. 89, 93.
31. Ibid., p. 110.
32. Ibid., pp. 123-159.
33. Ibid., pp. 129-130.
34. Ibid., p. 131, 150.
35. Ibid., p. 159.
36. Ibid., p. 200.
37. Ibid., p. 253. The italics in the last sentence are the author's, not Kardiner's.

Chapter 9

1. René Huyghe, Art and the Spirit of Man (N.Y.: Abrams, 1962), p. 64.
2. Ernest Van den Haag, "Is Pornography a Cause of Crime?" Encounter (December, 1967), p. 55.
3. Will Durant, The Life of Greece (N.Y.: Simon and Schuster, 1939), p. 523.
4. Horace M. Kallen, Art and Freedom (N.Y.: Duell, Sloan and Pearce, 1942), vol. 1, p. 3.
5. Ibid., p. 65.
6. Will Durant, Caesar and Christ (N.Y.: Simon and Schuster, 1944), pp. 256-258.
7. Iredell Jenkins, "The Laissez-Faire Theory of Artistic Censorship," Journal of the History of Ideas (January, 1944), p. 83.
8. W. P. Trent, "Some Remarks on Modern Book-Burning," in his: Greatness in Literature and Other Papers (N.Y.: Books for Libraries, c1905, repr. 1967), pp. 206, 217.
9. Ludwig Lewisohn, The Story of American Literature (N.Y.: Modern Library, 1939), pp. 44, 48.
10. Ibid., p. 59.
11. Cited in: ibid., p. 66.
12. Ibid., p. 94.
13. Norman O. Brown, Life Against Death (N.Y.: Vintage Books, 1959), p. 60.
14. Abraham Kaplan, "Obscenity As an Aesthetic Category," in: John Phelan, ed., Communications Control (N.Y.: Sheed and Ward, 1969), pp. 127-152.
15. George Santayana, Reason in Art (N.Y.: Charles Scribner's Sons, 1905), p. 171.
16. Kaplan, op. cit., p. 150.
17. Ibid.

18. Ibid., pp. 130-1.
19. Freidrich Schlegel, Aphorisms, in: The German
       Classics (N.Y.: German Publications Society,
       1913), vol. 4, pp. 175, 179.
20. Kaplan, op. cit., pp. 139-150.
21. Ibid., p. 150.
22. Susan Sontag, Styles of Radical Will (N.Y.: Farrar,
       Straus, and Giroux, 1969), p. 39.
23. Ibid., p. 41.
24. Ibid.
25. Ibid., p. 66, 71-72.
26. Peter Michelson, The Aesthetics of Pornography (N.Y.:
       Herder and Herder, 1971), p. 20.
27. Peter S. Prescott, "Hard Cores and Soft," Newsweek
       (March 15, 1971), pp. 113-114.
28. Michelson, op. cit., p. 21.
29. Ibid., p. 28-29.
30. Ibid., p. 29.
31. Harvey Cox, The Feast of Fools, (N.Y.: Harper and
       Row, 1969), p. viii.
32. Ibid., pp. 4-5.
33. Ibid., p. 6.
34. Ibid., pp. 11-12.
35. Ibid., p. 16.
36. Ibid., p. 83.
37. Henry Miller, Remember To Remember (Norfolk,
       Conn.: New Directions, 1947), pp. 283, 290.
38. Steven Marcus, The Other Victorians: a Study of
       Sexuality and Pornography in Mid-Nineteenth-Cen-
       tury England (N.Y.: Basic Books, 1966), pp. 279-
       281, 285.
39. Morse Peckham, Art and Pornography (N.Y.: Basic
       Books, 1969).
40. Ibid., unnumbered prefatory page [vii].
41. Ibid., pp. 5, 7-8.
42. Ibid., p. 36, 47.
43. Ibid., p. 21.
44. Ibid., p. 31.
45. Malcolm Cowley, Think Back on Us (Carbondale, Ill.:
       Southern Illinois University Press, 1967), p. 156.
46. Erich Kahler, Out of the Labyrinth: Essays in Clari-
       fication (N.Y.: George Braziller, 1967), p. 202.
47. Ibid., p. 207, 210.
48. Ibid., p. 226.
49. Ibid.
50. Charles Baudelaire, The Temple of Naline, in: Richard
       Ellmann and Charles Feidelson, Jr., eds., The

Modern Tradition (N. Y. : Oxford University Press, 1965), p. 59.

51. Anton Chekhov, "Dunghills As Artistic Material," in: Ellmann and Feidelson, op. cit., p. 245.

52. Arthur Rimbaud, "The Poet As Revolutionary Seer," in: Ellmann and Feidelson, op. cit., p. 204.

53. Ibid., p. 205.

54. Jean-Paul Sartre, "Commitment," in: Ellmann and Feidelson, op. cit., p. 288.

55. Emile Zola, "The Novel As Social Science," in: Ellmann and Feidelson, op. cit., p. 288.

56. Quoted in: Herbert J. Muller, Freedom in the Modern World (N. Y. : Harper and Row, 1966), p. 258.

57. John Dewey, Art As Experience (N. Y. : Minton, Balch, 1934), p. 21.

58. Ibid., pp. 21-22.

59. George Santayana, The Sense of Beauty (1896), quoted in: Albert W. Levi, Varieties of Experience (N. Y. : Ronald Press, 1957), pp. 412-413.

60. Ibid., p. 413.

61. Dewey, op. cit., p. 189.

62. Ibid., p. 190.

63. Walter Allen, "The Writer and the Frontiers of Tolerance," in: John Chandos, ed., 'To Deprave and Corrupt ...": Original Studies in the Nature and Definition of Obscenity (N. Y. : Association Press, 1962), p. 151.

64. Horace M. Kallen, op. cit., vol. 2, p. 907.

65. George Santayana, Reason in Art (N. Y. : Charles Scribner's Sons, 1905), p. 171.

66. Samuel Butler, Erewhon (N. Y. : Modern Library, 1955; first printed 1872), pp. 165-166.

Chapter 10

1. Ronald Pearsall, The Worm in the Bud: the World of Victorian Sexuality (N. Y. : Macmillan, 1969), pp. 294-295.

2. William J. Hempl and Patrick M. Wall, "Extralegal Censorship of Literature," in: Herbert W. Hildebrandt, ed., Issues of Our Time (N. Y. : Macmillan, 1963), p. 134.

3. Ibid., pp. 134-135.

4. Robert W. Haney, Comstockery in America: Patterns of Censorship and Control (Boston: Beacon Press, 1960), p. 80.

5.   Ibid.
6.   Kai T. Erikson, Wayward Puritans (N.Y.: John Wiley, 1966), p. 6.
7.   Ibid.
8.   Ibid., p. 4.
9.   Ibid., p. 14.
10. Knights of Columbus Religious Information Bureau, "Who's Responsible for Public Morals?," Family Weekly (February 7, 1971), p. 4. (Advertisement).
11. Harold C. Gardiner, Catholic Viewpoint on Censorship (Garden City, N.Y.: Hanover House, 1958), pp. 120-121.
12. Oscar E. Feucht, ed., op. cit., p. 231-232.
13. William Albig, Modern Public Opinion (N.Y.: McGraw-Hill, 1956), pp. 240-241.
14. Ibid., p. 245.
15. Graham Wallas, The Great Society (N.Y.: Macmillan, 1923), pp. 196-197.
16. Albig, op. cit., p. 268.
17. Leon A. Jakobovitz, in: Edward Karmack, ed., "Censorship and the Arts," Arts and Society (summer, 1967), p. 269.

Chapter 11

1.   Haney, op. cit., p. 16.
2.   Norman St. John-Stevas, op. cit., p. 23.
3.   Ibid., p. 24.
4.   Ibid., p. 38.
5.   Ibid., p. 67.
6.   Ibid., p. 68.
7.   Ibid., p. 70.
8.   Lord Birkett, "The Changing Law," in: John Chandos, ed., op. cit., p. 73.
9.   "The Case Against Obscenity Laws," New Statesman (August 8, 1969), pp. 172-177.
10. James Q. Wilson, "Violence, Pornography and Social Science," The Public Interest (Winter, 1971), p. 55.
11. Ibid., p. 58-60.
12. Quoted in: Chandos, ed., op. cit., pp. 31-32.
13. St. John-Stevas, op. cit., p. 169.
14. Ibid., pp. 169-170.
15. Quoted in: Michael Keeling, Morals in a Free Society (N.Y.: Seabury Press, 1968), p. 57.
16. Ibid.
17. Ibid., pp. 57-58.

18. Ibid., pp. 100-101.
19. Patrick Devlin, The Enforcement of Morals (N. Y.: Oxford University Press, 1965), p. 12.
20. Ibid., p. 14.
21. Ibid., p. 16.
22. Ibid., p. ix.
23. Ibid., p. 18.
24. Ibid., pp. 88, 100.
25. H. L. A. Hart, Law, Liberty, and Morality (N. Y.: Vintage, 1963), p. 50.
26. Ibid., pp. 71-73.
27. Ibid., p. 77.
28. Ernest Nagel, "The Enforcement of Morals," in: Paul Kurtz, ed., Moral Problems in Contemporary Society (Englewood Cliffs, N. J.: Prentice-Hall, 1969), pp. 137-160.
29. Ibid., pp. 149-150.
30. Ibid., p. 152.
31. Ibid., p. 159.
32. Alec Craig, "Censorship of Sexual Literature," in: Ellis and Abarbanel, eds., op. cit., pp. 235-246.
33. Eberhard and Phyllis Kronhausen, op. cit., p. 155.
34. Ibid., p. 17.
35. Herbert L. Packer, The Limits of the Criminal Sanctions (Stanford, Calif.: Stanford University Press, 1968), p. 324.
36. Huntington Cairns, "Sex and the Law," in: V. F. Calverton and S. D. Schmalhausen, eds., op. cit., p. 218.
37. Ibid., p. 216.
38. Robert B. Cairns, James C. Paul, and John Wishner, "Sex Censorship: the Assumptions of Anti-Obscenity Laws and the Empirical Evidence," Minnesota Law Review (May, 1967), p. 1013.
39. Geoffrey May, Social Control of Sex Expression (N. Y.: Morrow, 1931), p. 270.
40. Ibid., pp. 272-273.
41. St. John-Stevas, op. cit., p. 202.
42. Quoted in: Geoffrey May, op. cit., p. 63.
43. Ibid., pp. 77, 78 (footnote 69).
44. Ibid., p. 78.
45. Salt Lake Tribune (Salt Lake City, Utah, February 24, 1971), p. 2.
46. May, op. cit., pp. 79-80.
47. Ibid., p. 82.
48. Ibid., pp. 83, 84 (footnote 80).
49. Op. cit., pp. 104-106.

50.   Ibid., p. 112.
51.   Ibid., pp. 175-176.
52.   Cited in: Alexander Bickel, et al., "On Pornography:
      II, Dissenting and Concurring Opinions," The Public
      Interest (Winter, 1971), p. 25.
53.   Ibid., pp. 26, 28.
54.   Herbert L. Packer, "The Pornography Caper," Com-
      mentary (February, 1971), pp. 72-77.
55.   Ibid., pp. 76-77.
56.   Herbert L. Packer, The Limits of the Criminal Sanc-
      tion (Stanford, Calif.: Stanford University Press,
      1968), p. 324.
57.   Ibid., p. 326.
58.   Ibid., p. 316.
59.   St. John-Stevas, op. cit., p. 203.
60.   AP dispatch from Washington, D.C., in: Salt Lake
      Tribune (May 27, 1971), p. A9.
61.   Ronald Dworkin, "On Not Prosecuting Civil Disobedi-
      ence," in: Noam Chomsky, et al., Trials of the
      Resistance (N.Y.: Random House, 1970), p. 64.
62.   Craig, op. cit., p. 245.

Chapter 12

1.   Joseph Fletcher, Situation Ethics: the New Morality
      (Philadelphia: Westminster Press, 1966), p. 62.
2.   John Dewey and James Tufts, Ethics (N.Y.: Henry
      Holt, 1908), p. 212.
3.   Joseph Fletcher, Moral Responsibility: Situation Ethics
      at Work (Philadelphia: Westminster Press, 1967).
4.   Ibid., p. 70.
5.   Ibid., pp. 84-85.
6.   Ibid., p. 88.
7.   Ibid., p. 89.
8.   Abraham J. Heschel, The Insecurity of Freedom (N.Y.:
      Noonday Press, 1967).
9.   William Phillips, A Sense of the Present (N.Y.: Chil-
      mark Press, 1968), pp. 30-43.
10.   Henry David Thoreau, A Week on the Concord and
      Merrimack Rivers (N.Y.: New American Library,
      1961), p. 89.
11.   Quoted in: John Roeburt, The Wicked and the Banned
      (N.Y.: Macfadden-Bartell, 1963), p. 11.
12.   Anthony Comstock, Frauds Exposed (N.Y.: J. H.
      Brown, 1880), as quoted in: Heywood Brown and
      Margaret Leech, Anthony Comstock: Roundsman of
      the Lord (N.Y.: Boni, 1927), p. 86.

Chapter 13

1. The Report of the Commission on Obscenity and Por-
      nography (N.Y.: Bantam Books, 1970), p. 62.
2. Ibid., p. 85.
3. Ibid., p. 23.
4. Ibid., p. 148.
5. Quoted in: Lester Kinsolving, "The World of Religion:
      Clergymen Split on Smut Report," Idaho State Jour-
      nal, Pocatello (January 8, 1971), Section D., p. 7.
6. Congressional Record, October 13, 1970, pp. S17903-
      17922. The whole of the Senatorial discussion re-
      printed in that day's issue is well worth reading by
      any student of either American politics or American
      "morality"--or both.
7. Report (as the C.O.P. Report will be cited herein from
      now on), p. 49.
8. A June, 1971 Gallup Poll on "what is the top problem
      facing the U.S. now" showed that only 2% (the same
      as the C.O.P. figure!) saw "lack of religion, moral
      decay" as the number one problem with which our
      country now must deal.
9. Report, p. 190.
10. Ibid., footnote 8, p. 287.
11. Ibid., p. 32.
12. Ibid., p. 190.
13. Ibid., pp. 36-37.
14. Ibid., p. 38.
15. Ibid., p. 41.
16. Charles H. Keating, Jr. "The Report That Shocked the
      Nation," (Reader's Digest, January, 1971), pp. 37-
      41.
17. Report, p. 231.
18. Ibid., p. 287.
19. John G. Schmitz, "The Presidential Commission on
      Obscenity and Pornography," (Congressional Record,
      October 14, 1970), Extension of Remarks, pp.
      E9236-9237.
20. Thaddeus J. Dulski, "House Needs To Register Its Op-
      position to Smut Report," (Congressional Record,
      December 19, 1970), Extension of Remarks, p.
      E10596.
21. Eugene C. Kennedy, "Kind Words for the Porno-Re-
      searchers," (Commonweal, December 18, 1970), pp.
      292-293.
22. Kinsolving, op. cit.
23. Cf. Eli M. Oboler, "The Politics of Pornography,"

Library Journal (December 15, 1970), pp. 4225-
4228; also American Libraries (March, 1971) for
report of American Library Association action on
the C.O.P. 's Report.

24. Malcolm Cowley, "Ethics in the Arts," in: Ethical
Problems for the Sixties (New Britain, Conn.:
Central Connecticut State College, 1962), p. 15.

25. Ira L. Reiss, ed., "The Sexual Renaissance in America," Journal of Social Issues (April, 1966), pp. 1-
140.

26. "Sex as a Spectator Sport," Time (July 11, 1969), pp.
61-66.

27. Vance Packard, The Sexual Wilderness (N.Y.:   McKay,
1968).

28. Ira L. Reiss, "The Sexual Renaissance: a Summary
and an Analysis," in: Reiss, op. cit., p. 140.

29. Alex Comfort, Sex in Society (N.Y.: Citadel Press,
1966), p. 73.

30. Ibid., pp. 74-75.

31. Ibid., p. 76.

32. Ibid., p. 70.

33. Helena Wright, Sex and Society (Seattle: University of
Washington Press, 1969), p. 39.

34. Ibid., p. 83-84.

Chapter 14

1.   Quoted from Antonia Sertillanges, in: Marc Oraison,
Morality for Our Time (Garden City, N.Y.: Doubleday, 1968), p. 22.

2.   John Wilson, Logic and Sexual Morality (Baltimore,
Md.: Penguin Books, 1963), p. 237.

3.   Oraison, op. cit., p. 37.

4.   Ibid., pp. 40, 47.

5.   Ibid., p. 59, 60.

6.   Ibid., p. 61, 62.

7.   Ibid., p. 68, 71.

8.   Martin Buber, I and Thou (N.Y.: Charles Scribner's
Sons, 1958), 2nd edition.

9.   Ibid., pp. 133-134.

10. Ibid., p. 18.

11. Richard Boyd Ballou, The Individual and the State: the
Modern Challenge to Education (Boston: Beacon
Press, 1953), pp. 85, 93.

12. Ibid., pp. 95-98.

13. Ibid., p. 283.

14. Paul Ramsey, Nine Modern Moralists (Englewood
    Cliffs, N.J.: Prentice-Hall, 1962), p. 71.
15. Ibid., pp. 105, 108.
16. René Guyon, The Ethics of Sexual Acts (N.Y.: Knopf,
    1935), pp. 258-259.
17. Ibid., p. 276.
18. Ibid., p. 62.
19. Ibid., pp. 88, 90.
20. Ibid., p. 113.
21. Ibid., pp. 380-381.
22. Robert M. Frumkin, "Freedom, Sexual," in: Ellis
    and Abarbanel, eds., op. cit., pp. 439-449.
23. Ibid., p. 439.
24. Ibid., p. 448.
25. Havelock Ellis, On Life and Sex (N.Y.: New American
    Library, 1957), pp. 79, 81.
26. Ibid., pp. 82, 86-87.
27. Ibid., p. 188.
28. Phillippe Aries, Centuries of Childhood: a Social His-
    tory of Family Life (N.Y.: Knopf, 1962), p. 106,
    109.
29. St. Jean-Baptiste de La Salle, La Civilité Chritienne,
    quoted in: ibid., p. 116.
30. Aries, op. cit., p. 103, 411.
31. Ellis, op. cit., p. 191, 194.
32. William Joynson-Hicks Brentford, Do We Need a Cen-
    sor? (London: Faber & Faber, 1929).
33. Ibid., pp. 5-7.
34. Ibid., pp. 11-12.
35. Quoted in: ibid., p. 18.
36. Ibid.
37. Ibid., p. 24.
38. Ibid.
39. Lewis A. Coser, Men of Ideas (Glencoe, Illinois: Free
    Press, 1965), pp. 91-92.
40. Ibid., p. 93.
41. Ibid., p. 96.
42. Crane Brinton, op. cit., p. 142.
43. John Macmurray, Reason and Emotion (N.Y.: Barnes
    and Noble, 1962), pp. 124-125.
44. Ibid., p. 132.
45. Ibid., pp. 139-140.
46. Ibid., p. 143.
47. John Wilson, op. cit., pp. 10-15.
48. Ibid., pp. 34-35.
49. Ibid., p. 43.
50. Ibid., pp. 47, 50.

51.   Ibid., pp. 51-52.
52.   Ibid., p. 51.
53.   Ibid., p. 59.
54.   Ibid., p. 60.
55.   Ibid., p. 61.
56.   Ibid., p. 78.
57.   Ibid., pp. 82-85.
58.   (Nashville, Tenn.: Abingdon Press, 1970).
59.   Ibid., p. 80.

Chapter 15

1.   Samuel Krislov, The Supreme Court and Political Free-
         dom (N.Y.: Free Press, 1968), p. 19.
2.   Henry J. Abraham, Freedom and the Court: Civil
         Rights and Liberties in the United States. 2d ed.
         (N.Y.: Oxford University Press, 1972), Footnote
         1, p. 181.
3.   David L. Shapiro, ed., The Evolution of a Judicial
         Philosophy: Selected Opinions and Papers of Justice
         John M. Harlan (Cambridge: Harvard University
         Press, 1969), p. 118.
4.   U.S. National Advisory Commission on Criminal Justice
         Standards and Goals, A National Strategy to Reduce
         Crime (Washington, D.C.: U.S. Government Print-
         ing Office, 1973), p. 202.
5.   Ibid., pp. 203-204.
6.   James H. Breasted, The Dawn of Conscience (N.Y.:
         Charles Scribner's Sons, 1933), p. 37.

APPENDIX F

BIBLIOGRAPHY

This is an alphabetical listing of all items cited in the
chapter footnotes. A vast literature exists in the fields of
censorship and anti-censorship, a literature which certainly
is important to the subject of this volume, but the items
listed below are those containing material bearing directly
on the origins of censorship.

Abraham, Henry J. Freedom and the Court: Civil Rights
    and Liberties in the United States. 2nd ed. New York:
    Oxford University Press, 1972.

Adams, Michael. Censorship: the Irish Experience. Uni-
    versity, Alabama: University of Alabama Press, 1968.

Adorno, T. W., Else Frankel-Brunswick, et al. The Au-
    thoritarian Personality. New York: Harper and Row,
    1950.

Albig, William. Modern Public Opinion. New York: Mc-
    Graw-Hill, 1956.

The American Heritage Dictionary of the English Language.
    Boston: American Heritage Publishing and Houghton
    Mifflin, 1969.

Aries, Phillippe. Centuries of Childhood: a Social History
    of Family Life. New York: Knopf, 1962.

Astrov, Margo. The Winged Serpent. New York: John
    Day, 1946.

Bailey, Derrick Sherwin. Sexual Relations in Christian
    Thought. New York: Harper and Row, 1959.

311

Ballou, Richard Boyd. The Individual and the State: the
    Modern Challenge to Education. Boston: Beacon Press,
    1953.

Barnes, Harry Elmer. An Intellectual and Cultural History
    of the Western World. New York: Random House,
    1937.

Bataille, Georges. Death and Sensuality. New York: Bal-
    lantine Books, 1969.

Baudelaire, Charles. "The Temple of Naline. " In: The
    Modern Tradition.   Edited by Richard Ellmann and
    Charles Feidelson. New York: Oxford University
    Press, 1965.

Bennett, John C. , et al. Storm Over Ethics. New York:
    United Church Press, 1967.

Berdyaev, Nicolas. The Destiny of Man. New York:
    Harper & Row, 1960.

The New English Bible. New York: Oxford University
    Press, 1961.

Bickel, Alexander, et al. "On Pornography II.   Dissenting
    and Concurring Opinions. " The Public Interest, Winter,
    1971.

Birket-Smith, Kaj. The Paths of Culture. Madison, Wis-
    consin: University of Wisconsin Press, 1965.

Boynton, Percy H. Literature and American Life. Boston:
    Ginn, 1936.

Breasted, James Henry. The Dawn of Conscience. New
    York: Charles Scribner's Sons, 1933.

Brentford, William Joynson-Hicks. Do We Need a Censor?
    London: Faber & Faber, 1929.

Brinton, Crane. A History of Western Morals. New York:
    Harcourt, Brace, 1959.

Brinton, Crane, et al. A History of Civilization. New
    York: Harcourt, Brace, 1959.

Broun, Heywood, and Margaret Leech. Anthony Comstock: Roundsman of the Lord. New York: Boni, 1927.

Brown, Norman O. Life Against Death. New York: Vintage Books, 1959.

Brown, Peter. Augustine of Hippo. Berkeley, California: University of California Press, 1967.

Buber, Martin. I and Thou. New York: Charles Scribner's Sons, 1958. 2nd edition.

Bultmann, Rudolf. Jesus and the Word. New York: Charles Scribner's Sons, 1934.

Burke, Redmond. What Is the Index? Milwaukee, Wisconsin: Bruce, 1952.

Butler, Samuel. Erewhon. New York: Modern Library, 1955; first printed 1872.

Cairns, Robert B., James C. Paul, and John Wishner. "Sex Censorship: the Assumptions of Anti-Obscenity Laws and the Empirical Evidence." Minnesota Law Review, 46, May, 1962, pp. 1009-41.

Calverton, V. F. and Schmalhausen, S. D., eds. Sex in Civilization. Garden City, New York: Garden City Publishing, 1929.

Calvin, John. Institutes of the Christian Religion. Philadelphia: Presbyterian Board of Christian Education, 1928.

"The Case Against Obscenity Laws." New Statesman, August 8, 1969, pp. 172-177.

Chandos, John, ed. 'To Deprave and Corrupt': Original Studies in the Nature and Definition of Obscenity. New York: Association Press, 1962.

Chekhov, Anton. "Dunghills As Artistic Material." In: The Modern Tradition. Edited by Richard Ellmann and Charles Feidelson. New York: Oxford University Press, 1965, pp. 244-245.

Childe, V. Gordon. Man Makes Himself. New York: New American Library, 1951.

Churchill, Winston S. The New World. New York: Dodd,
    Mead, 1962. vol. 2, The History of the English-Speak-
    ing Peoples.

Clark, Sydney. All the Best in Switzerland. New York:
    Dodd, Mead, 1954.

Cole, William Graham. Sex in Christianity and Psychoanaly-
    sis. New York: Oxford University Press, 1966.

Comfort, Alex. Sex in Society. New York: Citadel Press,
    1966.

Condon, John C. Semantics and Communication. Macmil-
    lan, 1966.

Coser, Lewis A. Men of Ideas. Glencoe, Illinois: Free
    Press, 1965.

Coulton, G. C. Five Centuries of Religion. Cambridge:
    Cambridge University Press, 1923, vol. 1.

Cowley, Malcolm. "Ethics in the Arts." In: Ethical Prob-
    lems for the Sixties. New Britain, Connecticut: Cen-
    tral Connecticut State College, 1962.

_____. Think Back on Us. Carbondale, Illinois: South-
    ern Illinois University Press, 1967.

Cox, Harvey. The Feast of Fools. New York: Harper &
    Row, 1969.

Davies, W. D. Paul and Rabbinic Judaism. New York:
    Harper & Row, 1968.

Davis, William Stearns. Readings in Ancient History. Bos-
    ton: Allyn and Bacon, 1913, vol. II.

Degler, Carl N., ed. Pivotal Interpretations of American
    History. New York: Harper & Row, 1966. vol. 1.

Devlin, Patrick. The Enforcement of Morals. New York:
    Oxford University Press, 1965.

Dewey, John. Art As Experience. New York: Minton,
    Balch, 1934.

Dewey, John, and James Tufts. Ethics. New York: Henry
Holt, 1908.

Dickinson, G. Lowes. The Greek View of Life. Garden
City, New York: Doubleday, Doran, 1931.

Dodds, E. R. The Greeks and the Irrational. Berkeley:
University of California Press, 1951.

Downs, Robert B., ed. The First Freedom. Chicago:
American Library Association, 1960.

Dulski, Thaddeus J. "House Needs To Register Its Opposition to Smut Report." Congressional Record, December
19, 1970, p. E10596.

Dunphy, William, ed. The New Morality. New York:
Herder and Herder, 1967.

Durant, Will. The Story of Civilization. Vol. II: The
Life of Greece. New York: Simon and Schuster, 1939.

_____. The Story of Civilization. Vol. III: Caesar
and Christ. New York: Simon and Schuster, 1944.

_____. The Story of Civilization. Vol. IV: The Age of
Faith. New York: Simon and Schuster, 1950.

_____. The Story of Civilization. Vol. V: The Renais-
sance. New York: Simon and Schuster, 1955.

_____. The Story of Civilization. Vol. VI: The Re-
formation. New York: Simon and Schuster, 1957.

Durkheim, Emile. The Elementary Forms of the Religious
Life. Glencoe, Illinois: Free Press, 1947.

Dworkin, Ronald. "On Not Prosecuting Civil Disobedience."
In: Trials of the Resistance. Noam Chomsky, et al.
New York: Random House, 1970. pp. 50-73.

Ellis, Albert, and Albert Abarbanel, eds. The Encyclopedia
of Sexual Behavior. New York: Hawthorne Books, 1967.

Ellis, Havelock. On Life and Sex. New York: New American Library, 1957.

Erikson, Kai T. Wayward Puritans. New York: John
    Wiley, 1966.

Ernst, Morris L. , and William Seagle. To the Pure: A
    Study of Obscenity and the Censor. New York: Viking,
    1928.

Evans, Bergen, ed. Dictionary of Quotations. New York:
    Delacorte Press, 1968.

Feucht, Oscar E. , ed. Sex and the Church. St. Louis,
    Missouri: Concordia Publishing House, 1961.

Fletcher, Joseph. Moral Responsibility: Situation Ethics at
    Work. Philadelphia: Westminster Press, 1967.

_____. Situation Ethics: the New Morality. Philadel-
    phia: Westminster Press, 1966.

Flugel, J. C. Man, Morals and Society. New York: Vik-
    ing, 1961.

_____. "On the Biological Basis of Sexual Repression
    and Its Sociological Significance. " British Journal of
    Medical Psychology, I, 1927, pp. 225-280.

Frazer, Sir James. The Golden Bough. Vol. 3: Taboo
    and the Perils of the Soul. New York: Macmillan,
    1935. First published 1911.

Freud, Sigmund. 'Civilized' Sexual Morality and Modern
    Nervousness. Collected Papers. Vol. II. London:
    Hogarth Press, 1953. Article first published 1908. pp.
    76-99.

_____. Totem and Taboo. New York: Vintage, c1918.

Fromm, Erich. Escape from Freedom. New York: Avon
    Books, 1965. First published 1919. pp. 193-194.

Fryer, Peter. Private Case--Public Scandal. London:
    Secker & Warburg, 1966.

Garaudy, Roger. From Anathema to Dialogue. New York:
    Herder and Herder, 1966.

Gardiner, Harold C. Catholic Viewpoints on Censorship.
    Garden City, New York: Hanover House, 1958.

Gerth, H. H. and C. Wright Mills, eds. From Max Weber.
New York: Oxford University Press, 1946.

Gordis, Robert. Sex and the Family in the Jewish Tradition. New York: Burning Bush Press, 1967.

Guttmann, Julius. Philosophies of Judaism. Garden City,
New York: Anchor Books, Doubleday, 1966.

Guyon, René. The Ethics of Sexual Acts. New York:
Knopf, 1935.

A Handbook of Christian Theology. Cleveland: World Publishing, 1958.

Haney, Robert W. Comstockery in America: Patterns of
Censorship and Control. Boston: Beacon Press, 1960.

Hart, H. L. A. Law, Liberty, and Morality. New York:
Vintage Books, 1963.

Hawkins, Robert M. The Recovery of the Historical Past.
Nashville, Tennessee: Vanderbilt University Press,
1943.

Hempel, William J. , and Patrick M. Wall. "Extralegal
Censorship of Literature. " In: Issues of Our Time.
Edited by Herbert W. Hildebrandt. New York: Mac-
millan, 1963, pp. 133-135.

Heschel, Abraham J. The Insecurity of Freedom. New
York: Noonday Press, 1967.

Horn, Alastair, ed. Towards a Quaker View of Sex. London: Friends Home Service Committee, 1964. rev. ed.

Hunt, Morton M. The Natural History of Love. New York:
Grove Press, 1959.

Huyghe, René. Art and the Spirit of Man. New York:
Abrams, 1962.

Jakobovitz, Leon D. In: Edward Kamarck, ed. , "Censorship and the Arts, " Arts and Society (Summer, 1967),
p. 269.

Jenkins, Iredell. "The Laissez-Faire Theory of Artistic

Censorship. " Journal of the History of Ideas, January,
1944, pp. 71-90.

Jespersen, Otto. Language: its Nature, Development, and
Origin. New York: Norton, 1964. First published,
1921.

Kahler, Erich. Out of the Labyrinth: Essays in Clarification. New York: George Braziller, 1967.

Kallen, Horace M. Art and Freedom. New York: Duell,
Sloan and Pearce, 1942. 2 volumes.

Kardiner, Abram. Sex and Morality. Indianapolis, Indiana:
Bobbs-Merrill, 1962.

Keating, Charles H., Jr. "The Report That Shocked the
Nation. " Reader's Digest, January, 1971, pp. 37-41.

Keeling, Michael. Morals in a Free Society. New York:
Seabury Press, 1968.

Kennedy, Eugene C. "Kind Words for the Porno-Research-
ers. " Commonweal, December 18, 1970, pp. 292-293.

Kinsolving, Lester. "The World of Religion: Clergymen
Split on Smut Report. " Idaho State Journal. Pocatello,
January 8, 1971, Section D, p. 7.

Knights of Columbus Religious Information Bureau. "Who's
Responsible for Public Morals?" Family Weekly, February 7, 1971, p. 4.

Krislov, Samuel. The Supreme Court and Political Freedom.
New York: Free Press, 1968.

Kronhausen, Eberhard, and Phyllis. Pornography and the
Law. New York: Ballantine Books, 1959.

Krutch, Joseph Wood. "Introduction. " In: Eliseo Vivas.
The Moral Life and the Ethical Life. Chicago: Henry
Regnery, 1963, p. 9.

Kuhn, Alvin Boyd. Shadow of the Third Century. Elizabeth,
New Jersey: Academy Press, 1949.

The Lambeth Conference 1958. Greenwich, Connecticut:
Seabury Press, 1958.

Langdon-Davies, John. Sex, Sin and Sanctity. London:
Victor Gollancz, 1954.

Lévy-Bruhl, Lucien. Primitive Mentality. New York:
Macmillan, 1923.

Lewisohn, Ludwig. The Story of American Literature.
New York: Modern Library, 1939.

Lowie, Robert H. Primitive Society. New York: Horace
Liveright, 1920.

Mace, David R. The Christian Response to the Sexual Revolution. Nashville, Tennessee: Abingdon Press, 1970.

Macmurray, John. Reason and Emotion. New York:
Barnes and Noble, 1962.

Malinowski, Bronislaw. Coral Gardens and Their Magic.
New York: American Book, 1935. 2 volumes.

_____. Sex and Repression in Savage Society. Cleve-
land, Ohio: World Publishing, 1968.

_____. "Supplement I: the Problem of Meaning in Pri-
mitive Languages. " In: Edited by C. K. Ogden and
I. A. Richards. The Meaning of Meaning.

Marcus, Steven. The Other Victorians: a Study of Sexuality
and Pornography in Mid-Nineteenth Century England.
New York: Basic Books, 1966.

Marcuse, Herbert. Eros and Civilization: a Philosophical
Inquiry into Freud. New York: Vintage Books, 1962.
First published 1955 by Beacon Press.

_____. One-Dimensional Man; Studies in the Ideology of
Advanced Industrial Society. Boston: Beacon Press,
1964.

Marcuse, Ludwig. Obscene. London: MacGibbon and Kee,
1965.

Matthews, Shailer. The Social Teachings of Jesus. New
York: Macmillan, 1905.

May, Geoffrey. Social Control of Sex Expression. New
York: Morrow, 1931.

May, Rollo. Man's Search for Himself. New York: New American Library, 1967.

McClellan, John J., et al. "The Commission on Obscenity and Pornography." Congressional Record, October 13, 1970, pp. S17903-17922.

Michelson, Peter. The Aesthetics of Pornography. New York: Herder & Herder, 1971.

Miller, Henry. Remember to Remember. Norfolk, Connecticut: New Directions, 1947.

Murray, Gilbert. Greek Studies. London: Oxford University Press, 1946.

Nagel, Ernest. "The Enforcement of Morals." Moral Problems in Contemporary Society. Edited by Paul Kurtz. Englewood Cliffs, New Jersey: Prentice-Hall, 1969.

New Standard Jewish Encyclopedia. Garden City, New York: Doubleday, 1970.

Oates, Whitney J., ed. The Stoic and Epicurean Philosophers. New York: Random House, 1940.

Oboler, Eli M. "The Politics of Pornography." Library Journal, December 15, 1970, pp. 4225-4228.

Ogden, C. K. and I. A. Richards. The Meaning of Meaning. New York: Harcourt, Brace, 1956.

Ong, Walter J. The Presence of the Word. New York: Simon and Schuster, 1970.

Oraison, Marc. Morality for Our Time. Garden City, New York: Doubleday, 1968.

_____, et al. Sin. New York: Macmillan, 1962.

Packard, Vance. The Sexual Wilderness. New York: McKay, 1968.

Packer, Herbert L. The Limits of the Criminal Sanction. Stanford, Calif.: Stanford University Press, 1968.

_____. "The Pornography Caper." Commentary, February, 1971, pp. 72-77.

Pearsall, Ronald. The Worm in the Bud: the World of Victorian Sexuality. New York: Macmillan, 1969.

Peckham, Morse. Art and Pornography. New York: Basic Books, 1969.

Phelan, John, ed. Communications Control. New York: Shedd and Ward, 1969.

Phillips, William. A Sense of the Present. New York: Chilmark Press, 1968.

Prescott, Peter S. "Hard Cores and Soft." Newsweek, March 15, 1971, pp. 113-118.

Putnam, George Haven. The Censorship of the Church of Rome. New York: Benjamin Blom, 1967. 2 volumes.

Radin, Paul. Primitive Man As a Philosopher. New York: Appleton, 1920.

Ramsey, Paul. Nine Modern Moralists. Englewood Cliffs, New Jersey: Prentice-Hall, 1962.

The Random House Dictionary of the English Language. New York: Random House, 1967.

Rank, Otto. The Myth of the Birth of the Hero and Other Writings. New York: Vintage Books, 1959.

Read, David H. C. Christian Ethics. Philadelphia: Lippincott, 1969.

Reik, Theodor. Myth and Guilt. New York: Grosset & Dunlap, 1970.

Reiss, Ira L., ed. "The Sexual Renaissance in America." Journal of Social Issues, April, 1966, pp. 1-140.

The Report of the Commission on Obscenity and Pornography. New York: Bantam Books, 1970.

Ricoeur, Paul, ed. "Sexuality Today." Cross Currents, Spring, 1964. Entire issue.

Rimbaud, Arthur. "The Poet As Revolutionary Seer." In:
    The Modern Tradition. Edited by Richard Ellmann and
    Charles Feidelsen. New York: Oxford University
    Press, 1965.

Robinson, James Harvey. The Mind in the Making. New
    York: Harper, 1921.

Roeburt, John. The Wicked and the Banned. New York:
    Macfadden-Bartell, 1963.

Roeder, Ralph. The Man of the Renaissance. New York:
    Time, Inc., 1966.

Rubinstein, Richard L. After Auschwitz: Radical Theology
    and Contemporary Judaism. Indianapolis, Indiana:
    Bobbs-Merrill, 1966.

Sagarin, Edward. The Anatomy of Dirty Words. New
    York: Paperback Library, 1969.

_____. "An Essay on Obscenity and Pornography." Hu-
    manist, July-August, 1969, pp. 10-12.

St. John-Stevas, Norman. Obscenity and the Law. London:
    Secker & Warburg, 1956.

Sandmel, Samuel. The Genius of Paul. New York:
    Schocken Books, 1970. p. 22.

_____. A Jewish Understanding of the New Testament. Cin-
    cinnati: Hebrew Union College Press, 1957.

Santayana, George. Reason in Art. New York: Charles
    Scribner's Sons, 1905.

_____. The Sense of Beauty. New York: Charles
    Scribner's Sons, 1896.

Sartre, Jean-Paul. "Commitment." In: The Modern Trad-
    ition. Edited by Richard Ellmann and Charles Feidelson.
    New York: Oxford University Press, 1965, pp. 853-855.

Sattler, Henry V. Parents, Children, and the Facts of Life.
    Garden City, New York: Doubleday, 1956.

Schlegel, Freidrich. Aphorisms. In: The German Classics.

New York: German Publications Society, 1913. Vol. 4.

Schmitz, John G. "The Presidential Commission on Obscenity and Pornography." Congressional Record, October 14, 1970, pp. E9236-9237.

Sex and Morality: a Report to the British Council of Churches October 1966. Philadelphia: Fortress Press, 1966.

"Sex As a Spectator Sport." Time, July 11, 1969, pp. 61-66.

Shapiro, David L., ed. The Evolution of a Judicial Philosophy: Selected Opinions and Papers of Justice John M. Harlan. Cambridge: Harvard University Press, 1969.

Smith, Preserved. The Age of the Reformation. New York: Henry Holt, 1920.

Sontag, Susan. Styles of Radical Will. New York: Farrar, Straus and Giroux, 1969.

Steiner, Fritz. Taboo. Baltimore, Maryland: Penguin Books, 1967.

Suttie, Ian D. The Origins of Love and Hate. London: Kegan, Paul, Trench, Traebner, 1935.

Tambih, S. J. "The Magical Power of Words." Man, N.S. vol. 3, no. 2. June 2, 1968, pp. 175-208.

Tennant, F. R. The Sources of the Doctrines of the Fall and Original Sin. New York: Schocken Books, 1968.

Thilly, Frank. History of Philosophy. New York: Henry Holt, 1914. p. 153.

Thoreau, Henry David. A Week on the Concord and Merrimack Rivers. New York: New American Library, 1961. First published 1849.

Trachtenberg, Joshua. Jewish Magic and Superstition. Philadelphia: Meridian Books and Jewish Publication Society, 1961.

Trent, W. P. Greatness in Literature and Other Papers. New York: Books for Libraries, c1905.

Troeltsch, Ernst.   The Social Teaching of the Christian
     Church.   New York: Harper & Row, 1960.

U. S. National Advisory Commission on Criminal Justice
     Standards and Goals.   A National Strategy to Reduce
     Crime.   Washington, D. C.: U. S. G. P. O. , 1973.

Van den Haag, Ernest.   "Is Pornography a Cause of Crime?"
     Encounter, December, 1967, pp. 52-56.

Wallas, Graham.   The Great Society.   New York: Macmil-
     lan, 1923.

Weber, Max.   The Protestant Ethic and the Spirit of Capital-
     ism.   New York: Charles Scribner's Sons, 1958.

Wendel, Francois.   Calvin.   New York: Harper, 1963.

Westermarck, Edward.   Christianity and Morals.   Freeport,
     New York: Books for Libraries, 1969.   First pub. 1939.

_____ .   Ethical Relativity.   Paterson, New Jersey:
     Littlefield, Adams, 1960.   First published 1932.   .

White, Leslie A.   The Science of Culture.   New York:
     Grove Press, 1949.

Whiteley, C. H. and Winifred.   Sex and Morals.   New
     York: Basic Books, 1967.

Williams, Norman P.   The Ideas of the Fall and of Original
     Sin.   New York: Longmans, Green, 1927.

Wilson, James Q.   "Violence, Pornography and Social Sci-
     ence. " The Public Interest, Winter, 1971, pp. 45-61.

Wilson, John.   Logic and Sexual Morality.   Baltimore,
     Maryland: Penguin Books, 1963.

Wouk, Herman.   This is My God.   New York: Dell, 1964.

Wright, Helena.   Sex and Society.   Seattle, Washington:
     University of Washington Press, 1969.

Zola, Emile.   "The Novel As Social Science. " In The Mod-
     ern Tradition.   Edited by Richard Ellmann and Charles
     Feidelson.   New York: Oxford University Press, 1965,
     pp. 270-289.

INDEX

censorship and 39
Authoritarian personality (see Personality, authoritarian)
Authorship, censor's effect on 138

Bailey, Derrick Sherwin 75
Ballou, Richard 193-194
Balzac, Honore de 56
Barnes, Harry Elmer 50
Barth, Karl 192
Bataille, Georges 10, 14, 15
Baudelaire, Charles 121
Beauty
   identity of, with truth 110
   not identical with the good or true 114
Behold America! 129
Berdyaev, Nicolas 89
Berrigan brothers 88
Bible 22, 53, 57, 60, 64
   as not being basic for distrust of sexuality 82
   Geneva government based on 64
Bickel, Alexander 160
Birket-Smith, Kaj 11
Birmingham and Midland Counties Vigilance Association 130
Blackmun, Justice Harry 214
Blasphemy 22-23, 30
   fines for, by the Puritans 65
Boccaccio, Giovanni 56
Body, spirit and the 122
Bok, Judge Curtis 147-148
Bonfire of the Vanities 54
Bonjour Tristesse 177
Book-burning 54
Book selection, ethics of library 172, 174
Books
   reading of immoral, as cause of premarital sex relations
      17
   sales of sexually-oriented 94
Booksellers, censorship and 131
Booksellers Association 145
Bowdler, Thomas 67
Boycott, group censorship and the 131, 133
Boynton, Percy 66
Brave New World 213
Breasted, James Henry 27, 218
Brennan, Justice William 216
Brentford, Viscount (see Hicks, William Joynson)
Brinton, Crane 36, 38, 59, 63, 203

327

British Council of Churches 77
British Museum 94
British Society of Friends 77
Broun, Heywood 128
Brown, Norman O. 108-109
Buber, Martin 190, 192-194
Bultmann, Rudolf 28-29
Burger, Chief Justice Warren 214
Burke, Father Redmond 56
Burnett, Carol 139
Butler, Samuel 126-127

Cairns, Huntington 154-155
Caldwell, Erskine 148
"Calling, the" 62-63
Calvin, John 57, 60-64
    censorship and 60
    disagreement with interpretations of sex by 88
    original sin and 61-62
Calvinism 60-64
    effects of, on the West 63
Cassirer, Ernst 24
Catcher in the Rye 133, 145, 169, 207, 213
Catholic (see Roman Catholic)
Catholic Headmasters' Association 68
Catholic Truth Society of Ireland 68
Catholics (see Roman Catholic Church)
Cato, Marcus 32, 37-38
Catullus 106
Celibacy
    as preferred to marriage 51
    Jesus Christ and 45
    lifelong, as an ideal 50
    Luther and 56
    monasticism and 52
    St. Paul and 47
Censor
    aestheticism and 104
    aims of the 93
    applause for 67
    as limiting individual 193
    as negative influence 187-188
    as neurotic 95
    authoritative personality and the 96
    Calvin as prototypical 62
    Catholic as 84
    childhood of 96

329

Censorship (cont.)
American literary criticism and 107
American Puritan and 66
anthropology and 5-6
as an outdated human aberration 209
as effort to build up sexual mores 101
as example of preventive approach to life 81-82
as making pornography attractive 190
as sex stimulant 204
as sexual disability 186
as source of mankind's "minimal" satisfaction 98
basis for 109
British censor's views on 200-201
British Quaker attitude toward 78
Calvinism and 60-69
cause of 16
cave man and 8
change and 207-208
Chekhov's comments on 122
civil rights and 87
classics and 120
continence and 17
conventional wisdom on 2-3
Council of Trent and 53, 55
cowardice and 127
criticism and, contrasted 104
criticism as replacement for 176
democracy and 3
deviance and 134-135
"dominant consciousness" and 137
earliest known 8
education as preventative of 201-202
encouragement of 95
ethics and 5
eventual end of 201
extralegal 86-87, 130-140
family 138
first legal Anglo-American 143
free world and 194
freedom and 208
future of 187-188
Gaelic language and 70
government and 81, 132-133
Greek opposition to 36
group 130, 137-138, 182
historical positive values of 208
history and 5
human progress and 194

335

Kronhausen, Eberhard and Phyllis 29-30, 153
Krutch, Joseph Wood 3
Ku Klux Klan 138
Kuhn, Alvin Boyd 50
Kutz, Stanley 81

Lady Chatterley's Lover 6, 169
Lambeth Conference 76
Langdon-Davies, John 71
Language
    censorship and 17
    obscene 30, 145, 157
    significance of 23
Law
    and censorship 142-167
    and censorship in England 142-146, 156-159
    and censorship in the U.S. 147-148
    and individual 148-149, 158
    and morals 154
    and society 148-153
    as codifying of societal opinion 153
    as not controlling the inevitable 141
    as not guardian of morals 148
    as protector of society 148
    British common 142
    censorship, described 153
    ethics and 174
    function of 154, 210
    individual's protection by 148-149
    love and, Luther's dictum on 170
    obscenity and 167, 215
    pornography and the 210
    purpose of obscenity 160
    relationship of, to private morality 149-151
Lawrence, D. H. 85, 119, 201
Laws
    censorship, modifiability of 162-163
    failure of, to affect morals 38
    needed restriction on censorship 164-165
    obscenity, abolition of advocated 198
    obscenity, need for understandable 162
    obscenity, to protect Americans 215
    unenforced sex 173
    versus spirit, on censorship 204
Laws (of Plato) 105
League of Dramatists 145
Leaves of Grass 120

341

Radin, Paul 25
Ramsey, Paul 194
Rank, Otto 95-96
Rape, reading and 2, 17
Read, David H. X. 78
Read, Herbert 192
Reader as proper judge of obscenity 110
Reader's Digest 183
Reading
 about sex, lack of defense for 209
 about sex, relationship of, to sexual crime 209
 about sexual conduct 95
 about sexual intercourse 17
 as cause of homosexuality 2
 as cause of juvenile delinquency 2
 as cause of rape 2
 basic Catholic doctrine and 84
 censor and 95
 censorship of, as anachronism 186
 effect on conduct of 107
 erotic 94
 freedom of, for adults on sexual materials 181, 197
Reading of pornography, crime and 63
Reason
 Stoicism and 38
Reference, circular (see Circular reference)
Reformation, the 62, 64
Regina v. Hicklin (see Hicklin Case)
Rehnquist, Justice William 214
Reik, Theodor 44-45, 90
Religion
 censorship and 71
 sex and 77
Religious groups
 as censors 133-134
Repression
 as replacing taboo 18
 as universal innate capacity 100
 family life as remedy for 101
Repression, paternal, and authoritarian personality 93
Repression, psychology of 91-101
Repression, sexual, and need for moral code 95
Repression, Trobriand Islanders and 98
Repressions, societal 96
Reproduction, sex and 197
Republic 121
Restoration, the 66
Richards, I. A. 20

351

354

effects of 199
Sexual conduct, violation of church rules on 158
Sexual ethics
    unclarity of 1970's Judeo-Christian doctrine of 88
Sexual ethics, Christian 71
Sexual expression, community as hurt by 12
    freedom of, for individual, under English law 158
    results of repression of 71
Sexual frankness, society's attitude toward 76
Sexual freedom
    as not meaning license 149
    Frumkin's definition of 197
    today's increased 85
Sexual intercourse
    acceptance as God's gift to man of 88
    as a transcendent act 194
    as source of fear, shame, prudery 116
    ascetic view of 48
    Calvinist and 63
    Christian views on, and religious faith 75
    Church of England and 76
    denial of 10
    during menstrual period as unclean or dangerous 11
    for procreation only 14
    Jewish literature and 87
    Judaism and 88
    penance for 156-159
    permissibility of 46
    premarital, caused by reading immoral books 17
    reading about 17
    unmarried and 97
Sexual language, freedom of 175
Sexual literature, reasons for popularity of 186
Sexual materials
    exposure of adult Americans to 179-180
    exposure to, as not causing delinquency 181
Sexual morality (see Morality, sexual)
Sexual pleasure
    and non-marriage 86
    Guyon's philosophy of 196
    neural origin of 196
    sexual activity as cause of 195
Sexual relations (see Sexual intercourse)
Sexual relationships
    functions involved in 197
    Macmurray's definition of 204
Sexual standards, modern 168
Sexual techniques, society's attitude toward 76